"Ye will say
I am no
Christian"

"Ye will say I am no Christian"

The Thomas Jefferson/John Adams Correspondence
on Religion, Morals, and Values

Edited by **Bruce Braden**

 Prometheus Books
59 John Glenn Drive
Amherst, New York 14228-2197

Published 2006 by Prometheus Books

Inquiries should be addressed to
Prometheus Books
59 John Glenn Drive
Amherst, New York 14228–2197
VOICE: 716–691–0133, ext. 207
FAX: 716–564–2711
WWW.PROMETHEUSBOOKS.COM

10 09 08 07 06   5 4 3 2 1

Library of Congress Cataloging-in-Publication Data

Jefferson, Thomas, 1743–1826.
    "Ye will say I am no Christian" : the Thomas Jefferson/John Adams correspondence on religion, morals, and values / [edited by] Bruce Braden.
        p. cm.
    Includes bibliographical references and index.
    ISBN 1–59102–356–4 (hardcover : alk. paper)
    1. Jefferson, Thomas, 1743–1826—Correspondence. 2. Adams, John, 1735–1826—Correspondence. 3. Jefferson, Thomas, 1743–1826—Philosophy.
4. Adams, John, 1735–1826—Philosophy. 5. United States—Politics and government—1783–1865. 6. United States—Religion. 7. United States—Moral conditions. 8. Christianity and politics—United States—Correspondence. I. Adams, John, 1735–1826. II. Braden, Bruce. III. Title.

E332.88.A23 2005
973.4'6'0922—dc22

                                                                    2005020528

Printed in the United States on acid-free paper

To Paul F. Boller Jr., Gene Garman, and Lester J. Cappon

CONTENTS

ACKNOWLEDGMENTS   15

INTRODUCTION   17

THE CORRESPONDENCE   23

1. John Adams to Thomas Jefferson (December 10, 1787)   23
   Reformations

2. John Adams to Thomas Jefferson (February 10, 1812)   23
   Prophecies

3. Thomas Jefferson to John Adams (April 20, 1812)   25
   Richmond and Wabash prophets

4. John Adams to Thomas Jefferson (May 1, 1812)   27
   Charges of corruption

5. John Adams to Thomas Jefferson (May 3, 1812)   27
   Spreading delusions

6. Thomas Jefferson to John Adams (June 11, 1812)   28
   Indian traditions

7. John Adams to Thomas Jefferson (June 28, 1812)   32
    Indian metaphysical science

8. John Adams to Thomas Jefferson (October 12, 1812)   36
    New England histories/Wollaston

9. Thomas Jefferson to John Adams (December 28, 1812)   42
    Wollaston/Thomas Morton

10. Thomas Jefferson to John Adams (May 27, 1813)   48
    Death of Benjamin Rush/Indian origins

11. John Adams to Thomas Jefferson (May 29, 1813)   51
    Unitarians/Lindsey's memoirs

12. John Adams to Thomas Jefferson (June 10, 1813)   53
    Letter to Dr. Joseph Priestley

13. John Adams to Thomas Jefferson (June 11, 1813)   55
    The living and the dead

14. Thomas Jefferson to John Adams (June 15, 1813)   55
    Enemies of reform

15. John Adams to Thomas Jefferson (June 25, 1813)   58
    Spiritual tyranny beginning

16. John Adams to Thomas Jefferson (June 28, 1813)   60
    Denunciations of the priesthood

17. John Adams to Thomas Jefferson (June 30, 1813)   64
    Terrorism of the day

18. John Adams to Thomas Jefferson (July 1813)   68
    The most lying tongue

19. John Adams to Thomas Jefferson (July 9, 1813)   70
    Histories are annihilated

20. John Adams to Thomas Jefferson (July 13, 1813)   73
    Inequalities of mind and body

21. John Adams to Thomas Jefferson (July 15, 1813)   75
    The progress of the human mind

22. John Adams to Thomas Jefferson (July 16, 1813)   77
     Promise to Benjamin Rush

23. John Adams to Thomas Jefferson (July 18, 1813)   80
     More to say on religion

24. John Adams to Thomas Jefferson (July 22, 1813)   83
     Dr. Priestley says . . .

25. John Adams to Thomas Jefferson (August 9, 1813)   85
     Bible compared with other scripture

26. John Adams to Thomas Jefferson (August [14?] 1813)   86
     Theognis lived 540 years before Jesus

27. Thomas Jefferson to John Adams (August 22, 1813)   87
     The basis for my own faith

28. John Adams to Thomas Jefferson (September 14, 1813)   89
     Ye will say I am no Christian

29. John Adams to Thomas Jefferson (September 15, 1813)   93
     No mind, but one, can see

30. John Adams to Thomas Jefferson (September 22, 1813)   94
     Zeno and his disciples too Christian?

31. John Adams to Thomas Jefferson
     (September [or October 4], 1813)   96
     *How much of Judeo-Christianity was learned
     from Babylon, Egypt, and Persia*

32. Thomas Jefferson to John Adams (October 12, 1813)   98
     Cutting verse by verse out

33. Thomas Jefferson to John Adams (October 28, 1813)   101
     Natural versus artificial aristocracy

34. John Adams to Thomas Jefferson (November 14, 1813)   108
     A second set of Ten Commandments

35. John Adams to Thomas Jefferson (November 15, 1813)   111
     Aristocracies

36. John Adams to Thomas Jefferson (December 3, 1813)   118
      Honor the gods established by law

37. John Adams to Thomas Jefferson (December 25, 1813)   124
      I return to Priestley

38. Thomas Jefferson to John Adams (January 24, 1814)   129
      Such tricks have been played

39. John Adams to Thomas Jefferson (February 1814)   133
      Looking into Oriental history and Hindoo religion

40. Thomas Jefferson to John Adams (July 5, 1814)   138
      Use of Plato to construct artificial Christianity

41. John Adams to Thomas Jefferson (July 16, 1814)   140
      Platonic Christianity has received a mortal wound

42. John Adams to Thomas Jefferson (June 19, 1815)   142
      Science, religion, government need reform

43. John Adams to Thomas Jefferson (June 20, 1815)   144
      Whether priests and kings shall rule by fictional miracles

44. John Adams to Thomas Jefferson (June 22, 1815)   146
      Acts of the saints (Acta Sanctorum)

45. Thomas Jefferson to John Adams (August 10, 1815)   151
      Acta Sanctorum: A mass of lies, a farrago of falsehood

46. John Adams to Thomas Jefferson (August 24, 1815)   152
      *Acta Sanctorum: A most complete history of the
      corruption of Christianity*

47. John Adams to Thomas Jefferson (November 13, 1815)   152
      Another St. Bartholomew's Day threatened

48. Thomas Jefferson to John Adams (January 11, 1816)   154
      Arts and sciences soften and correct the manners and morals of men

49. John Adams to Thomas Jefferson (February 2, 1816)   156
      The people wish to be deceived

50. John Adams to Thomas Jefferson (March 2, 1816)   160
      Who and what is this Fate?

51. Thomas Jefferson to John Adams (April 8, 1816)   163
    A good world on the whole

52. John Adams to Thomas Jefferson (May 3, 1816)   166
    If "afterlife" is fraud, we shall never know it

53. John Adams to Thomas Jefferson (May 6, 1816)   170
    Use of grief/Grimm/Pascal/History of Jesus

54. Thomas Jefferson to John Adams (August 1, 1816)   174
    Dreams of the future better than history of the past

55. John Adams to Thomas Jefferson (August 9, 1816)   176
    Van der Kemp/Quality of life/Jesuits

56. John Adams to Thomas Jefferson (September 3, 1816)   178
    Cross most fatal example of abuse of grief

57. John Adams to Thomas Jefferson (September 30, 1816)   181
    Priestley on Dupuis's Origin of All Cults

58. Thomas Jefferson to John Adams (October 14, 1816)   182
    Essence of virtue is in doing good to others

59. John Adams to Thomas Jefferson (November 4, 1816)   185
    Purify Christendom from corruptions

60. Thomas Jefferson to John Adams (November 25, 1816)   186
    Bible societies

61. John Adams to Thomas Jefferson (December 12, 1816)   187
    Be just and good

62. John Adams to Thomas Jefferson (December 16, 1816)   188
    Greatest fictions immortalized in art

63. Thomas Jefferson to John Adams (January 11, 1817)   190
    They supposed they knew my religion

64. John Adams to Thomas Jefferson (February 2, 1817)   191
    Passions and interests generally prevail

65. John Adams to Thomas Jefferson (April 19, 1817)   192
    I never can be a misanthrope

66. Thomas Jefferson to John Adams (May 5, 1817)   194
    Resurrection of Connecticut to light

67. John Adams to Thomas Jefferson (May 18, 1817)   195
    You think Protestant Popedom is annihilated in America?

68. John Adams to Thomas Jefferson (May 26, 1817)   197
    Controversy between spiritualists and materialists

69. John Adams to Thomas Jefferson (July 15, 1817)   199
    I choose to laugh

70. John Adams to Thomas Jefferson (October 10, 1817)   199
    Will their religion allow it?

71. John Adams to Thomas Jefferson (January 28, 1818)   200
    A mind too inquisitive for Connecticut

72. Thomas Jefferson to John Adams (May 17, 1818)   201
    I am glad he is gone to Kentucky

73. John Adams to Thomas Jefferson (May 29, 1818)   202
    His system is founded in hope, not fear

74. John Adams to Thomas Jefferson (July 18, 1818)   202
    Dr. Mayhew

75. John Adams to Thomas Jefferson (October 20, 1818)   203
    The dear partner of my life lies in extremis

76. Thomas Jefferson to John Adams (November 13, 1818)   204
    I know well and feel what you have lost

77. John Adams to Thomas Jefferson (December 8, 1818)   204
    If I did not believe in a future state

78. John Adams to Thomas Jefferson (January 29, 1819)   205
    How has it happened?

79. John Adams to Thomas Jefferson (February 13, 1819)   205
    Abolish polytheism

80. Thomas Jefferson to John Adams (March 21, 1819)   206
    Eccentricities of planets

81. John Adams to Thomas Jefferson (May 21, 1819)   206
     The world is dead

82. Thomas Jefferson to John Adams (December 10, 1819)   207
     Follow truth, eschew error

83. John Adams to Thomas Jefferson (December 21, 1819)   207
     To render all prayer futile

84. John Adams to Thomas Jefferson (January 20, 1820)   208
     God: An essence we know nothing of

85. Thomas Jefferson to John Adams (March 14, 1820)   208
     The ablest metaphysicians

86. John Adams to Thomas Jefferson (May 12, 1820)   210
     The cause of all is beyond conception

87. Thomas Jefferson to John Adams (August 15, 1820)   211
     This heresy of immaterialism

88. Thomas Jefferson to John Adams (January 22, 1821)   213
     We prescribe a cure for others

89. John Adams to Thomas Jefferson (February 3, 1821)   215
     *Free government and the Roman Catholic religion
     can never exist together*

90. John Adams to Thomas Jefferson (May 19, 1821)   216
     Surrender hope

91. John Adams to Thomas Jefferson (September 24, 1821)   217
     Hope springs eternal

92. Thomas Jefferson to John Adams (June 1, 1822)   217
     When all our faculties are gone, is death an evil?/War

93. John Adams to Thomas Jefferson (June 11, 1822)   219
     Death is a blessing/Globe is a theater of war

94. John Adams to Thomas Jefferson (March 10, 1823)   219
     Right and justice have hard fare

95. Thomas Jefferson to John Adams (April 11, 1823)   220
     Virgin birth of Jesus classed with fable

96. John Adams to Thomas Jefferson (August 15, 1823)   224
    Dr. Priestley came to breakfast

97. Thomas Jefferson to John Adams (September 4, 1823)   226
    Art of printing changed the world

98. Thomas Jefferson to John Adams (October 12, 1823)   226
    The evening of our lives

99. Thomas Jefferson to John Adams (January 8, 1825)   227
    Experiments on the nervous system/Soul?

100. John Adams to Thomas Jefferson (January 22, 1825)   229
    This awful blasphemy

101. John Adams to Thomas Jefferson (January 23, 1825)   230
    Liberty of conscience, right of free inquiry

102. John Adams to Thomas Jefferson (February 25, 1825)   231
    I like him much for his curiosity

103. John Adams to Thomas Jefferson (December 1, 1825)   231
    Rather go forward, meet what is to come

104. Thomas Jefferson to John Adams (December 18, 1825)   232
    In favor of treading the ground over again

105. John Adams to Thomas Jefferson (January 14, 1826)   232
    Death: A transformation or an end?

106. Thomas Jefferson to John Adams (March 25, 1826)   233
    What he has heard and learnt of the Heroic Age

107. John Adams to Thomas Jefferson (April 17, 1826)   233
    More personal abuse than there used to be

ADDENDUM: A SAMPLING OF
JEFFERSON AND ADAMS WRITING TO OTHERS
ON RELIGION, PHILOSOPHY, AND MORALS   235

INDEX   245

ACKNOWLEDGMENTS

I offer my gratitude and appreciation to previous compilers and editors of Thomas Jefferson/John Adams writings. In particular, I want to thank the following:

Norman Cousins: *In God We Trust: The Religious Beliefs and Ideas of the American Founding Fathers*. New York: Harper & Row, 1958.

Norman Cousins: *The Republic of Reason: The Personal Philosophies of the Founding Fathers*. New York: Harper & Row, 1958, 1988.

Lester J. Cappon: *The Adams-Jefferson Letters: The Complete Correspondence between Thomas Jefferson and Abigail and John Adams*. Chapel Hill: University of North Carolina Press, 1959, 1987.

Edwin S. Gaustad: *A Documentary History of Religion in America*. 2 Vols. Grand Rapids, MI: Eerdman's, 1982–1983

Edwin S. Gaustad: *Faith of Our Fathers: Religion and the New Nation*. San Francisco: Harper & Row, 1987.

Edwin S. Gaustad: *Faith of the Founders: Religion and the New Nation, 1776–1826*. Waco, TX: Baylor University Press, 2004.

Leonard Kriegel: *Essential Works of the Founding Fathers*. New York: Bantam Books, 1964.

Merrill D. Peterson: *Jefferson*. New York: Library of America, 1984.

Albert Ellery Bergh, editor: *The Writings of Thomas Jefferson*. 19 Vols. Washington, DC: Thomas Jefferson Memorial Association, H-Bar Enterprises CD, 1905, 1996.

Albert Ellery Bergh, editor: *The Writings of Thomas Jefferson*. 20 Vols. Washington, DC: Thomas Jefferson Memorial Association, 1907.

Paul Leicester Ford: *The Works of Thomas Jefferson*. New York: G. P. Putnam and Sons/Knickerbocker Press, 1904–1905.

Andrew J. Lipscomb, editor-in-chief: *The Writings of Thomas Jefferson*. 20 Vols. Washington, DC: Thomas Jefferson Memorial Association, 1903–1904. Bank of Wisdom CD, 2000.

Charles Francis Adams, compiler and editor: *The Works of John Adams*. 10 Vols. Boston: Little, Brown, and Company, 1851–1865.

Paul Wilstach: *Correspondence of Thomas Jefferson and John Adams*. Indianapolis: Merrill, 1925.

SPECIAL THANKS

I want to offer my deepest gratitude to my mother, Veronica. She taught me to read. Before I started school, she walked me to the Mt. Pleasant Library in southwestern Pennsylvania to sign me up for my first library card. I still remember that walk, the sight, the smell of the library and a room full of books!

I want to thank my wife, Linda Davis, for all the reading she does and for the new ideas she brings to our relationship. I want to thank her for being comfortable in the quietness of our reading together. We both appreciate "what peace there may be in silence." My thanks go out to Vicky Wells, permissions department, University of North Carolina Press.

Finally, I want to thank Prometheus Books, particularly my editor, Steven L. Mitchell, for seeing the value and potential of this volume. I want to thank the Prometheus committee members and staff for bringing this work to print.

INTRODUCTION

I have been a letter carrier in Indianapolis, Indiana, for twenty years. Now, I carry letters of Thomas Jefferson and John Adams to you.

As a young man, like John Adams I gave some consideration to the ministry. John Adams was born into Protestant Calvinism; I was born into Roman Catholicism. Both of us dismissed ordination vows so that we might have more freedom of thought.

John Adams and Thomas Jefferson both enjoyed collecting and reading books. As do I.

So, it is not surprising that someday, though generations apart, the three of us should come together in what might be called a collaborative work.

As a teen, I enjoyed reading books like George Seldes's *Great Quotations*. There was something about discovering the ideas from ages past. I was intrigued that men and women, thousands of years before my time, nay, even thousands of years before Christ, could hold such marvelous, well-developed views on life and religion.

When I was thirty-one years old, I was a grad student in personality theory and religion at Christian Theological Seminary/Butler University in Indianapolis, Indiana. During that time, I served as a chaplain extern at Methodist Hospital. There, Rev. Glenn Caulkins, my adviser, after listening to me trying to remember and cite quotes I had read, recommended that I quote myself more often, offer up what I believed or knew from my own experience. Well, Glenn was right, to a degree. I did, indeed, need to know myself better, to trust myself better, and then offer my unique gifts to the world. But one of my unique gifts is my love for discovering and passing on the thoughts of men and women long gone. It is one thing to find your own values, loves, and beliefs. It is then a marvelous thing to discover those same values, loves, and beliefs in the past.

Thomas Jefferson and John Adams both had concerns that history might distort truth. Both complained that even the histories of their own day, those written about the American Revolution, were not always accurate. Jefferson's hope was that "the letters of the day," the actual letters and documents of people within a certain era, would later be discovered and laid open to the public to reveal the truth of an era, the truth of one person or another.

So it was that, when I received my masters degree in personality theory and religion in 1982, I made a decision. Rather than go on for a doctorate, where I would again be more or less directed in my studies and readings, I would venture into the reading and research I longed to do.

Like Thomas Jefferson and John Adams, through the purchase of new and used books, I assembled my own private library. I focused on early American history, religion, and mythology. Several times I read the Bible, visually from hard copies and audibly from books on tape. Likewise, I read religious texts, such as the Bhagavad Gita, Dharma-pada, Tao Te Ching, Koran, and Nag Hammadi Library. I studied mythology, especially Joseph Campbell's work. And, I finally went back to find the actual writings of America's Founding Fathers and their era, the primary source documents. I was back to the world of quotations, back to "the letters of the day."

As with the Bible, so, too, with the Founding Fathers, I had heard so much about what each allegedly stated, or required belief in, that I wanted to find out for myself. I was disappointed to find that the Bible was not infallible or not without contradiction, though it contains much of value. But I was surprised, no, I was elated, to find that some

Founders shared knowledge or beliefs I had finally come to on my own about the Bible, Christianity, and other religions. In fact, on one occasion, Adams tells Jefferson that the reason he found enjoyment and stimulation in their correspondence was because Adams felt that Jefferson would understand what Adams was talking about and where he was coming from.

Founders, like Thomas Jefferson, John Adams, Thomas Paine, and Ethan Allen, though they had respect for many aspects of Christianity, also admitted their own disbelief at some aspects of Christianity and the Bible. For their challenges to Christianity and Scripture, all these Founders and others bore the insults and defamation of the Fundamentalists of their day.

America was first settled by religious dissenters, who, once established, did not tolerate religious dissent from their views. Yet when one studies religion for any length of time, it becomes clear that the evolution of religion is but one long tale of religious dissent. Judaism arose in dissent of various pagan religions. Jesus himself was a dissenter of orthodox Judaism. Martin Luther rose in dissent of Roman Catholicism. Protestantism, too, has hundreds of "dissenting" denominations. No wonder it is difficult to define "Christian." Dissenters have been and will always be in the world. This book will reveal the "dissent" in Jefferson and Adams.

This book is intended to provide readers with a reference volume centered on the Jefferson-Adams correspondence relating to religion and philosophies to live by. By investing my time in research, I hope to save readers some discovery time. But I also hope readers will be inspired to follow leads found within the letters and the footnotes. "Like beams of light jumping all over," the ideas herein should lead readers to begin their own correspondence with others who seek the ascent of the mind, rather than its imprisonment. This book should give its readers insights, not only into the minds of Jefferson and Adams, but also into the minds and hearts of those they wrote about or quoted.

I thank my Prometheus Books editor, Steven L. Mitchell, for spurring me on to investigate and present the footnotes for the Adams-

Jefferson letters. As I prepared the footnotes, it dawned on me that (like myself, Jefferson, and Adams) many of the people you will find mentioned therein did their research and writing in their "spare time." Most did not earn their primary income from their writings on religion or philosophy. Their careers ran the gamut. There were farmers, statesmen, soldiers, clergy, mathematicians, scientists, teachers, explorers, lawyers, merchants, slaves. Most of these men and women were just curious thinkers and writers who took their experiences of the world and ventured out to find the thoughts of their contemporaries and predecessors. Then, in their own writings, they hoped to influence and shape, not only their own eras, but future ones as well. I hope this volume can do the same.

I look forward to the progress of the human mind, not its regression, in religion or government. I believe that revelation is ongoing. I believe revelation goes way beyond the Bible or any current "revealed" religion. Like Jefferson and Adams, I respect and appreciate what their generation and all those before them have accomplished.

But, like them, I expect my generation and those to come to find their own way in religion, philosophy, and morals.

Jefferson and Adams broke with tradition as much as they dared. But just as they lamented the loss of the "genuine" teaching of Jesus in the "corruptions of Christianity," we must guard against the loss of the teachings of our Founding Fathers owing to the corruptions of American history. (Some will say my work is such a corruption.) But it would be even worse to become so mired in the myths of our Founders that we fail to move America, the world, the human mind, heart, and soul beyond current accomplishments in thought and action.

There is a need for revisionist history, because, as Adams, Jefferson, and others of their era, like their friend Benjamin Rush, claimed, historians don't always give us accurate accounts.

When Jefferson and Adams were presidential candidates in 1800, a vote for Adams was said to be a vote for God, religion, law and order; a vote for Jefferson was a vote for "no god" and lawlessness. This religious test, in spite of the US Constitution's Article VI clause forbidding religious tests for public office, is still present today. The irony today is that even John Adams might not get the "religious" vote. It all depends on who is defining what it means to be Christian, what it means to be moral. American is not yet ready to elect "just and good" men regardless of their religious beliefs.

America will know that it has made greater steps toward freedom of, and freedom from, religion when John Adams and Thomas Jefferson can return to find that America has learned, after a few hundred years, that the whole of religion, philosophy, and morals, can be summed up simply in John Adams's words: "Be just and good."

Bruce Braden, MA
Carmel, Indiana
February 4, 2005

Th Jefferson

Painting by Gilbert Stuart,
Courtesy Bowdoin College Museum of Art

John Adams

Painting by Charles Willson Peale,
Courtesy of Independence National Historical Park

The Correspondence

1. JOHN ADAMS TO THOMAS JEFFERSON
GROSVENOR SQUARE
December 10, 1787

Corrections, Reformations, Improvements, are much wanted in all the Institutions of Europe, Ecclesiastical and Civil.

John Adams

2. JOHN ADAMS TO THOMAS JEFFERSON
February 10, 1812

Although you and I are weary of politics, you may be surprised to find me making a transition to such a subject as Prophecies. I find that Virginia produces Prophets as well as the Indian Territory. There have been lately sent me from Richmond two volumes, one written by Nimrod Hewes and the other by Christopher Macpherson; both, upon Prophecies, and neither ill written.

I should apprehend that two such Mulattoes might raise the Devil among the Negroes in that vicinity. For, though they are evidently cracked, they are not much more irrational than Dr. Towers[1] who wrote two ponderous volumes, near twenty years ago to prove that the French Revolution was the commencement of the Millennium, and the decapitation of the king of France but the beginning of a series, immediately to follow, by which all the Monarchies were to be destroyed and succeeded by universal Republicanism over all Europe.

Nor than Dr. Priestley[2] who told me soberly, coolly, and deliberately that though he knew of nothing in human nature or in the History of Mankind to justify the opinion, yet he fully believed upon the Authority of Prophecy that the French nation would establish a free government and that the king of France, who had been executed, was the first of the Ten Horns of the great Beast, and that all the other Nine Monarchs were soon to fall off after him.

Nor than the Reverend Mr. Faber[3] who has lately written a very elegant and learned volume to prove that Napoleon is Antichrist; nor than our worthy friend, Mr. Joseph Wharton[4] of Philadelphia, who in consequence of great reading and profound study has long since settled his opinion that the city of London is, or is to be, the Headquarters of Antichrist.

Nor than the Prophet of the Wabash (Tenskwatawa),[5] of whom I want to know more than I do, because I learn that the Indians, the Sons

---

1. Joseph Towers (1737–1799). English biographer, minister, pamphleteer, and editor. Wrote *Thoughts on the Commencement of a New Parliament* (1790) and biographies of Dr. Samuel Johnson and King Frederick the Great.

2. (1733–1804). English-born chemist and Unitarian minister. Wrote *History of the Corruptions of Christianity* (1782).

3. George Stanley Faber. Author of several works on Apocalyptic End-Times, including *Dissertations on the Prophecies* in 2 volumes (1808). Critiqued James Bicheno's *Signs of the Times*.

4. (1733–1816). While living in France after being forced to leave England because of his writings, Wharton befriended artist Benjamin West. He suggested bringing West's painting "Christ Healing the Sick" to Philadelphia's hospital. The painting arrived in 1817.

5. Shawnee prophet (c. 1768–1834). Together with his brother, Tecumseh, he urged a Northwest Indian confederacy. He claimed to receive messages from God commanding rejection of White Men and a return to Indian racial purity. He was a participant in the Battle of Tippecanoe (1811).

of the Forest, are as superstitious as any of the great learned men aforesaid, and as firm believers in Witchcraft as all Europe and America were in the Seventeenth Century, and as frequently punish witches by splitting their skulls with the tomahawk, after a solemn trial and adjudication by the sachems and warriors in council.

The Crusades were commenced by the prophets and every age since, whenever any great turmoil happens in the world, has produced fresh prophets. The continual refutation of all their prognostications by time and experience has no effect in extinguishing or damping their ardor.

I think these prophecies are not only unphilosophical and inconsistent with the political safety of states and nations, but that most sincere and sober Christians in the world ought, upon their own principles, to hold them impious. For, nothing is clearer from their scriptures than that their prophecies were not intended to make us prophets.

Pardon this strange vagary. I want only to know something more than I do about the Richmond and Wabash prophets.

John Adams

3. THOMAS JEFFERSON TO JOHN ADAMS
MONTICELLO, April 20, 1812

You wish to know something of the Richmond and Wabash prophets. Of Nimrod Hews, I never heard before. Christopher Macpherson I have known for twenty years. He is a man of color, brought up as a book-keeper by a merchant, his master, and afterwards enfranchised. He had understanding enough to post up his ledger from his journal, but not enough to bear up against hypochondriac affections, and the gloomy forebodings they inspire. He became crazy, foggy, his head always in the clouds, and rhapsodizing what neither himself nor any one else could understand.

I think he told me he had visited you personally while you were in the administration, and wrote you letters, which you have probably forgotten in the mass of the correspondences of that crazy class, of whose complaints, and terrors, and mysticisms, the several Presidents have been the regular depositories. Macpherson was too honest to be molested by anybody, and too inoffensive to be a subject for the mad-house. Although, I believe, we are told in the old book, that "every man that is mad, and maketh himself a prophet, thou shouldest put him in prison and in the stocks."

The Wabash prophet is a very different character, more rogue than fool, if to be a rogue is not the greatest of all follies. He arose to notice while I was in the administration, and became, of course, a proper sub-ject of inquiry for me. The inquiry was made with diligence. His declared object was the reformation of his red brethren, and their return to their pristine manner of living. He pretended to be in constant communication with the Great Spirit; that he was instructed by him to make known to the Indians that they were created by him distinct from the whites, of different natures, for different purposes, and placed under different circumstances, adapted to their nature and destinies; that they must return from all the ways of the whites to the habits and opinions of their forefathers; they must not eat the flesh of hogs, of bullocks, of sheep, etc., the deer and buffalo having been created for their food; they must not make bread of wheat, but of Indian corn; they must not wear linen nor woolen, but dress like their fathers in the skins and furs of animals; they must not drink ardent spirits, and I do not remember whether he extended his inhibitions to the gun and gun-powder, in favor of the bow and arrow.

I concluded from all this, that he was a visionary, enveloped in the clouds of their antiquities, and vainly endeavoring to lead back his brethren to the fancied beatitudes of their golden age. I thought there was little danger of his making many proselytes from the habits and comfort they had learned from the whites, to the hardships and priva-tions of savagism, and no great harm if he did. We let him go on, there-fore, unmolested. But his followers increased till the English thought him worth corruption and found him corruptible.

I suppose his views were then changed; but his proceedings in consequence of them were after I left the administration, and are, therefore, unknown to me; nor have I ever been informed what were the particular acts on his part which produced an actual commencement of hostilities on ours. I have no doubt, however, that his subsequent proceedings are but a chapter apart, like that of Henry and Lord Liverpool, in the Book of the Kings of England.

This letter, with what it encloses, has given you enough, I presume, of law and the prophets.

Thomas Jefferson

4. JOHN ADAMS TO THOMAS JEFFERSON
May 1, 1812

Good God! Is a President of the U.S. to be subject to a private action of every individual?

This will soon introduce the axiom that a President can do no wrong; or, another equally curious, that a President can do no right.

I have run over this pamphlet[6] with great pleasure, but must read it with more attention. I have uniformly treated the charges of corruption, which I have read in the newspapers and pamphlets, and, heard from the pulpit against you and Mr. Madison with contempt and indignation. I believe in the integrity of both, at least as undoubtingly as in that of Washington. In the measures of administration, I have neither agreed with you or Mr. Madison. Whether you or I were right, Posterity must judge.

John Adams

5. JOHN ADAMS TO THOMAS JEFFERSON
May 3, 1812

I thank you for the account of the Wabash Prophet. MacPherson, Parson Austin, and Abraham Brown[7] made themselves sufficiently known to me when I was in the Government. They all assumed the Character of Ambassadors extraordinary from the Almighty. But, as I

---

6. Pamphlet that deals with President Jefferson's repossession as public property some New Orleans beach batture purchased by Edward Livingston.

7. Religious leaders/ministers.

required miracles in proof of their credentials, and they did not perform any, I never gave public audience to either of them.

Though I have long acknowledged your superiority in most
branches of Science and Literature, I little thought of being compelled
to confess it in Biblical Knowledge. I had forgotten the custom of putting prophets in the stocks, and was obliged to have recourse to the
Concordance to discover Jer. 29.26 for your text, and found at the
same time Jer. 20.2–3 that Jeremiah himself had been put in the stocks.

It may be thought impiety by many, but I could not help wishing that
the ancient practice had been continued down to more modern times and
that all the prophets, at least from Peter the Hermit, to Nimrod Hewes
inclusively, had been confined in the stocks and prevented from
spreading so many delusions and shedding so much blood.

Could you believe that the mad rant of Nimrod, which was sent to
me by Christopher [Macpherson] with his own and which I sent to a
neighbor in whose house it was seen and read by some visitors, spread
a great deal of terror and a serious apprehension that one third of the
human race would be destroyed on the fourth day of next month?

As my neighbors are far from being remarkably superstitious, I
could not have believed what has appeared in experience. The transition from one set of crazy people to another is not unnatural.

                                                        John Adams

6. THOMAS JEFFERSON TO JOHN ADAMS
    MONTICELLO, June 11, 1812

You ask if there is any book that pretends to give any account of the
traditions of the Indians, or how one can acquire an idea of them.
Some scanty accounts of their traditions, but fuller of their customs
and characters, are given us by most of the early travellers among
them; these you know were mostly French Lafitau,[8] among them, and

---

8. Joseph Francis Lafitau (1681?–1746). A French missionary who made two
trips to America and discovered ginseng in North America. Wrote *Mores of American
Savages Compared with Mores of the First Times.*

Adair[9] an Englishman, have written on this subject; the former two volumes, the latter one, all in 4to [meaning quarto].[10]

But unluckily Lafitau had in his head a preconceived theory on the mythology, manners, institutions and government of the ancient nations of Europe, Asia and Africa, and seems to have entered on those of America only to fit them into the same frame, and to draw from them a confirmation of his general theory. He keeps up a perpetual parallel, in all those articles, between the Indians of America and the ancients of the other quarters of the globe. He selects, therefore, all the facts and adopts all the falsehoods which favor this theory, and very gravely [retells] such absurdities as zeal for a theory could alone swallow. He was a man of much classical and scriptural reading, and has rendered his book not unentertaining. He resided five years among the Northern Indians, as a Missionary, but collects his matter much more from the writings of others, than from his own observation.

Adair too had his kink. He believed all the Indians of America to be descended from the Jews; the same laws, usages, rites and ceremonies, the same sacrifices, priests, prophets, fasts and festivals, almost the same religion, and that they all spoke Hebrew. For, although he writes particularly of the Southern Indians only, the Catawbas, Creeks, Cherokees, Chickasaws and Choctaws, with whom alone he was personally acquainted, yet he generalizes whatever he found among them, and brings himself to believe that the hundred languages of America, differing fundamentally every one from every other, as much as Greek from Gothic, yet have all one common prototype. He was a trader, a man of learning, a self-taught Hebraist, a strong religionist, and of as sound a mind as Don Quixote in whatever did not touch his religious chivalry. His book contains a great deal of real instruction on its subject, only requiring the reader to be constantly on his guard against the wonderful obliquities of his theory.

The scope of your inquiry would scarcely, I suppose, take in the

---

9. James Adair (1709?–1783). American trader and writer who lived forty years among Indians, mostly the Chickasaw of Southeastern America. Wrote *History of American Indians* (1775). He claimed Jewish origins for American Indians.

10. A small book since its pages are cut four from a sheet.

three folio volumes of Latin of De Bry.[11] In these, facts and fable are mingled together, without regard to any favorite system. They are less suspicious, therefore, in their complexion, more original and authentic, than those of Lafitau and Adair. This is a work of great curiosity, extremely rare, so as never to be bought in Europe, but on the breaking up and selling some ancient library. On one of these occasions a bookseller procured me a copy, which, unless you have one, is probably the only one in America.

You ask further, if the Indians have any order of priesthood among them, like the Druids, Bards or Minstrels of the Celtic nations? Adair alone, determined to see what he wished to see in every object, metamorphoses their Conjurers into an order of priests, and describes their sorceries as if they were the great religious ceremonies of the nation. Lafitau called them by their proper names, Jongleurs, Devins, Sortileges; De Bry praestigiatores; Adair himself sometimes Magi, Archimagi, cunning men, Seers, rain makers; and the modern Indian interpreters call them conjurers and witches. They are persons pretending to have communications with the devil and other evil spirits, to foretell future events, bring down rain, find stolen goods, raise the dead, destroy some and heal others by enchantment, lay spells, etc.

And Adair, without departing from his parallel of the Jews and Indians, might have found their counterpart much more aptly, among the soothsayers, sorcerers and wizards of the Jews, their Jannes and Jambres, their Simon Magus, Witch of Endor, and the young damsel whose sorceries disturbed Paul so much; instead of placing them in a line with their high-priest, their chief priests, and their magnificent hierarchy generally. In the solemn ceremonies of the Indians, the persons who direct or officiate are their chiefs, elders and warriors, in civil ceremonies or in those of war; it is the head of the cabin in their private or particular feasts or ceremonies; and sometimes the matrons, as in their corn feasts.

---

11. Theodore De Bry (1528–1598). Made text and copper plate engravings of Indian life in Virginia and Florida based on John White's time in Virginia and Jacques Le Moyne's work in Florida. De Bry had to use imagination and creativity since the Spanish had destroyed much of Le Moyne's works. Born a Calvinist, De Bry's work was driven to spread "Truth" in light of Catholic Spain's persecution of European Protestants.

And even here, Adair might have kept up his parallel, with ennobling his conjurers. For the ancient patriarchs, the Noahs, the Abrahams, Isaacs and Jacobs, and even after the consecration of Aaron, the Samuels and Elijahs, and we may say further, every one for himself offered sacrifices on the altars. The true line of distinction seems to be, that solemn ceremonies, whether public or private, addressed to the Great Spirit, are conducted by the worthies of the nation, men or matrons, while conjurers are resorted to only for the invocation of evil spirits.

The present state of the several Indian tribes, without any public order of priests, is proof sufficient that they never had such an order. Their steady habits permit no innovations, not even those which the progress of science offers to increase the comforts, enlarge the understanding, and improve the morality of mankind. Indeed, so little idea have they of a regular order of priests, that they mistake ours for their conjurers, and call them by that name.

So much in answer to your inquiries concerning Indians, a people with whom, in the early part of my life, I was very familiar, and acquired impressions of attachment and commiseration for them which have never been obliterated. Before the Revolution, they were in the habit of coming often and in great numbers to the seat of government, where I was very much with them. I knew much the great Ontassete, the warrior and orator of the Cherokees. He was always the guest of my father, on his journeys to and from Williamsburg. I was in his camp when he made his great farewell oration to his people the evening before his departure for England. The moon was in full splendor, and to her he seemed to address himself in his prayers for his own safety on the voyage, and that of his people during his absence. His sounding voice, distinct articulation, animated action, and the solemn silence of his people at their several fires, filled me with awe and veneration, although I did not understand a word he uttered.

Thomas Jefferson

7. JOHN ADAMS TO THOMAS JEFFERSON
QUINCY, June 28, 1812

DEAR SIR,

I know not what, unless it were the prophet of Tippecanoe, had turned my curiosity to inquiries after the metaphysical science of the Indians, their ecclesiastical establishments, and theological theories; but your letter, written with all the accuracy, perspicuity, and elegance of your youth and middle age, as it has given me great satisfaction, deserves my best thanks.

It has given me satisfaction, because, while it has furnished me with information where all the knowledge is to be obtained that books afford, it has convinced me that I shall never know much more of the subject than I do now. As I have never aimed at making my collection of books upon this subject, I have none of those you abridged in so concise a manner. Lafitau, Adair, and De Bry, were known to me only by name.

The various ingenuity which has been displayed in inventions of hypothesis, to account for the original population of America, and the immensity of learning profusely expended to support them, have appeared to me for a longer time than I can precisely recollect, what the physicians call the Literae nihil Sanantes [Writings correcting nothing]. Whether serpents' teeth were sown here and sprang up men; whether men and women dropped from the clouds upon this Atlantic Island; whether the Almighty created them here, or whether they emigrated from Europe, are questions of no moment to the present or future happiness of man. Neither agriculture, commerce, manufactures, fisheries, science, literature, taste, religion, morals, nor any other good will be promoted, or any evil, averted, by any discoveries that can be made in answer to these questions.

The opinions of the Indians and their usages, as they are represented in your obliging letter of the 11th of June, appear to me to resemble the Platonizing Philo,[12] or the Philonizing Plato,[13] more than the genuine system of Indianism.

---

12. Philo Judaeus, aka Philo of Alexandria (c. 20 BCE–50 CE). Jewish Hellenistic philosopher who conceived of God as without attributes, so exalted that an

The philosophy both of Philo and Plato are at least as absurd. It is indeed less intelligible.

Plato borrowed his doctrines from Oriental and Egyptian philosophers, for he had traveled both in India and Egypt.

The Oriental philosophy, imitated and adopted, in part, if not the whole, by Plato and Philo, was

1. One God the good.
2. The ideas, the thoughts, the reason, the intellect, the logos, the ratio of God.
3. Matter, the universe, the production of the logos, or contemplations of God. This matter was the source of evil.

Perhaps the three powers of Plato, Philo, the Egyptians, and Indians, cannot be distinctly made out, from your account of the Indians, but

1. The great spirit, the good, who is worshipped by the kings, sachems, and all the great men, in their solemn festivals, as the Author, the Parent of good.
2. The Devil, or the source of evil. They are not metaphysicians enough as yet to suppose it, or at least to call it matter, like the Wiseacres of Antiquity, and like Frederick the Great,[14] who has written a very silly essay on the origin of evil, in which he

---

intermediary class of beings (each called Logos) was required to contact him. For Philo, Logos was not identical with God, but unique and separate from God as an instrument of creation. Philo's works dealt with allegorical interpretations of Genesis, expositions on the Law of Moses, and Ten Commandments for Gentiles.

13. Plato (c. 428–347 BCE). Greek philosopher whose concepts of Ideas, Forms, and Demiurge (Father, Builder, Maker, Framer, Artisan of the Universe) influenced early Jewish thinkers like Philo Judaeus and early Christians, such as Clement of Alexandria, Origen, and St. Augustine. These concepts later impacted Islamic thought.

14. Frederick II (1712–1786). King of Prussia. Wrote *Philosophical Works from Sans Souci (Oeuvres du Philosophe de Sanssouci)* (1750). Sans Souci was Frederick's rococo palace near Potsdam, where Frederick entertained the likes of Voltaire.

ascribes it all to matter, as if this was an original discovery of his own.

The Watchmaker has in his head an idea of the system of a watch before he makes it. The Mechanician of the universe had a complete idea of the universe before he made it; and this idea, this logos, was almighty, or at least powerful enough to produce the world, but it must be made of matter which was eternal; for, creation out of nothing was impossible. And matter was unmanageable. It would not, and could not be fashioned into any system, without a large mixture of evil in it; for matter was essentially evil.

The Indians are not metaphysicians enough to have discovered this idea, this logos, this intermediate power between good and evil, God and matter. But of the two powers, the good and the evil, they seem to have a full conviction; and what son or daughter of Adam and Eve has not?

This Logos of Plato seems to resemble, if it was not the prototype of, the Ratio and its Progress of Manilius,[15] the astrologer; of the Progress of the Mind of Condorcet,[16] and the Age of Reason of Tom Paine.[17]

I could make a system too. The seven hundred thousand soldiers of Zingis,[18] when the whole: or any part of them went to battle, they

---

15. Roman poet first century CE. Of his didactic poem on astrology, *Astronomica*, five books remain. "For I shall sing of God, silent-minded monarch of nature, who, permeating sky and land and sea, controls with uniform compact the mighty structure."

16. Marquis de Condorcet, Marie Jean Antoine Nicholas de Caritat (1743–1794). French philosopher, mathematician, and political revolutionary chiefly remembered for his theory that the human race, having risen from barbarism, would continue to progress toward moral, intellectual, and physical perfection.

17. (1737–1809). Author of *Common Sense* and *The Rights of Man*. He drew criticism for his 1794 *Age of Reason*, a critique of the Bible and religion.

18. Zingis Khan, or Genghis Khan (1155–1227). Founder of Mongol Empire, of whom Edward Gibbon had this to say in chapter 64 of *The Decline and Fall of the Roman Empire*: "But it is the religion of Zingis that best deserves our wonder and applause. The Catholic inquisitors of Europe, who defended nonsense by cruelty, might have been confounded by the example of a Barbarian, who anticipated the lessons of philosophy, and established by his laws a system of pure theism and perfect toleration. His first and only article of faith was the existence of one God, the Author

sent up a howl, which resembled nothing that human imagination has conceived, unless it be the supposition that all the devils in hell were let loose at once to set up an infernal scream, which terrified their enemies; and never failed to obtain them victory. The Indian yell resembles this; and, therefore, America was peopled from Asia.

Another system. The armies of Zingis, sometimes two or three or four hundred thousand of them, surrounded a province in a circle, and marched towards the centre, driving all the wild beasts before them, lions, tigers; wolves; bears, and every living thing, terrifying them with their howls and yells, their drums, trumpets, etc., till they terrified and tamed enough of them to victual the whole army. Therefore, the Scotch Highlanders, who practice the same thing in miniature, are emigrants from Asia. Therefore, the American Indians, who, for anything I know, practice the same custom, are emigrants from Asia or Scotland.

I am weary of contemplating nations from the lowest and most beastly degradations of human life, to the highest refinement of civilization. I am weary of Philosophers, Theologians, Politicians; and Historians. They are an immense mass of absurdities, vices, and lies. Montesquieu[19] had sense enough to say in jest, that all our knowledge might be comprehended in twelve pages in duodecimo, and I believe him in earnest. I could express my faith in shorter terms. He who loves the workman and his work, and does what he can to preserve and improve it, shall be accepted of him.

I have also felt an interest in the Indians, and a commiseration for them from my childhood. Aaron Pomham, the priest, and Moses Pomham, the king of the Punkapaug and Neponsit tribes, were frequent visitors at my father's house, at least seventy years ago. I have

---

of all good; who fills by his presence the heavens and earth, which he has created by his power. The Tartars and Moguls were addicted to the idols of their peculiar tribes; and many of them had been converted by the foreign missionaries to the religions of Moses, of Mahomet, and of Christ. These various systems in freedom and concord were taught and practiced within the precincts of the same camp."

19. Charles Louis de Secondat Montesquieu (1689–1755). French political philosopher. His theory that governmental powers should be separated into legislative, executive, and judicial bodies to safeguard personal liberty was developed in *The Spirit of the Laws* (1748), which influenced the US Constitution.

a distinct remembrance of their forms and figures. They were very aged, and the tallest and stoutest Indians I have ever seen. The titles of king and priest, and the names of Moses and Aaron, were given them no doubt by our Massachusetts divines and statesmen. There was a numerous family in this town, whose wigwam was within a mile of this house. This family was frequently at my father's house, and I, in my boyish rambles, used to call at their wigwam, where I never failed to be treated with whortleberries, blackberries, strawberries or apples, plums, peaches, etc., for they had planted a variety of fruit trees about them. But the girls went out to service, and the boys to sea, till not a soul is left. We scarcely see an Indian in a year. I remember the time when Indian murder, scalpings, depredations and conflagrations, were as frequent on the Eastern and Northern frontier of Massachusetts, as they are now in Indiana, and spread as much terror. But since the conquest of Canada, all has ceased; and I believe with you that another conquest of Canada will quiet the Indians forever, and be as great a blessing to them as to us.

The instance of Aaron Pomham made me suspect that there was an order of priesthood among them. But, according to your account, the worship of the good spirit was performed by the kings, sachems, and warriors, as among the ancient Germans, whose highest rank of nobility were priests.

I am, Sir, with an affectionate respect, yours,

John Adams

8. JOHN ADAMS TO THOMAS JEFFERSON
October 12, 1812

I have a curiosity to learn something of the character, life, and death of a gentleman, whose name was Wollaston,[20] who came from England with a company of a few dozen persons in the year 1622, took possession of a height on Massachusetts Bay, built houses there for his

---

20. Captain Wollaston, "a man of pretty parts," as described in chapter 19 of William Bradford's *Of Plymouth Plantation*.

people, and after looking about him and not finding the face of Nature smiling enough for him, went to Virginia to seek a better situation, leaving the government of his little band in the hands of Thomas Morton. As I have not found any account of him after his departure from his little flock in any history or record of New England, I should be very much obliged to you for any information you can give me of any notice that remains of him in Virginia.

My curiosity has been stimulated by an event of singular oddity. John Quincy Adams, at Berlin, purchased at an auction a volume containing three pamphlets bound together:

Woods Prospect, Wonder Working Providence of Zion's savior in New England, and The New English Canaan, or New Canaan, containing an Abstract of New England, composed in three books. The first book setting forth the Origin of the natives, their manners and customs together with their tractable nature and love towards the English. The second book setting forth the natural endowments of the country, and what staple commodities it yieldeth. The third book setting forth what people are planted there, their prosperity, what remarkable accidents have happened since the first planting of it, together with their tenets and practice of their Church.

"Written by Thomas Morton of Cliffords Inne Gentleman[21] upon ten years knowledge and experiment of the country." "Printed at Amsterdam by Jacob Frederick Stam in the year 1637." The book is dedicated to the commissioners of the privy council, for the government of all his Majesties foreign provinces.

To add a trifle to the whimsical circumstances attending the adventure of this volume, there are a few words in manuscript on a blank leaf, which, had it been in any other place, I should have sworn were in the handwriting of my father.

The design of the Writer appears to have been to promote two Objects:

---

21. Clifford's Inn was one of at least ten English inns, located near Chancery Lane. Societies of men in the legal profession would meet at inns like Clifford's and Furnival's.

1. To spread the fame and exaggerate the Advantages of New England;
2. To destroy the Characters of the English Inhabitants, and excite the Government to suppress the Puritans, and send over Settlers in their Stead, from among the Royalists and the disciples of Archbishop Laud.[22]

That such a Work had been written, has been known by tradition, and I have enquired for it, more than half a Century, but have never been able to learn that any Copy of it ever was seen in this Country. The Berlin Adventurer is I believe the only one in America. It is possible however that some straggling Copy of it may be in Virginia, and if you have ever seen or heard of it, I shall be obliged to you for the information.

I know not whether you have in your library, extensive and well chosen as it is, any of our New England Histories. If you have and feel any inclination to know any Thing of this Cliffords Inn man, this incendiary instrument of spiritual and temporal domination, you may find it in Neals Hist. New England III,[23]1. Hutchinson 8. 31,[24] Winthrop's Journal 20. 27. 321. 352,[25] 2 Belknap's Biography 332.[26]

He hints at his Objects in his Preface: "I have observed how diverse Persons not so well affected to the Weal public in mine Opinion, out of respect to their own private ends, have labored to keep, both the prac-

---

22. William Laud (1573–1645). Arminian appointed Archbishop of Canterbury and chief advisor of Charles I. He restored ritual and High Church beliefs to liturgy and persecuted Puritans and Presbyterians. He was impeached and executed for treason.

23. Daniel Neal (1678–1742). English clergymen who, in 1720, authored *The History of New England Containing an Impartial Account of the Civil and Ecclesiastical Affairs of the Colony to the Year 1700.*

24. Thomas Hutchinson was descended from Mrs. Anne Hutchinson, who was exiled from Massachusetts in 1638 because she defied the Puritan hierarchy. He published volume I of *History of the Colony of Massachusetts Bay* in 1764, volume II in 1767, and volume III in 1828.

25. One of three John Winthrops (1588–1649). He came to Salem in 1630 and founded Boston. He was also governor of Massachusetts Bay Colony and author of the journal *The History of New England.*

26. Jeremy Belknap (1744–1798). Massachusetts clergyman. In 1794 and 1798 he published two volumes of *American Biographies.*

tice of the People there, and the real worth of that eminent Country, concealed from public Knowledge, both which I have abundantly in this discourse laid open."

Sir Christopher Gardiner,[27] Knight, as he calls him, tho he was only a Cavalier of St. Iago de Compostella, a Roman Catholick and another Tool of Archbishop Laud as well as a Companion and fellow labourer in the pious Work of destroying the first Planters of Plymouth and Massachusetts: writes in laudem Authoris,[28] and in the despicable Verse of that Age:

> This Work a matchless mirror is that shows
> The humors of the Separatists, and those
> So truly personated by thy Pen,
> I was amaz'd to see it.
> Nothing but Opposition, 'gainst the Right
> Of sacred Majesty Men; full of Spight
> Goodness abusing, turning Virtue out
> Of doors, to whipping, Stocking, and full bent
> To plotting mischief 'gainst the innocent
> Burning their Houses, as if ordained by fate
> In Spight of Law to be made ruinate.

Another "In laudem Authoris, by F. C. Armiger" shows the high Church and high State Principles of this group of Laudians and their inveterate hatred of that Opposition to Priestcraft and Kingcraft which animated the first Settlers of New England:

---

27. When Puritans arrived in 1630, Gardiner was already present, living out of wedlock, and he had several wives in Europe. In addition, he was an agent for Ferdinado Gorges (Maine), who was trying to lay claim to Massachusetts. Gardiner was a member of the Knights of St. James, a Catholic organization named after James, the brother of Jesus. Legend has him buried in Compostela, Spain.

28. Francis Beaumont's sardonic tribute poem to Thomas Coryate (1577–1617), travel writer and autobiographer, *Coryats Crudites*. Coryate, a Protestant, on his travels through France, considered Catholic worship full of idolatry and superstition, that is, the "mutilated sacrament."

But that I rather pitty I confesse
The Practice of their Church, I could expresse
Myself a Satyrist, whose smarting fanges
Should strike it with a Palsy, and the Pangs
Beget a fear, to tempt the Majesty,
Of those, our mortal Gods, will they defy
The thundering Jove, like children they desire,
Such is their Zeal, to sport themselves with fire
So have I seen an angry fly presume
To strike a burning taper, and consume
His feeble Wings. Why is an Air so milde
Are they so monstrous grown up? and so vilde?
That Savages can of themselves espy
Their Errors, brand their names with infamy
What is their Zeale for blood, like Cyrus thirst
Will they be over head and ears accurst
A cruel Way to found a Church On? Noe
T'is not their Zeal, but fury blinds them so.
And pricks their malice on, like fire to joyne
And offer up the Sacrifice of Kain;
Jonas! thou hast done well, to call these men
Home, to repentance, with thy painful Pen.

Then comes the Authors prologue in a similar Strain of Panegyrick upon his New English Canaan and of Phillippic against the Inhabitants.

If Art and Industry should do as much
As Nature hath for Canaan, not such
Another place, for benefit and rest
In all the Universe can be possess'd
The more We prove it by discovery
The more delight each Object to the Eye
Discovers etc.

In page 15 is a high wrought Eulogium of Sir Ferdinand Gorges to whom he ascribes all the Glory of discovering and Settling in fine Country situated in the middle of the Golden mean, the temperate Zone. Then he discovers the wondrous Wisdom and love of God, in sending his Minister, the plague, among the Indians, to sweep away by heaps the Savages, and in giving Sir Ferdinando length of days, to see the same performed, after his enterprize was begun, for the propagation of the Church of Christ, i.e., as I understand him, the Church of Archbishop Laud and Sir Ferdinando Gorges.

In Chapter 2: p. 17, he says, "In the Year since the Incarnation of Christ 1622, it was my Chance to be landed in the parts of New England, where I found two Sorts of People, the one Christians, the other Infidels; these I found most full of humanity and more friendly than the other: as shall hereafter be made apparent in due course, by their several Actions from time to time, after my Arrival among them."

In no part of the Work has he said any thing of Mr. Wollaston, his Commander in Chief, to whom he was only second, in command of the Party. But it was of Wollaston I was most interested to enquire. I knew enough of Morton, and was therefore much disappointed in perusing the Book.

The Original Indian Name of the Spot possest by the Party was Passonagesset, but the People of the Company changed it to Mount Wollaston by which Name it has been called to this day. Morton, however, after the departure of his Leader for Virginia, chose to alter the Name, and call it Mare Mount from its Position near the Sea and commanding the prospect of Boston Harbour and Massachusetts Bay.

In his 132 page He gives us a History of the Ceremonies instituted by him in honor of this important Nomination. Several Songs were composed to be sung. A Pine Tree, Eighty feet long, was erected with a pair of Bucks Horns nailed on the Top. On May Day this mighty May Pole was drawn to its appointed Place on the Summit of the Hill by the help of Savages males and females, with Sound of Guns, Drums, Pistols and other Instruments of Musick.

A Barrel of excellent Beer was brewed, and a Case of Bottles (of

Brandy I suppose) with other good Cheer. English Men and Indians, Sannups and Squaws, danced and sang and reveled round the Maypole till Bacchus and Venus, I suppose, were satiated. The Separatists called it an Idol, the Calf of Horeb, Mount Dagon,[29] threatening to make it a woeful mount and not a merry Mount.

It is whimsical that this Book, so long lost, should be brought to me, for this Hill is in my Farm. There are curious Things in it, about the Indians and the Country. If you have any Inclination, I will send you more of them. Yours as Usual

John Adams

9. THOMAS JEFFERSON TO JOHN ADAMS
MONTICELLO, December 28, 1812

DEAR SIR,

An absence of five or six weeks, on a journey I take three or four times a year, must apologize for my late acknowledgment of your favor of October 12th. After getting through the mass of business which generally accumulates during my absence, my first attention has been bestowed on the subject of your letter. I turned to the passages you refer to in Hutchinson and Winthrop, and with the aid of their dates, I examined our historians to see if Wollaston's migration to this State was noticeably them.

It happens, unluckily, that Smith[30] and Stith,[31] who alone of them go into minute facts, bring their histories, the former only to 1623, and the latter to 1624. Wollaston's arrival in Massachusetts was in

---

29. Dagon was a Philistine god.

30. John Smith (1580–1631). English founder of Jamestown. In 1616 he published *A Description of New England*. He also wrote *A General History of Virginia, New England, and the Summer Isles*.

31. Rev. William Stith, who was connected with prominent persons in the Jamestown colony and had been president of William and Mary College. His *History of the First Discovery and Settlement of Virginia* was published in 1747.

1625, and his removal to this State was "some time" after. Beverly[32] & Keith,[33] who came lower down, are nearly superficial, giving nothing but those general facts which every one knew as well as themselves.

If our public records of that date were not among those destroyed by the British on their invasion of this State, they may possibly have noticed Wollaston. What I possessed in this way have been given out to two gentlemen, the one engaged in writing our history, the other in collecting our ancient laws; so that none of these resources are at present accessible to me.

Recollecting that Nathaniel Morton,[34] in his New England memorial, gives with minuteness the early annals of the colony of New Plymouth, and occasionally interweaves the occurrences of that on Massachusetts Bay, I recurred to him, and under the year 1628, I find he notices both Wollaston and Thomas Morton, and gives with respect to both, some details which are not in Hutchinson or Winthrop. As you do not refer to him, and so possibly may not have his book, I will transcribe from it the entire passage, which will prove at least my desire to gratify your curiosity as far as the materials within my power will enable me. Extract from Nathaniel Morton's New England's Memorial, pp. 93 to 99, Anno 1628:

"Whereas about three years before this time, there came over one Captain Wollaston, a man of considerable parts, and with him three or four more of some eminency who brought with them a great many servants, with provisions and other requisites for to begin a plantation,

---

32. Robert Beverley was a wealthy planter who saw while in London a poor account of the colony by the British historian and pamphleteer John Oldmixon and undertook to write a better one. His book, *A History of Virginia* (1705), was hastily prepared without any study of documents or other respectable sources. Its chief value lies in the shrewd and just observations the author made on Virginia life and history out of his own knowledge.

33. George Keith (1639?–1716). Wrote *New England's Spirit of Persecution Transmitted to Pennsilvania*.

34. Nathaniel Morton was a trusted nephew of Gov. William Bradford and became secretary of the Plymouth colony. In 1669 he published *New England's Memorial*, a history of the colony.

and pitched themselves in a place within the Massachusetts Bay, which they called afterwards by their captain's name, Mount Wollaston; which place is since called by the name of Braintry.

Amongst others that came with him, there was one Mr. Thomas Morton, who, it should seem, had some small adventure of his own or other men's amongst them, but had little respect, and was slighted by the meanest servants they kept. They having continued some time in New England, and not finding things to answer their expectation, nor profit to arise as they looked for, the said Captain Wollaston takes a great part of the servants and transports them to Virginia, and disposed of them there, and writes back to one Mr. Rasdale, one of his chief partners, (and accounted then merchant,) to bring another part of them to Virginia, likewise intending to put them off there as he had done the rest; and he, with the consent of the said Rasdale, appointed one whose name was Filcher, to be his Lieutenant, and to govern the remainder of the plantation until he or Rasdale should take further order thereabout.

But the aforesaid Morton, (having more craft than honesty,) having been a petty-fogger[35] at Furnival's Inn, he, in the other's absence, watches an opportunity, (commons being put hard among them,) and got some strong drink and other junkets, and made them a feast, and after they were merry, he began to tell them he would give them good counsel. 'You see,' he says, 'that many of your fellows are carried to Virginia, and if you stay still until Rasdale's return, you will also be carried away and sold for slaves with the rest. Therefore I would advise you to thrust out Lieutenant Filcher, and I having a part in the plantation, will receive you as my partners, and consociates, so you may be free from service, and we will converse, plant, trade and live together as equals (or to the like effect).'

This counsel was easily followed; so they took opportunity, and thrust Lieutenant Filcher out of doors, and would not suffer him to come any more amongst them, but forced him to seek bread to eat and other necessaries amongst his neighbors, till he would get passage for England. (See the sad effect of want of good government.)

---

35. A petty-fogger is an unscrupulous/shyster lawyer. In this case, the attorney belongs to a legal society of England's Furnival Inn.

After this they fell to great licentiousness of life, in all prophaneness, and the said Morton became lord of misrule, and maintained (as it were) a school of Atheism, and after they had got some goods into their hands, and got much by trading with the Indians, they spent it as vainly, in quaffing and drinking both wine and strong liquors in great excess, (as some have reported,) ten pounds worth in a morning, setting up a May pole, drinking and dancing about like so many fairies, or furies rather, yea and worse practices, as if they had anew revived and celebrated the feast of the Roman goddess Flora, or the beastly practices of the mad Bacchanalians.

The said Morton likewise to show his poetry, composed sundry rhymes and verses, some tending to licentiousness, and others to the detraction and scandal of some persons' names, which he affixed to his idle or idol May-pole; they changed also the name of their place, and instead of calling it Mount Wollaston, they called it the Merry Mount, as if this jollity would have lasted always. But this continued not long, for shortly after that worthy gentleman Mr. John Endicott, who brought over a patent under the broad seal of England for the government of the Massachusetts, visiting those parts, caused that Maypole to be cut down, and rebuked them for their prophaneness, and admonished them to look to it that they walked better; so the name was again changed and called Mount Dagon.

Now to maintain this riotous prodigality and profuse expense, the said Morton thinking himself lawless, and hearing what gain the fishermen made of trading of pieces, powder, and shot, he as head of this consortship, began the practice of the same in these parts; and first he taught the Indians how to use them, to charge and discharge 'em, and what proportion of powder to give the piece, according to the size of bigness of the same, and what shot to use for fowl, and what for deer; and having instructed them, he employed some of them to hunt and fowl for him; so as they became somewhat more active in that employment than any of the English, by reason of their swiftness of foot, and nimbleness of body, being also quick-sighted, and by continual exercise, well knowing the haunt of all sorts of game; so as when they saw the execution that a piece would do, and the benefit that might come by the same, they became very eager after them, and would not stick to give any price they could attain to for them; accounting their bows and arrows but baubles in comparison of them.

And here we may take occasion to bewail the mischief which came by this wicked man, and others like unto him; in that notwithstanding laws for the restraint of selling ammunition to the natives, that so far base covetousness prevailed, and doth still prevail, as that the Savages became amply furnished with guns, powder, shot, rapiers, pistols, and also well skilled in repairing of defective arms: yea some have not spared to tell them how gunpowder is made, and all the materials in it, and they are to be had in their own land; and would (no doubt, in case they could attain to the making of Saltpeter) teach them to make powder, and what mischief may fall out unto the English in these parts thereby, let this pestilent fellow Morton (aforenamed) bear a great part of the blame and guilt of it to future generations.

But lest I should hold the reader too long in relation to the particulars of his vile actings; when as the English that then lived up and down about the Massachusetts, and in other places, perceiving the sad consequences of his trading, so as the Indians became furnished with the English arms and ammunition, and expert in the improving of them, and fearing that they should at one time or another get a blow thereby; and also taking notice, that if he were let alone in his way, they should keep no servants for him, because he would entertain any, how vile so ever, sundry of the chief of the straggling plantations met together, and agreed by mutual consent to send to Plimouth, who were then of more strength to join with them, to suppress this mischief; who considering the particulars proposed to them to join together to take some speedy course to prevent (if it might be) the evil that was accruing towards them; and resolved first to admonish him of his wickedness respecting the premises, laying before him the injury he did to their common safety, and that his acting considering the same was against the King's proclamation; but he insolently persisted on in his way, and said the King was dead, and his displeasure with him, and threatened them that if they come to molest him, they should look to themselves.

So that they saw that there was no way but to take him by force; so they resolved to proceed in such a way, and obtained of the Governor of Plymouth to send Capt. Standish[36] and some other aid with him, to take the said Morton by force, the which accordingly was done; but they found him to stand stiffly on his defense, having made fast his doors, armed his consorts, set powder and shot ready upon the table; scoffed and scorned at them, he and his complices being filled with strong drink, were desperate in their way; but he himself coming out of doors to make a shot at Capt. Standish, he stepping to him put by his piece and took him, and so little hurt was done; and so he was brought prisoner to Plymouth, and continued in durance till an opportunity of sending him for England, which was done at their common charge, and letters also with him, to the honorable council for New England, and returned again into the country in some short time, with less punishment than his demerits deserved (as was apprehended).

The year following he was again apprehended, and sent for England, where he lay a considerable time in Exeter jail; for besides his miscarriage here in New England, he was suspected to have murdered a man that had ventured monies with him when he came first into New England; and a warrant was sent over from the Lord Chief Justice to apprehend him, by virtue whereof, he was by the Governor of Massachusetts sent into England, and for other of his misdemeanors amongst them in that government, they demolished his house, that it might no longer be a roost for such unclean birds.

Notwithstanding he got free in England again, and wrote an infamous and scurrilous book against many godly and chief men of the country, full of lies and slanders, and full fraught with prophane calumnies against their names and persons, and the way of God. But to the intent I may not trouble the reader any more with mentioning of him in this history; in fine, sundry years after he came again into the country, and was imprisoned at Boston for the aforesaid book and other things, but denied sundry things therein, affirming his book was adulterated. And soon after being grown old in wickedness, at last

---

36. Captain Miles Standish, assistant governor and treasurer of the Plymouth colony.

ended his life at Piscataqua. But I fear I have held the reader too long about so unworthy a person, but hope it may be useful to take notice how wickedness was beginning, and would have further proceeded, had it not been prevented timely."

So far, Nathaniel Morton, the copy you have of Thomas Morton's New English Canaan, printed in 1637 by Stam of Amsterdam, was a second edition of that "infamous and scurrilous book against the godly." The first had been printed in 1632, by Charles Green, in a quarto of 188 pages, and is the one alluded to by N. Morton. Both of them made a part of the American library given by White Kennett in 1713 to the Society for the propagation of the Gospel in foreign parts. This society being a chartered one, still, as I believe, existing, and probably their library also, I suppose that these and the other books of that immense collection, the catalogue of which occupies 275 pages quarto, are still to be found with them. If any research I can hereafter make should ever bring to my knowledge anything more of Wollaston, I shall not fail to communicate it to you.

Ever and affectionately yours,

Thomas Jefferson

10.   THOMAS JEFFERSON TO JOHN ADAMS
   MONTICELLO, May 27, 1813

Another of our friends of seventy-six is gone, my dear sir, another of the co-signers of the Independence of our country. And a better man than Rush[37] could not have left us, more benevolent, more learned, of finer genius, or more honest. We too must go; and that ere long. I believe we are under half a dozen at present; I mean the signers of the Declaration. Yourself, Gerry, Carroll, and myself, are all I know to be living. I am the only one south of the Potomac. Is Robert Treat Payne

---

37. Dr. Benjamin Rush (1746–1813). Mainly responsible for the 1812 renewal of Adams-Jefferson correspondence. A Founder of the Philadelphia Bible Society, his works include *Essays, Literary, Moral, and Philosophical* (1798) and *Medical Enquiries and Observations upon the Diseases of the Mind* (1812).

or Floyd living? It is long since I heard of them, and yet I do not recollect to have heard of their deaths.

Morton's deduction of the origin of our Indians from the fugitive Trojans, stated in your letter of January the 26th, and his manner of accounting for the sprinkling of their Latin with Greek, is really amusing. Adair makes them talk Hebrew. Reinold Forster[38] derives them from the soldiers sent by Kouli Khan to conquer Japan. Brerewood,[39] from the Tartars, as well as our bears, wolves, foxes, etc., which, he says, "must of necessity fetch their beginning from Noah's ark, which rested, after the deluge in Asia, seeing they could not proceed by the course of nature, as the imperfect sort of living creatures do, from putrefaction." Bernard Romans[40] is of opinion that God created an original man and woman in this part of the globe. Doctor Barton[41] thinks they are not specifically different from the Persians; but taking afterwards a broader range, he thinks, "that in all the vast countries of America, there is but one language, nay, that it may be proven, or rendered highly probable, that all the languages of the earth bear some affinity together."

This reduces it to a question of definition, in which every one is free to use his own: to wit, what constitutes identity, or difference in two things, in the common acceptation of sameness? All languages may be called the same, as being all made up of the same primitive sounds, expressed by the letters of the different alphabets. But, in this sense, all things on earth are the same as consisting of matter. This

38. *Travels into North America* (1722) by Peter Kalm. Translated into English by John Reinhold Forster.

39. In 1614 Edward Brerewood, an English scholar, also noted similarities between Asian Mongols and Native Americans. He believed in a migration from northeast Asia by way of "some narrow channel of the ocean."

40. Military engineer and cartographer who wrote *A Concise Natural History of East and West Florida* (1775). Romans posited a separate creation for American Indians.

41. Benjamin Smith Barton. Wrote *Observations on Some Parts of Natural History* (London, 1787), *New Views on the Origin of the Tribes of America* (1797), *Elements of Botany* (Philadelphia, 1803; 2nd ed., 2 vols., 1812–1814), and an edition of Cullen's *Materia Medica, . . . Eulogy on Dr. Priestley.*

gives up the useful distribution into genera and species, which we form, arbitrarily indeed, for the relief of our imperfect memories.

To aid the question, from whence our Indian tribes descended, some have gone into their religion, their morals, their manners, customs, habits, and physical forms. By such helps it may be learnedly proved, that our trees and plants of every kind are descended from those of Europe, because, like them, they have no locomotion, they draw nourishment from the earth, they clothe themselves with leaves in spring, of which they divest themselves in autumn for the sleep of winter, etc. Our animals too must be descended from those of Europe, because our wolves eat lambs, our deer are gregarious, our ants hoard, etc.

But, when for convenience we distribute languages, according to common understanding, into classes originally different, as we choose to consider them, as the Hebrew, the Greek, the Celtic, the Gothic; and these again into genera, or families, as the Icelandic, German, Swedish, Danish, English, and these last into species, or dialects, as English, Scotch, Irish, we then ascribe other meanings to the terms "same" and "different." In some one of these senses, Barton, and Adair, and Forster, and Brerewood, and Morton, may be right, every one according to his own definition of what constitutes "identity." Romans, indeed, takes a higher stand and supposes a separate creation. On the same unscriptural ground, he had but to mount one step higher, to suppose no creation at all, but that all things have existed without beginning in time, as they now exist, and may forever exist, producing and reproducing in a circle, without end. This would very summarily dispose of Mr. Morton's learning, and show that the question of Indian origin, like many others, pushed to a certain height must receive the same answer, "Ignoro."

You ask if the usage of hunting in circles has ever been known among any of our tribes of Indians. It has been practiced by them all; and is to this day, by those still remote from the settlements of the whites. But their numbers not enabling them, like Genghis Khan's seven hundred thousand, to form themselves into circles of one hundred miles diameter, they make their circle by firing the leaves fallen on the ground, which gradually forcing the animals to a centre, they there slaughter them with arrows, darts, and other missiles. This is called fire hunting, and has been practiced in this State within my time, by the white inhabitants. This is the most probable cause of the origin and extension of the vast prairies in the western country, where the grass having been of extraordinary luxuriance, has made a conflagration sufficient to kill even the old as well as the young timber.

Thomas Jefferson

11. JOHN ADAMS TO THOMAS JEFFERSON
QUINCY, May 29, 1813

DEAR SIR,

To leave the Pettifogger of Furnivals Inn, or Cliffords Inn, his Archbishop Laud, and his Chevalier of St. Iago of Compostella, Sir Christopher Gardiner, for the present; Paulo Multo majora canamus.[42]

There has been put into my hands, within a few days a gross Volume in octavo, of 544 Pages, with the Title of "Memoirs of the late reverend Theophilus Lindsey, M. A."[43] including a brief "Analysis of his Works; together with Anecdotes and Letters of eminent Persons, his Friends and Correspondents: also a general View of the progress of the Unitarian doctrine in England and America. By Thomas Belsham,[44] Minister of the Chapel in Essex Street [London, 1812]."

Whether you have seen this Work, I know not. But this I know, the Author, and his Friends ought to have sent you a Copy of it; and therefore I conclude they have.

---

42. "Let us chant of the highest things." A poem by William Walsh (1663–1708) in imitation of Vergil's fourth pastoral, supposed to have been taken from Sybelline prophecy. Reference to Laud: "a high church progeny from heaven descends."

43. Theophilus Lindsey. Unitarian minister.

44. Thomas Belsham (1750–1829). English Unitarian minister. Published *Lindsey's Memoirs*. He was a colleague of Joseph Priestley and pastor of Essex Street Chapel (1805–1829), a chapel attended by John Adams. Wrote *Evidences of Christianity*, *Epistles of St. Paul*, and *Elements/Philosophy of the Human Mind*.

With Lindsey, Disney, Price,[45] Priestley, Jebb, Kippis[46] etc. and their Connections, whom I could name, I was much Acquainted in London from 1785 to 1788. These Characters, with Cappe,[47] Farmer,[48] and a multitude of others, figure in this Work.

The Religion, the Philosophy, the Morality, the Politicks which these People teach, have been Objects of my anxious Attention for more than Three Score Years, as I could demonstrate to you, if I could give you a brief Sketch of my Life. But my Life has been too trifling and my Actions too insignificant for me to write or the Public to read. In my wandering romantic Life, with my incessant Res angusta Domi,[49] and my numerous unfortunate Family, of Children and Grand Children without the honour, which you have attained of being a great grandfather, tho' I have a near prospect of it; it has been impossible for me to pursue such Inquiries with any thing like Learning.

What may be the Effect, of these "Memoirs" in the U.S. if they should become public I know not; and I will add I care not, for I wish every Subject to be discussed at all Events. The human Mind is awake: Let it not Sleep. Let it however consider. Let it think, Let it pause.

This Work must produce a noise in U.S. Fiat Justitia ["Let justice be done"]. The 12th. Article in the Appendix is "Letters from Dr. Priestley to Mr. Lindsey: and from Thomas Jefferson Esq. President of the United States to Dr. Priestley. p. 525." The first Letter from you is

---

45. Richard Price (1723–1791). English minister. Author of *Review of the Principal Questions of Morals* (1758) and *The Evidence for a Future Period of Improvement in the State of Mankind* (1787). He was a friend to Joseph Priestley and Mary Wollstonecraft (1759–1797) (who authored *Vindication of the Rights of Man* and *Vindication of the Rights of Women*). Price was a member of Unitarian Society, but could not question the divinity of Jesus.

46. Andrew Kippis (1778–1793). Author of *Essays on the Case of Balaam*.

47. Catherine Cappe (1744–1821). Unitarian philanthropist and author of *Observations on Charity Schools, Female Friendly Societies, and Other Subjects*.

48. Hugh Farmer (1714–1787?). Wrote *An Inquiry into the Nature and Design of Christ's Temptation in the Wilderness, Essay on the Demoniacs of the New Testament* (1775) and *The General Prevalence of the Worship of Human Spirits in the Ancient Heathen Nations, Asserted and Proved* (1783).

49. Limited means/narrowed circumstances at home.

dated March 21, 1801, at Washington. The second April 9, 1803, at Washington. Dr. Priestley's Letter to Mr. Lindsey, containing remarks upon Mr. Jeffersons Letter is dated Northumberland April 23, 1803.

I wish to know, if you have seen this Book. I have much to say on the Subject. And you may depend upon it, I will discuss the Subject with as much Candour, as much Friendship, as much Freedom, as Price, Priestley, Lindsey, Cappe or Farmer ever displayed in their Controversies. I have not time to enlarge at present.

I will only Add, have you seen the Naval History by Mr. Clark, published by Mathew Carey at Philadelphia? I wish I had time and Eyes and fingers to write much to you on this Subject.

I lament the death of my dear Friend of 38 Years, Dr. Benjamin Rush, much the more since I have seen Lindseys Memoirs. I am, with unalterable Esteem and Affection your old Friend

John Adams

12. JOHN ADAMS TO THOMAS JEFFERSON
QUINCY, June 10, 1813

DEAR SIR,

In your Letter to Dr. Priestley of March 21, 1801, you ask "What an Effort of Bigotry in politics and religion have We gone through! The barbarians really flattered themselves, they should be able to bring back the times of Vandalism, when ignorance put every thing into the hands of power and priestcraft. All Advances in Science were proscribed as innovations; they pretended to praise and encourage education, but it was to be the education of our ancestors; We were to look backwards, not forwards, for improvement; *the President himself* declaring, in one of his Answers to addresses, that We were never to expect to go beyond them in real Science." I shall stop here. Other parts of this Letter, may hereafter be considered if I can keep the Book long enough: but only four Copies have arrived in Boston, and they have spread terror, as yet, however in secret.

"The President himself declaring, that 'We were never to expect to go beyond them in real Science.'" This Sentence shall be the theme of the present Letter.

I would ask, what President is meant? I remember no such Sentiment in any of Washingtons Answers to addresses. I, myself must have been mean'd. Now I have no recollection of any such Sentiment ever issued from my Pen, or my tongue, or of any such thought in my heart for, at least sixty Years of my past life. I should be obliged to you, for the Words of any Answer of mine, that you have thus misunderstood. A man of 77 or 78 cannot commonly be expected to recollect promptly every passage of his past life, or every trifle he has written. Much less can it be expected of me, to recollect every Expression of every Answer to an Address, when for six months together, I was compelled to answer Addresses of all Sorts from all quarters of the Union. My private Secretary has declared that he has copied fifteen Answers from me in one morning. The greatest Affliction, distress, confusion of my Administration arose from the necessity of receiving and Answering those Addresses. Richard Cromwells Trunk, did not contain so many of the Lives and Fortunes of the English Nati[on] as mine of those in the United States. For the hon[or] of my Country I wish these Addresses and Answers [to be] annihilated. For my own Character and repu[tation I] wish every Word of every Address and every Answer were published.

The Sentiment, that you have attributed to me in your letter to Dr. Priestley I totally disclaim and demand in the French sense of the word demand of you the proof. It is totally incongruous to every principle of my mind and every Sentiment of my heart for Threescore Years at least.

You may expect, many more expostulations from one who has loved and esteemed you for Eight and thirty Years.

John Adams

When this Letter was ready to go, I recd your favour of May 27th. came to hand, I can only thank you for it, at present.

13. JOHN ADAMS TO THOMAS JEFFERSON
QUINCY, June 11, 1813

DEAR SIR,

I received yesterday your favour of May 27th. I lament with you the loss of Rush. I know of no Character living or dead, who has done more real good in America. Robert Treat Paine still lives, at 83 or 84, alert, droll, and witty, though deaf. Floyd, I believe, yet remains. Paine must be very great; Philosopher and Christian; to live under the Afflictions of his Family.

Sons and Daughters with Genius and qualities and Connections and prospects the most pleasing, have been signally unfortunate. A Son, whose name was altered, from Thomas to Robert Treat has left a Volume of Prose and Verse, which will attract the Attention of Posterity to his Father, more than his Signature of Independence. It is the History of a Poet, in Genius Excentricity, Irregularity Misfortune and Misery, equal to most in Johnsons Lives.

To your ignoro, I add non curo. I should as soon suppose that the Prodigal Son, in a frolic with one of his Girls made a trip to America in one of Mother Careys Eggshels, and left the fruits of their Amours here, as believe any of the grave hypotheses and solemn reasonings of Philosophers or Divines upon the Subject of the peopling of America. If my Faith in Moses or Noah depended on any of these Speculations, I would give it up.

John Adams

14. THOMAS JEFFERSON TO JOHN ADAMS
MONTICELLO, June 15, 1813

DEAR SIR,

I wrote you a letter on the 27th of May, which probably would reach you about the 3d instant, and on the 9th I received yours of the 29th of

May. Of Lindsay's Memoirs, I had never before heard, and scarcely indeed of himself. It could not, therefore, but be unexpected, that two letters of mine should have anything to do with his life. The name of his editor was new to me, and certainly presents itself for the first time under unfavorable circumstances. Religion, I suppose, is the scope of his book; and that a writer on that subject should usher himself to the world in the very act of the grossest abuse of confidence, by publishing private letters which passed between two friends, with no views to their ever being made public, is an instance of inconsistency as well as of infidelity, of which I would rather be the victim than the author.

By your kind quotation of the dates of my two letters, I have been enabled to turn to them. They had completely vanished from my memory. The last is on the subject of religion, and by its publication will gratify the priesthood with new occasion of repeating their comminations against me. They wish it to be believed that he can have no religion who advocates its freedom. This was not the doctrine of Priestley; and I honored him for the example of liberality he set to his order. The first letter is political. It recalls to our recollection the gloomy transactions of the times, the doctrines they witnessed, and the sensibilities they excited. It was a confidential communication of reflections on these from one friend to another, deposited in his bosom, and never meant to trouble the public mind.

Whether the character of the times is justly portrayed or not, posterity will decide. But on one feature of them they can never decide, the sensations excited in free yet firm minds by the terrorism of the day. None can conceive who did not witness them, and they were felt by one party only. This letter exhibits their side of the medal. The federalists, no doubt, have presented the other in their private correspondences as well as open action. If these correspondences should ever be laid open to the public eye, they will probably be found not models of comity towards their adversaries. The readers of my letter should be cautioned not to confine its view to this country alone. England and its alarmists were equally under consideration.

Still less must they consider it as looking personally towards you. You happen, indeed, to be quoted, because you happened to express more pithily than had been done by themselves, one of the mottoes of the party. This was in your answer to the address of the young men of Philadelphia. One of the questions, you know, on which our parties took different sides, was on the improvability of the human mind in science, in ethics, in government, etc.

Those who advocated reformation of institutions, pari passu with the progress of science, maintained that no definite limits could be assigned to that progress. The enemies of reform, on the other hand, denied improvement, and advocated steady adherence to the principles, practices and institutions of our fathers, which they represented as the consummation of wisdom, and acme of excellence, beyond which the human mind could never advance.

Although in the passage of your answer alluded to, you expressly disclaim the wish to influence the freedom of inquiry, you predict that that will produce nothing more worthy of transmission to posterity than the principles, institutions and systems of education received from their ancestors. I do not consider this as your deliberate opinion. You possess, yourself, too much science, not to see how much is still ahead of you, unexplained and unexplored. Your own consciousness must place you as far before our ancestors as in the rear of our posterity. I consider it as an expression lent to the prejudices of your friends; and although I happened to cite it from you, the whole letter shows I had them only in view.

In truth, my dear Sir, we were far from considering you as the author of all the measures we blamed. They were placed under the protection of your name, but we were satisfied they wanted much of your approbation. We ascribed them to their real authors, the Pickerings, the Wolcotts, the Tracys, the Sedgwicks,[50] and all of their kind, with whom we supposed you in a state of duress. I well remember a conversation with you in the morning of the day on which you nominated to the Senate a substitute for Pickering, in which you expressed a just impa-

---

50. Timothy Pickering, Oliver Wolcott, Uriah Tracy, and Theodore Sedgewick. They were Adams's Federalist political opponents, though not always known by Adams as such. Pickering and Sedgewick were members of Essex Junto, a group of Eastern secessionists.

tience under "the legacy of secretaries which General Washington had left you," and whom you seemed, therefore, to consider as under public protection. Many other incidents showed how differently you would have acted with less impassioned advisers; and subsequent events have proved that your minds were not together. You would do me great injustice, therefore, by taking to yourself what was intended for men who were then your secret, as they are now your open enemies. Should you write on the subject, as you propose, I am sure we shall see you place yourself farther from them than from us.

As to myself, I shall take no part in any discussions. I leave others to judge of what I have done, and to give me exactly that place which they shall think I have occupied. Marshall[51] has written libels on one side; others, I suppose, will be written on the other side; and the world will sift both and separate the truth as well as they can. I should see with reluctance the passions of that day rekindled in this, while so many of the actors are living, and all are too near the scene not to participate in sympathies with them. About facts you and I cannot differ; because truth is our mutual guide. And if any opinions you may express should be different from mine, I shall receive them with the liberality and indulgence which I ask for my own, and still cherish with warmth the sentiments of affectionate respect, of which I can with so much truth tender you the assurance.

Thomas Jefferson

15. JOHN ADAMS TO THOMAS JEFFERSON
June 25, 1813

Be not surprised or alarmed. Lindseys Memoirs will do no harm to you or me. You have the right and reason to feel and to resent the breach of confidence. I have had enough of the same kind of treachery and perfidy practiced upon me, to know how to sympathize with you. I will agree with you in unqualified censure of such abuses. They are

---

51. John Marshall, Supreme Court chief justice and George Washington biographer. He ruled against President Jefferson in the Burr Conspiracy case.

the worst species of tyranny over private judgment and free inquiry. They suppress the free communication of soul to soul.

There are critical moments when faction, whether in Church or State will stick at nothing. Confidence of friendship the most sacred is but a cobweb tie. How few! Oh, how few are the exceptions! I could name many cases of the rule. . . . My reputation has been so much the sport of the public for fifty years and will be for posterity, that I hold it a bubble, a gossamer, that idles in the wanton summer air.

I wish you could live a year in Boston, hear the Divines, read their publications, especially the Repository. You would see how spiritual tyranny and ecclesiastical domination are beginning in our country: at least struggling for birth.

Now, for your political letter. No, I have not done with spiritual pride in high places and low. I would trust these liberal Christians in London and in Boston with power just as soon as I would Calvin[52] or Cardinal Lorrain;[53] just as soon as I would the Quakers of Pennsylvania; just as soon as I would the Methodists or Moravians;[54] just as soon as I would Rochefoucault[55] and Condorcet; just as soon as I would the Economists of France; just as soon as I would Bolingbroke[56] and Voltaire,[57] Hume,[58] and Gibbon;[59] nay just as soon as I

52. John Calvin (1509–1564). Founder of Calvinistic Protestantism. He believed in predestination and focused on man's depravity.

53. In 1562 Lorrain proposed a Catholic holy league whose members were to defend the Church by all means and at any cost from Protestants, such as the Hugenots.

54. Protestant sect founded by John Hus in 1457.

55. François, Duc de la Rochefoucauld (1613–1680). Wrote *Maxims and Moral Reflections*, published in 1663 and 1665.

56. Viscount Henry St. John Bolingbroke (1678–1751). English statesman. Used Conformity and Schism acts to weaken Whig opponents. Wrote *Letters on the Study and Use of History* (1735–1736) and *Idea of a Patriot King* (1749).

57. Pen name of François-Marie Arouet (1694–1778). French writer and historian. His *Letters Concerning the English Nation* praised religious and political toleration. He was a friend to Frederick the Great and a contributor to Diderot's *Encylopedia*.

58. David Hume (1711–1776). Scottish Enlightenment philosopher. Wrote *Dialogues Concerning Natural Religion* and *Treatise on Human Nature*.

59. Edward Gibbon (1737–1794). Author of *History of the Decline and Fall of the Roman Empire*, a work considered skeptical of Christianity.

would Robespierre[60] or Brissot.[61] I can go no higher, unless I add the League[62] and the Fronde[63] in France, or Charles the First and the Archbishop Laud in England and Ireland.

Checks and Balances, Jefferson, however you and your Party may have ridiculed them, are our only security for the progress of Mind, as well as security of body. Every species of these Christians would persecute Deists,[64] as soon as either sect would persecute another, if it had unchecked and unbalanced power. Nay, the Deists would persecute Christians, and Atheists would persecute Deists, with as unrelenting cruelty, as any Christians would persecute them or one another. Know thyself, human nature!

John Adams

16. JOHN ADAMS TO THOMAS JEFFERSON
QUINCY, June 28, 1813

DEAR SIR,

It is very true that the denunciations of the priesthood are fulminated against every advocate for a complete freedom of religion. Comminations, I believe, would be plenteously pronounced by even the most liberal of them, against Atheism, Deism, against every man who disbelieved or doubted the resurrection of Jesus, or the miracles of the New Testament. Priestley himself would denounce the man who

---

60. Maximilien François Marie Isodore de Robespierre (1758–1794). Idealist leader of French Revolution's Jacobins. He initiated Reign of Terror mass executions of Girondins and other political/religious opponents in an effort to establish a Reign of Virtue. He was arrested, tried, and executed after also introducing new religious cult of the "Supreme Being."

61. Jacques Pierre Brissot, de Warville (1754–1793). French Girondist, executed during Reign of Terror.

62. See Cardinal Lorraine, footnote 53.

63. Series of uprisings against the French crown (1648–1653).

64. Believed in a Creator God, but rejected providence, revelation, and the supernatural. Truth was to be known through reason and nature.

should deny the Apocalypse, or the Prophecies of Daniel. Priestley and Lindsay both have denounced as idolaters and blasphemers all the Trinitarians, and even the Arians.[65]

Poor weak man, when will thy perfection arrive? Thy perfectibility I shall not deny; for a greater character than Priestley or Godwin[66] has said, "Be ye perfect," etc. For my part I can not deal damnation round the land on all I judge the foes of God and man. But I did not intend to say a word on this subject in this letter. As much of it as you please hereafter, but let me return to politics. With some difficulty I have hunted up, or down, the "address of the young men of the city of Philadelphia, the district of Southwark, and the Northern Liberties," and the answer.[67]

The addresses say, "Actuated by the SAME PRINCIPLES on which our forefathers achieved their independence, the recent attempts of a foreign power to derogate from the dignity and rights of our country, awaken our liveliest sensibility, and our strongest indignation."

Huzza, my brave boys! Could Thomas Jefferson or John Adams hear those words with insensibility, and without emotion? These boys afterwards add, "We regard our liberty and independence as the richest portion given us by our ancestors."

And who were those ancestors? Among them were Thomas Jefferson and John Adams. And I very coolly believe that no two men among those ancestors did more towards it than those two. Could either hear this like statues? If, one hundred years hence, your letters and mine should see the light, I hope the reader will hunt up this address, and read it all; and remember that we were then engaged, or on the point of engaging, in a war with France. I shall not repeat the

---

65. Followers of Arianism, which held that Christ was not coequal and coeternal with God the Father. Named after Arian, a fourth-century CE Alexandrian priest.

66. William Godwin (1756–1836). English political theorist and novelist who rejected all government as corrupting. He expressed his belief that humans are rational beings able to live without laws and institutions. Wrote *Enquiry Concerning Political Justice* (1793).

67. The May 1798 published letter from the youth of Philadelphia to President John Adams concerning the threat of war with France, followed on May 7, 1798, by Adams's answer.

answer till we come to the paragraph upon which you criticized to Dr.
Priestley, though every word of it is true, and I now rejoice to see it
recorded, and though I had wholly forgotten it.

The paragraph is, "Science and morals are the great pillars on
which this country has been raised to its present population, opulence
and prosperity, and these alone can advance, support, and preserve it.
Without wishing to damp the ardor of curiosity, or influence the
freedom of inquiry, I will hazard a prediction that, after the most
industrious and impartial researches, the longest liver of you all will
find no principles, institutions, or systems of education more fit, IN
GENERAL, to be transmitted to your posterity than those you have
received from your ancestors."

Now, compare the paragraph in the answer with the paragraph in
the address, as both are quoted above, and see if we can find the extent
and the limits of the meaning of both.

Who composed that army of fine young fellows that was then
before my eyes? There were among them Roman Catholics, English
Episcopalians, Scotch and American Presbyterians, Methodists, Moravians, Anabaptists, German Lutherans, German Calvinists, Universalists,[68] Arians, Priestleyans, Socinians,[69] Independents, Congregation-
alists, Horse Protestants and House Protestants,[70] Deists and Atheists;
and "Protestans qui ne croyent rien [Protestants who believe
nothing]." Very few however of several of these species. Nevertheless,
all educated in the GENERAL PRINCIPLES of Christianity; and the
general principles of English and American liberty.

Could my answer be understood by any candid reader or hearer, to
recommend to all the others the general principles, institutions, or systems of education of the Roman Catholics? Or those of the Quakers?
Or those of the Presbyterians? Or those of the Menonists? Or those of

---

68. Religious sect that believes that all people will be saved and that Hell does
not exist.

69. Socinianism was the sixteenth-century religious doctrine developed in
Poland by Italians Laelius Socinus and his nephew Faustus. It rejected the idea of
Trinity and the divinity of Jesus.

70. Itinerant, circuit-riding Protestants versus meetinghouse Protestants.

the Methodists? Or those of the Moravians? Or those of the Universalists? Or those of the Philosophers? No.

The GENERAL PRINCIPLES, on which the fathers achieved independence, were the only principles in which that beautiful assembly of young gentlemen could unite, and these principles only could be intended by them in their address, or by me in my answer.

And what were these GENERAL PRINCIPLES? I answer, the general principles of Christianity, in which all those sects were united; and the GENERAL PRINCIPLES of English and American liberty, in Which all these young men united, and Which had united all parties in America, in majorities sufficient to assert and maintain her independence.

Now I will avow that I then believed, and now believe, that those general principles of Christianity are as eternal and immutable as the existence and attributes of God; and that those principles of liberty are as unalterable as human nature, and our terrestrial mundane system. I could, therefore safely say, consistently with all my then and present information that I believed they would never make discoveries in contradiction to these GENERAL PRINCIPLES. In favor of these GENERAL PRINCIPLES in philosophy, religion and government, I would fill sheets of quotations from Frederick of Prussia, from Hume, Gibbon, Bolingbroke, Rousseau[71] and Voltaire, as well as Newton[72] and Locke;[73] not to mention thousands of divines and philosophers of inferior fame.

I might have flattered myself that my sentiments were sufficiently known to have protected me against suspicions of narrow thoughts,

---

71. Jean Jacques Rousseau (1712–1778). Authored essays on how arts and sciences corrupt human behavior. Wrote *Origin of the Inequality of Man* in 1755 and *The Social Contract* in 1762, laying out an authoritarian premise that religion exists for state purposes and detailing punishments for heretics of his secular church.

72. Isaac Newton (1642–1726). Philosopher-scientist who wrote theological and scientific treatises. Arian in his approach, Newton viewed the world as having divine origin or creation, with that creator playing an active, ongoing role in Nature.

73. John Locke (1632–1704). English philosopher. Wrote *Essay Concerning Human Nature* (1690), stressing the limitations of human knowledge; *A Letter Concerning Toleration* (1689); and *The Reasonableness of Christianity* (1695). He valued ethics of religion rather than dogmas and ceremonies.

contracted sentiments, bigoted, enthusiastic, or superstitious principles, civil, political, philosophical, or ecclesiastical. The first sentence of the preface to my defense of the constitution, volume 1st, printed in 1787, is in these words:

"The arts and sciences, in general, during the three or four last centuries, have had a regular course of progressive improvement. The inventions in mechanic arts, the discoveries in natural philosophy, navigation, and commerce, and the advancement of civilization and humanity, have occasioned changes in the condition of the world and the human character, which would have astonished the most refined nations of antiquity, etc."

I will quote no farther; but request you to read again that whole page, and then say whether the writer of it could be suspected of recommending to youth "to look backward instead of forward" for instruction and improvement.

This letter is already too long. In my next I shall consider the Terrorism of the day. Meantime I am, as ever, your friend.

John Adams

17. JOHN ADAMS TO THOMAS JEFFERSON
QUINCY, June 30, 1813

DEAR SIR,

But to return for the present to "The sensations excited in free, yet firm minds by the Terrorism of the day." You say none can conceive them who did not witness them; and they were felt by one party only. Upon this subject I despair of making myself understood by posterity, by the present age, and even by you. To collect and arrange the documents illustrative of it, would require as many lives as those of a cat.

You never felt the terrorism of Shay's Rebellion in Massachusetts.[74] I believe you never felt the terrorism of Gallatin's insurrection

---

74. Daniel Shays led an armed uprising (1786–1787) in Massachusetts to protest high taxes and legal actions against debtors.

in Pennsylvania.[75] You certainly never realized the terrorism of Fries's most outrageous riot and rescue,[76] as I call it. Treason rebellion—as the world, and great judges, and two juries pronounce it. You certainly never felt the terrorism excited by Genet[77] in 1793, when ten thousand people in the streets of Philadelphia, day after day, threatened to drag Washington out of his house, and effect a revolution in the government, or compel it to declare war in favor of the French Revolution, and against England.

The coolest and the firmest minds, even among the Quakers in Philadelphia, have given their opinions to me, that nothing but the yellow fever, which removed Dr. Hutchinson and Jonathan Dickenson Sargent[78] from this world, could have saved the United States from a total revolution of government. I have no doubt you were fast asleep in philosophical tranquility when ten thousand people, and perhaps many more, were parading the streets of Philadelphia, on the evening of my Fast Day.

When even Governor Mifflin himself, thought it his duty to order a patrol of horse and foot, to preserve the peace; when Market Street was

---

75. Whiskey Rebellion in southwestern Pennsylvania (1794) against federal excise tax on whiskey. President Washington ordered 13,000–15,000 militia in to quell the rebellion. Ironically, Albert Gallatin helped quell the rebellion peacefully, but, perhaps, because as a congressman Gallatin opposed some of President Adams's actions, such as the Alien-Sedition Act and a treaty with Great Britain, he engendered the ire of Adams to such a degree that Adams would in this letter attribute the Whiskey Rebellion to Gallatin.

76. John Fries (not Tries, as copies of Adams's letter reads). Fries led citizen army in 1799 to Quakertown and Bethlehem, Pennsylvania, to free other citizens arrested for refusal to pay a House/Hearth/Window tax instituted to fund possible war with France. Fries was arrested, tried, convicted, and sentenced to hang, but was pardoned by John Adams.

77. Edmond Genet (1763–1834). French diplomat and minister to the United States (1792–1794). Genet tried to bring the United States into war against Great Britain during the French Revolution. This brought about crisis and confrontation in the United States as Americans were split in their loyalties to France and Great Britain following the American Revolution, wherein France was a critical, and it could be said, indispensable, ally to America.

78. Hutchinson and Sargent were both doctors, who also seem to have incurred Adams's ire.

as full as men could stand by one another, and even before my door; when some of my domestics, in frenzy, determined to sacrifice their lives in my defense; when all were ready to make a desperate sally among the multitude, and others were with difficulty and danger dragged back by the others; when I myself judged it prudent and necessary to order chests of arms from the War Office, to be brought through by lanes and back doors; determined to defend my house at the expense of my life, and the lives of the few, very few, domestics and friends within it.

What think you of terrorism, Mr. Jefferson? Shall I investigate the causes, the motives, the incentives to these terrorisms? Shall I remind you of Philip Freneau, of Lloyd, of Ned Church? Of Peter Markoe, of Andrew Brown, of Duane? Of Callender, of Tom Paine, of Greenleaf, of Cheatham, of Tennison at New York, of Benjamin Austin at Boston?[79]

But above all, shall I request you to collect circular letters from members of Congress in the Middle and Southern States to their con-stituents? I would give all I am worth for a complete collection of all those circular letters. Please to recollect Edward Livingston's motions and speeches, and those of his associates, in the case of Jonathan Rob-bins.[80] The real, terrors of both parties have always been, and now are, the fear that they shall lose the elections, and consequently the loaves and fishes; and that their antagonists will obtain them. Both parties have excited artificial terrors, and if I were summoned as a witness to say, upon oath, which party had excited, like Machiavelli,[81] the most terror, and which had really felt the most, I could not give a more sin-cere answer than in the vulgar style, put them in a bag and shake them, and then see which comes out first.

---

79. Writers and newspaper editors opposed to Federalist Party/John Adams.

80. Jonathan Robbins, alias Thomas Nash, was extradited to England by John Adams. There Robbins was tried and executed for mutiny. Robbins had argued that he was American-born Thomas Nash. While he was held in South Carolina jails, Charles Pinckney and Edward Livingston had written in his defense. Republican efforts to censure President Adams failed in March 1800, thanks in part to a John Marshall speech in Adams's behalf.

81. Niccolo Machiavelli (1469–1527). French statesman and political theorist. Wrote *Discourses on Livy* (1531) and *The Prince*, which details how an unscrupulous "ideal" prince keeps his power.

Where is the terrorism now, my friend? There is now more real terrorism in New England than there ever was in Virginia: the terror of a civil war, a La Vendee,[82] a division of the States, etc., etc., etc. How shall we conjure down this damnable rivalry between Virginia and Massachusetts? Virginia had recourse to Pennsylvania and New York. Massachusetts has now recourse to New York. They have almost got New Jersey and Maryland, and they are aiming at Pennsylvania. And, all this in the midst of a war with England, when all Europe is in flames.

I will give you a hint or two more on the subject of terrorism. When John Randolph in the House and Stephens Thompson Mason in the Senate were treating me with the utmost contempt, when Ed Livingston was threatening me with impeachment for the murder of Jonathan Robbins, the native of Danvers in Connecticut, when I had certain information, that the daily language in an Insurance Office in Boston was, even from the mouth of Charles Jarvis:[83] "We must go to Philadelphia and drag that John Adams from his chair!"

I thank God that terror never yet seized on my mind.

But I have had more excitements to it, from 1761 to this day, than any other man. Name the other if you can. I have been disgraced and degraded, and I have a right to complain. But as I always expected it, I have always submitted to it; perhaps often with too much tameness. The amount of all the speeches of John Randolph in the House, for two or three years is, that himself and myself are the only two honest and consistent men in the United States, himself eternally in opposition to government, and myself as constantly in favor of it. He is now in correspondence with his friend Quincy. What will come of it, let Virginia and Massachusetts judge. In my next you may find something upon correspondences; Whig and Tory; Federal and Democratic; Virginian and Novanglain; English and French; Jacobin and Despotic, etc.

Mean time I am as ever, your friend,

John Adams

---

82. In 1794 Robespierre's Republican Convention called for the complete extermination of all men, women, and children of the Vendeen (area of western France) revolt.

83. Charles Jarvis (1748–1807). Massachusetts Republican physician, legislator, and orator.

18. JOHN ADAMS TO THOMAS JEFFERSON
QUINCY, July 1813

DEAR SIR,

Correspondences! The letters of Bernard, Hutchinson,[84] Oliver,[85] and Paxton,[86] etc., were detected and exposed before the Revolution. There are, I doubt not, thousands of letters now in being (but still concealed from their party) to their friends, which will, one day, see the light. I have wondered for more than thirty years that so few have appeared; and have constantly expected that a Tory History of the rise and progress of the Revolution would appear; and wished it. I would give more for it than for Marshall, Gordon,[87] Ramsay,[88] and all the rest.

Private letters of all parties will be found analogous to the newspapers, pamphlets, and historians of the times. Gordon's and Marshall's histories were written to make money; and fashioned and finished to sell high in the London market. I should expect to find more truth in a history written by Hutchinson, Oliver, or Sewel;[89] and I

---

84. Sir Francis Bernard (1714–1779) and Thomas Hutchinson (1711–1780). Loyalist governors of Massachusetts Bay. Bernard's "Letter Books," written after his removal from America, were published by Jared Sparks in 1848 and given to Harvard.

85. Thomas Oliver (1734–1815). Loyalist lieutenant governor of Massachusetts by recommendation of Gov. Thomas Hutchinson.

86. Charles Paxton (1704–1788). Boston Commissioner of Customs, burned several times in effigy, once between pope and devil as "Every man's servant, but no man's friend." He was one of the writers of the "Hutchinson letters," Loyalist letters leaked from England to Boston by Benjamin Franklin.

87. William Gordon (1730–1807). Minister. Wrote *History of the Rise, Progress, and Establishment of Independence in America*. He was dismissed as chaplain to Massachusetts provincial congress because many felt his prayers were too dictatorial rather than Divine guidance requests.

88. David Ramsay (1749–1815). Wrote *The History of the American Revolution* (1789) and in 1819 published *Universal History Americanized*, with one emphasis being on religion.

89. Jonathan Sewall (1728–1796). Defended England's coercion by force in Tory newspapers. After signing an address to Gov. Thomas Hutchinson, his property in Cambridge was attacked and later confiscated.

doubt not, such histories will one day appear. Marshall's is a Mausoleum, 100 feet square at the base, and 200 feet high. It will be as durable as the monuments of the Washington benevolent societies.

Your character in history may easily be foreseen. Your administration will be quoted by philosophers as a model of profound wisdom; by politicians, as weak, superficial, and shortsighted. Mine, like Pope's[90] woman, will have no character at all. The impious idolatry to Washington destroyed all character. His legacy of ministers was not the worst part of the tragedy; though by his own express confession to me, and by Pickering's confession to the world in his letters to Sullivan, two of them, at least, were fastened upon him by necessity, because he could get no other.

The truth is, Hamilton's[91] influence over him was so well known, that no man fit for the office of State or War would accept either. He was driven to the necessity of appointing such as would accept; and this necessity was, in my opinion, the real cause of his retirement from office; for you may depend upon it, that retirement was not voluntary.

My friend, you and I have passed our lives in serious times. I know not whether we have ever seen any moments more serious than the present. The Northern States are now retaliating upon the Southern States their conduct from 1797 to 1800. It is a mortification to me to see what servile mimics they are. Their newspapers, pamphlets, hand-bills, and their legislative proceedings, are copied from the examples set them, especially by Virginia and Kentucky. I know not which party has the most unblushing front, the most lying tongue, or the most impudent and insolent, not to say the most seditious and rebellious pen.

If you desire explanation on any of the points in this letter, you shall have them. This correspondence, I hope, will be concealed as

---

90. Alexander Pope (1688–1744). English poet and satirist. Authored essays on moral philosophy, including *An Essay on Man* and *Moral Essays*.

91. Alexander Hamilton (c. 1755–1804). Secretary of treasury under George Washington. In 1802, with the Federalist Party in disarray, he proposed the formation of the Christian Constitutional Society to support the Christian religion and the Constitution, and to use "all lawful means in concert to promote the election of fit men."

long as Hutchinson's and Oliver's; but I should have no personal objection to the publication of it in the National Intelligencer.

I am, and shall be for life, your friend.

John Adams

19. JOHN ADAMS TO THOMAS JEFFERSON
QUINCY, July 9, 1813

Whenever I sit down to write to you, I am precisely in the situation of the wood-cutter on Mount Ida. I cannot see wood for trees. So many subjects crowd upon me that I know not with which to begin. But I will begin, at random, with Belsham; who is, as I have no doubt, a man of merit. He had no malice against you, nor any thought of doing mischief; nor has he done any, though he has been imprudent. The truth is, the dissenters of all denominations in England, and especially the Unitarians,[92] are cowed, as we used to say at college. They are ridiculed, insulted, persecuted. They can scarcely hold their heads above water. They catch at straws and shadows to avoid drowning.

Priestley sent your letter to Lindsay, and Belsham printed it from the same motive, i.e., to derive some countenance from the name of Jefferson. Nor has it done harm here. Priestley says to Lindsay, "You see he is almost one of us, and he hopes will soon be altogether such as we are." Even in our New England, I have heard a high federal divine say, your letters had increased his respect for you.

"The same political parties which now agitate the United States, have existed through all time." Precisely! And this is precisely the complaint in the preface to the first volume of my defense. While all other sciences have advanced, that of government is at a stand; little better understood; little better practiced now, than three or four thousand years ago. What is the reason? I say, parties and factions will not suffer, or permit improvements to be made. As soon as one man hints at an improvement, his rival opposes it.

No sooner has one party discovered or invented an amelioration of

---

92. Belief in One God, not Trinity. Jesus, human only.

the condition of man, or the order of society, than the opposite party belies it, misconstrues it, misrepresents it, ridicules it, insults it, and persecutes it. Records are destroyed. Histories are annihilated, or interpolated, or prohibited: sometimes by popes, sometimes by emperors, sometimes by aristocratical, and sometimes by democratical assemblies, and sometimes by mobs.

Aristotle wrote the history of eighteen hundred republics which existed before his time. Cicero[93] wrote two volumes of discourses on government, which, perhaps, were worth all the rest of his works. The works of Livy[94] and Tacitus,[95] etc., that are lost, would be more interesting than all that remain. Fifty gospels have been destroyed, and where are St. Luke's world of books that have been written? If you ask my opinion who has committed all the havoc, I will answer you candidly, "Ecclesiastical and Imperial despotism has done it, to conceal their frauds!"

Why are the histories of all nations, more ancient than the Christian era lost? Who destroyed the Alexandrian library?[96] I believe that Christian priests, Jewish rabbis, Grecian sages, and emperors, had as great a hand in it as Turks and Mahometans. Democrats, Rebels and Jacobins, when they possessed a momentary power, have shown a disposition both to destroy and forge records as vandalical as priests and despots. Such has been and such is the world we live in.

I recollect, near some thirty years ago, to have said carelessly to you that I wished I could find time and means to write something upon aristocracy. You seized upon the idea, and encouraged me to do it with all that friendly warmth that is natural and habitual to you. I soon

---

93. Marcus Tullius Cicero (106–43 BCE). Roman orator. Author of *On the Nature of God*, *On Divination*, *On Old Age*, and *On Friendship*.

94. Livy, or Titus Livius (c. 59 BCE–17 CE). Roman historian. His *History of Rome* extolled ancient republican virtues.

95. Cornelius Tacitus (c. 55–c. 120 CE). Roman historian. Wrote *Histories* and *Annals*.

96. Library of Alexandria, Egypt, commenced under Ptolemy Soter. It stored volumes of knowledge collected from many parts of the known world. Portions were destroyed by fires between 47 BCE and the final fall of the city in 646 CE.

began, and have been writing upon that subject ever since. I have been so unfortunate as never to be able to make myself understood.

Your aristocrats are the most difficult animals to manage of anything in the whole theory and practice of government. They will not suffer themselves to be governed. They not only exert all their own subtlety, industry and courage, but they employ the commonalty to knock to pieces every plan and model that the most honest architects in legislation can invent to keep them within bounds. Both patricians and plebeians are as furious as the workmen in England, to demolish labor-saving machinery.

But who are these aristocrats? Who shall judge? Who shall select these choice spirits from the rest of the congregation? Themselves? We must first find out and determine who themselves are. Shall the congregation choose? Ask Xenophon.[97] Perhaps hereafter I may quote you Greek. Too much in a hurry at present, English must suffice. Xenophon says that the ecclesia always choose the worst men they can find, because none others will do their dirty work. This wicked motive is worse than birth or wealth.

Here I want to quote Greek again. But the day before I received your letter of June 27th, I gave the book to George Washington Adams, going to the academy at Hingham. The title is Moralia ex Poetis, a collection of moral sentences from all the most ancient Greek poets. In one of the oldest of them, I read in Greek, that I cannot repeat, a couplet, the sense of which was: "Nobility in men is worth as much as it is in horses, asses, or rams; but the meanest blooded puppy in the world, if he gets a little money, is as good a man as the best of them."

Yet birth and wealth together have prevailed over virtue and talents in all ages. The many will acknowledge no other aristocrats. Your experience of this truth will not much differ from that of your best friend.

John Adams

---

97. Greek soldier and author (431–355 BCE). Wrote *Anabasis*, memoirs of Socrates, an account of Cyrus the Great's education, and political works.

20. JOHN ADAMS TO THOMAS JEFFERSON
QUINCY, July 13, 1813

DEAR SIR,

Let me allude to one circumstance more in one of your letters to me, before I touch upon the subject of religion in your letters to Priestley.

The first time that you and I differed in opinion on any material question, was after your arrival from Europe, and that point was the French Revolution. You were well persuaded in your own mind that the nation would succeed in establishing a free republican government. I was as well persuaded in mine, that a project of such a government over five and twenty millions of people, when four and twenty millions and five hundred thousand of them could neither read nor write, was as unnatural, irrational and impracticable as it would be over the elephants, lions, tigers, panthers, wolves and bears in the royal menagerie at Versailles.

Napoleon has lately invented a word which perfectly expresses my opinion, at that time and ever since. He calls the project Ideology; and John Randolph, though he was, fourteen years ago, as wild an enthusiast for equality and fraternity as any of them, appears to be now a regenerated proselyte to Napoleon's opinion and mine, that it was all madness.

The Greeks, in their allegorical style, said that the two ladies, Aristocracy and Democracy, always in a quarrel, disturbed every neighborhood with their brawls. It is a fine observation of yours that "Whig and Tory belong to natural history." Inequalities of mind and body are so established by God Almighty, in His constitution of human nature, that no art or policy can ever plane them down to a level.

I have never read reasoning more absurd, sophistry more gross, in proof of the Athanasian Creed, or Transubstantiation,[98] than the subtle labors of Helvetius[99] and Rousseau, to demonstrate the natural

98. The Athanasian Creed upheld dogma of the Divine Birth of Jesus and the Trinity. Transubstantiation is the belief that Communion bread and wine turn into the actual body and blood of Jesus.

99. Claude Adrian Helvetius (1715–1771). French philosopher and Encyclopedist. His *The Mind* (1758) was considered godless in France. He was attacked by

equality of mankind. Justice for everyone, the golden rule, do as you would be done by, is all the equality that can be supported or defended by reason, or reconciled to common sense.

It is very true, as you justly observe, I can say nothing new on this or any other subject of government. But when Lafayette harangued you and me and John Quincy Adams, through a whole evening in your hotel in the Cul de Sac at Paris, and developed the plans then in operation to reform France, though I was as silent as you were, I then thought I could say something new to him. In plain truth, I was astonished at the grossness of his ignorance of government and history, as I had been for years before, at that of Turgot,[100] Rochefoucauld, Condorcet and Franklin. This gross Ideology of them all, first suggested to me the thought and the inclination which I afterwards hinted to you in London, of writing something upon aristocracy. I was restrained for years, by many fearful considerations.

Who, and what was I? A man of no name or consideration in Europe. The manual exercise of writing was painful and distressing to me, almost like a blow on the elbow or knee. My style was habitually negligent, unstudied, unpolished; I should make enemies of all the French patriots, the Dutch patriots, the English republicans, dissenters, reformers, call them what you will; and what came nearer home to my bosom than all the rest, I knew I should give offence to many if not all of my best friends in America, and very probably destroy all the little popularity I ever had, in a country where popularity had more omnipotence than the British Parliament assumed.

Where should I get the necessary books? What printer or bookseller would undertake to print such hazardous writings? But when the French assembly of notables met, and I saw that Turgot's "government in one centre, and that centre the nation," a sentence as mysterious or as con-

---

Rousseau and Voltaire, but later incorporated by Utilitarianism (Jeremy Bentham), a theory of ethics that the right or wrong of an action depends on the happiness its consequences bring for the greatest number of people.

100. Jacques Turgot (1727–1781). French economist and reformer. Favored free trade (laissez-faire, let it be) and a land tax, anticipated the law of diminishing returns, and pressed for an end to compulsory labor. As one of François Quesnay's physiocrats, he, like early Thomas Jefferson, but unlike Alexander Hamilton, believed that agriculture rather than industry or commerce was the basis of a nation's prosperity.

tradictory as the Athanasian creed, was about to take place, and when I saw that Shay's rebellion was about breaking out in Massachusetts, and when I saw that even my obscure name was often quoted in France as an advocate for simple democracy, which I saw that the sympathies in America had caught the French flame, I was determined to wash my own hands as clean as I could of all this foulness. I had then strong forebodings that I was sacrificing all the honors and emoluments of this life, and so it has happened, but not in so great a degree as I apprehended.

In truth, my defense of the constitutions and "discourses on Davila,"[101] laid the foundation for that immense unpopularity which fell, like the tower of Siloam, upon me. Your steady defense of democratical principles, and your invariable favorable opinion of the French revolution, laid the foundation of your unbounded popularity.

Sic transit gloria mundi! Now I will forfeit my life, if you can find one sentence in my defense of the constitutions, or the discourses on Davila, which by a fair construction, can favor the introduction of hereditary monarchy or aristocracy into America.

They were all written to support and strengthen the constitutions of the United States.

The wood-cutter on Ida, though he was puzzled to find a tree to chop at first, I presume knew how to leave off when he was weary. But I never know when to cease when I begin to write to you.

John Adams

21. JOHN ADAMS TO THOMAS JEFFERSON
QUINCY, July 15, 1813

Never mind it, my dear sir, if I write four letters to your one, your one is worth more than my four.

David Hume had made himself so fashionable with the aid of the

---

101. John Adams wrote 3 volumes of *Defense of the Constitutions of the United States of America* in 1787. In 1790 Philadelphia newspapers he wrote the *Discourses on Davila*, arguing for a strong executive. Many readers were angered by *Davila*, thinking that Adams was in favor of hereditary monarchy.

court and clergy, Atheist, as they called him, and by his elegant lies against the republicans and gaudy daubings of the courtiers, that he had nearly laughed into contempt Rapin,[102] Sydney,[103] and even Locke. It was ridiculous and even criminal in almost all Europe to speak of constitutions, or writers upon the principles or the fabrics of them.

The nations of Europe appeared to me, when I was among them, from the beginning of 1778, to 1785, i.e., to the commencement of the troubles in France, to be advancing by slow but sure steps towards an amelioration of the condition of man in religion and government, in liberty, equality, fraternity, knowledge, civilization and humanity.

The French Revolution I dreaded, because I was sure it would not only arrest the progress of improvement, but give it a retrograde course, for at least a century, if not many centuries. The French patriots appeared to me like young scholars from a college, or sailors flushed with recent pay or prize money mounted on wild horses, lashing and spurring till they would kill the horses, and break their own necks.

Let me now ask you very seriously, my friend, where are now, in 1813, the perfection and the perfectibility of human nature? Where is now the progress of the human mind? Where is the amelioration of society? Where the augmentations of human comforts? Where the diminutions of human pains and miseries? I know not whether the last day of Dr. Young[104] can exhibit to a mind unstaid by philosophy and religion, for I hold there can be no philosophy without religion, more terrors than the present state of the world.

When, where, and how is the present chaos to be arranged into order? There is not, there cannot be, a greater abuse of words than to call the writings of Callender,[105] Paine, Austin[106] and Lowell,[107] or, the

---

102. Rene Rapin (1621–1687). French Jesuit poet and writer. Author of several theological and ascetic works.

103. Algernon Sydney (1622–1683). English politician executed for alleged attempt to overthrow Charles II. His *Discourses Concerning Government* influenced the American Revolution.

104. Dr. Thomas Young. Revolutionary ideologue, deist, mentor of Ethan Allen, poet, and writer.

105. James Callender. Scots-born political writer. Wrote *The Prospect before Us* and *Sketches of American History. Prospect* ridiculed George Washington as a traitor,

speeches of Ed Livingston and John Randolph, public discussions. The ravings and rantings of Bedlam merit the character as well; and yet Joel Barlow was about to record Tom Paine as the great author of the American Revolution! If he was, I desire that my name may be blotted out forever from its records.

You and I ought not to die before we have explained ourselves to each other.

I shall come to the subject of religion by-and-bye. Your friend,

John Adams

22. JOHN ADAMS TO THOMAS JEFFERSON
QUINCY, July 16, 1813

DEAR SIR,

Your letters to Priestley have increased my grief, if that were possible, for the loss of Rush. Had he lived, I would have stimulated him to insist on your promise to him, to write him on the subject of religion. Your plan I admire.

In your letter to Priestley of March 21st, 1801, dated at Washington, you call "The Christian Philosophy, the most sublime and benevolent, but the most perverted system that ever shone upon man." That it is the most sublime and benevolent, I agree. But whether it has

---

thief, and perjurer, while also lambasting John Adams. His *History of the US for 1796* exposed Alexander Hamilton's Maria Reynolds affair. Later, Callender tendered the Sally Hemings allegations against Thomas Jefferson.

106. Benjamin Austin (1752–1820). Boston merchant who wrote fierce Republican newspaper articles during the John Adams administration.

107. John Lowell (1769–1840). Lawyer pamphleteer opposed to Democratic Party and "Mr. Madison's War." He used pseudonyms of "Boston Rebel" and "The Roxbury Farmer." Wrote *New England Patriot, Being a Candid Comparison of the Principles and Conduct of the Washington and Jefferson Administrations.*

108. (630–550 BCE). Persian prophet. Founder of Zoroastrian religion and *Avesta/Gathas* scripture. His ideas probably influenced Judeo-Christian demonology and eschatology.

been more perverted than that of Moses, of Confucius, of Zoroaster,[108] of Sanchoniathan,[109] of Numa,[110] of Mahomet, of the Druids, of the Hindoos, etc., etc., I cannot as yet determine, because I am not sufficiently acquainted with these systems, or the history of their effects to form a decisive opinion of the result of the comparison.

In your letter dated Washington, April 9, 1803, you say:

"In consequence of some conversations with Dr. Rush, in the years 1798–99, I had promised some day to write to him a letter, giving him my view of the Christian system. I have reflected often on it since, and even sketched the outline in my own mind. I should first take a general view of the moral doctrines of the most remarkable of the ancient philosophers, of whose ethics we have sufficient information to make an estimate; say of Pythagoras,[111] Epicurus,[112] Epictetus,[113] Socrates,[114]

109. Or Sanchoniathon. Author of a *Phoenician History* sometime between 2000 and 1200 BCE, which contains Phoenician account of Creation by "Wind" and "Darkness." Also wrote about Serpent Worship and Remnants in Eusebius. Detractors say his works are forgeries by Philo of Byblus (76–130 CE) or Porphyry (233 CE) to discredit the Bible and Christianity.

110. Numa Pompilius. Legendary second king of Rome. Given sacred prophetic shield by god, Mars. This shield and eleven duplicates (*ancilia*) were carried in procession each year by the Salii ("jumping priests") of Mars. He died in 673 BCE.

111. (582–496 BCE). Ionian mathematician and philosopher. He and his disciples believed in reincarnation of the soul.

112. Epicurus (341–270 BCE). Greek philosopher. Broke from god-fearing worship and admitted women and slaves to his school. He put Matter over Form, relying on Senses, and cited as essential the pursuit of "life, liberty, and safety."

113. Epictetus (55–135 CE). Greek Stoic philosopher. Wrote *Enchiridon* (*Handbook*), a collection of maxims by which to guide one's life. Also wrote *Discourses*. His ethics pursued "happiness."

114. (470–399 BCE). Greek philosopher. Taught that *virtue is knowledge* and that vice was the result of ignorance. He was charged in 399 BCE with neglecting the gods of the state and introducing new ones because of his teachings on *daemonion*, an inner guide.

115. Seneca the Younger (4 BCE–65 CE). Spanish-born Roman philosopher. Wrote *Naturales Quaestiones*, seven books on ancient theories of cosmology, as well as *Epistulae Morales*, 124 letters on morals.

116. Marcus Aurelius Antoninus (121–180 CE). Roman emperor. Wrote *Meditations*. Advocated virtue, reason, and positive thinking and persecuted Christians as disrupters of government rule.

Cicero, Seneca,[115] and Antoninus.[116] I should do justice to the branches of morality they have treated well, but point out the importance of those in which they are deficient.

I should then take a view of the Deism[117] and Ethics of the Jews, and show in what a degraded state they were, and the necessity they presented of a reformation. I should proceed to a view of the life, character, and doctrines of Jesus, who, sensible of the incorrectness of their ideas of the Deity, and of morality, endeavored to bring them to the principles of a pure Deism, and juster notions of the attributes of God to reform their moral doctrines to the standard of reason, justice, and philanthropy, and to inculcate the belief of a future state. This view would purposely omit the question of his Divinity, and even of his inspiration.

To do him justice, it would be necessary to remark the disadvantages his doctrines have to encounter, not having been committed to writing by himself, but by the most unlettered of men, by memory, long after they had heard them from him, when much was forgotten, much misunderstood, and presented in very paradoxical shapes; yet such are the fragments remaining, as to show a master workman, and that his system of morality was the most benevolent and sublime, probably, that has been ever taught, and more perfect than those of any of the ancient philosophers.

His character and doctrines have received still greater injury from those who pretend to be his special disciples, and who have disfigured and sophisticated his actions and precepts from views of personal interest, so as to induce the unthinking part of mankind to throw off the whole system in disgust, and to pass sentence, as an impostor, on the most innocent, the most benevolent, the most eloquent and sublime character that has ever been exhibited to man. This is the outline!"

"Sancte Socrate, ora pro nobis!" ["Holy Socrates, pray for us."] —Erasmus.[118]

---

117. Rationalistic movement asserting belief in one God Creator and relying on Reason, not Revelation. Revelation viewed as man-made fabrications.

118. (1466–1536). Dutch Roman Catholic. Published edition of Greek New Testament and *In Praise of Folly*, a satire on Church corruption. Wrote *Diatribe on Free Will* (1524) opposing Martin Luther.

Priestley in his letter to Lindsay, enclosing a copy of your letter to him, says:

"He is generally considered an unbeliever; if so, however, he cannot be far from us, and I hope in the way to be not only almost, but altogether what we are. He now attends public worship very regularly, and his moral conduct was never impeached."

Now, I see not but you are as good a Christian as Priestley and Lindsay. Piety and morality were the end and object of the Christian system, according to them, and according to you. They believed in the resurrection of Jesus, in his miracles, and in his inspiration. But what inspiration? Not all that is recorded in the New Testament, nor the Old. They have not yet told us how much they believe, or how much they doubt or disbelieve. They have not told us how much allegory, how much parable, they find, nor how they explain them all, in the Old Testament or the New.

John Quincy Adams[119] has written for years to his two sons, boys of ten and twelve, a series of letters, in which he pursues a plan more extensive than yours, but agreeing in most of the essential points. I wish these letters could be preserved in the bosoms of his boys, but women and priests will get them and I expect, if he makes a peace, he will be obliged to retire like a Jay, to study prophecies to the end of his life. I have more to say on this subject of religion.

John Adams

23. JOHN ADAMS TO THOMAS JEFFERSON
QUINCY, July 18, 1813

DEAR SIR,

I have more to say on religion. For more than sixty years I have been attentive to this great subject. Controversies between Calvinists and Arminians,[120] Trinitarians and Unitarians, Deists and Christians, Athe-

---

119. (1767–1848). John Adams's son. More conservative in his religion and a Trinitarian. Not in favor of forced orthodoxy.

120. Emphasis on man's free will. Challenged Calvin's predestination.

ists and both, have attracted my attention, whenever the singular life I have led would admit to all these questions. The history of this little village of Quincy, if it were worth recording, would explain to you how this happened.

I think I can now say I have read away bigotry, if not enthusiasm. What does Priestley mean by an unbeliever, when he applies it to you? How much did he "unbelieve" himself? Gibbon had him right, when he determined his creed "scanty." We are to understand, no doubt, that he believed the resurrection of Jesus; some of his miracles; his inspiration, but in what degree? He did not believe in the inspiration of the writings that contain his history, yet he believed in the Apocalyptic beast, and he believed as much as he pleased in the writings of Daniel and John.

This great, excellent, and extraordinary man, whom I sincerely loved, esteemed, and respected, was really a phenomenon; a comet in the system, like Voltaire, Bolingbroke, and Hume. Had Bolingbroke or Voltaire taken him in hand, what would they have made of him and his creed?

I do not believe you have read much of Priestley's "Corruptions of Christianity,"[121] his history of early opinions of Jesus Christ, his predestination, his no-soul system, or his controversy with Horsley.

I have been a diligent student for many years in books whose titles you have never seen: in Priestley's and Lindsay's writings; in Farmer, in Cappe, in Tucker's or Edward Search's Light of Nature pursued;[122] in Edwards[123]

---

121. (1782). Attacked Roman Catholicism, calling for a return to pure faith in Christ and his teachings.

122. Abraham Tucker, pen name Edward Search (1705–1774). Wrote *The Light of Nature Pursued*. Believed reason and revelation could work together and that reason alone was not sufficient for moral theory. Like Locke, he rejected innate ideas. He rejected doctrine of endless punishment in Hell and believed all men would know eternal happiness due to Goodness of God.

123. Jonathan Edwards (1703–1758). Clergyman. Wrote *Freedom of the Will*. Opposed Half-Way Covenant, which allowed baptized persons not professing conversion to be church members, but not communicants.

and Hopkins,[124] and lately in Ezra Styles Ely;[125] his reverend and learned panegyrists, and his elegant and spirited opponents.

I am not wholly uninformed of the controversies in Germany, and the learned researches of universities and professors, in which the sanctity of the Bible and the inspiration of its authors are taken for granted, or waived, or admitted, or not denied. I have also read Condorcet's Progress of the Human Mind.

Now, what is all this to you? No more, than if I should tell you that I read Dr. Clark,[126] and Dr. Waterland,[127] and Emlyn,[128] and Leland's[129] view or review of the Deistical writers more than fifty years ago; which is a literal truth. I blame you not for reading Euclid[130] and Newton, Thucydides[131] and Theocritus;[132] for I believe you will find as much entertainment and instruction in them, as I have found in my theological and ecclesiastical instructors; or even as I have found in a profound investigation of the life, writings, and doctrines of Erasmus, whose disciples were Milton,[133] Harrington,[134] Selden,[135] St.

---

124. Samuel Hopkins (1721–1803). Clergyman and follower of Jonathan Edwards. Wrote *Inquiry into the Nature of Holiness* (1773) and *System of Doctrines* (1793). Believed self-love was the root of all sin.

125. (1786–1861). Clergyman. Wrote *Contrast between Calvinism and Hopkinsianism* (1811).

126. Samuel Clarke (1675–1729). Wrote *Scripture Doctrine of the Trinity* (1712).

127. Daniel Waterland (1683–1740). Rebutted Clarke, defending Trinitarian beliefs. Wrote *Vindication of Christ's Divinity, Review of the Doctrine of the Eucharist, and History of the Athanasian Creed* (1723).

128. Thomas Emlyn (1663–1741). Unitarian minister. Imprisoned in England in 1702 for publishing a book defending Arianism.

129. John Leland (1754–1841). Baptist minister to Massachusetts and Virginia and religious liberty proponent with Thomas Jefferson and James Madison. Wrote *The Rights of Conscience Inalienable* (1802) and *The History of Jack Nips: The Yankee Spy* (1794).

130. (c. 300 BCE). Alexandrian mathematician. Wrote *Elements*, *Phaenomena*, a description of the heavens, and *Optics*.

131. (c. 460–c. 400 BCE). Greek historian. Wrote *History of the Peloponnesian War*.

132. (c. 300–250 BCE). Alexandrian Greek poet of the *Idylls*.

133. John Milton (1608–1674). Wrote pamphlets that attacked Episcopal form of church government. Author of *Of Reformation in England* (1641) and *The Reason of Church Government Urged against Prelaty*.

John, the Chief Justice, father of Bolingbroke, and others; the choicest spirits of their age; or in Le Harpe's history of the philosophy of the eighteenth century,[136] or in Van der Kemp's[137] vast map of the causes of the revolutionary spirit in the same and preceding centuries. These things are to me, at present, the marbles and nine-pins of old age; I will not say the beads and prayer-books.

I agree with you, as far as you go, most cordially, and I think solidly. How much farther I go, how much more I believe than you, I may explain in a future letter. Thus much I will say at present, I have found so many difficulties, that I am not astonished at your stopping where you are; and so far from sentencing you to perdition, I hope soon to meet you in another country.

John Adams

24. JOHN ADAMS TO THOMAS JEFFERSON
QUINCY, July 22, 1813

DEAR SIR,

Dr. Priestley, in a letter to Mr. Lindsay, Northumberland, November 4, 1803, says:

> "As you were pleased with my comparison of Socrates and Jesus, I have begun to carry the same comparison to all the heathen moralists. I have all the books that I want for the purpose except Simpli-

---

134. James Harrington (1611–1677). Wrote *The Commonwealth of Oceana* (1656) and *Outline of a Plan for Republican Government.*

135. John Selden (1584–1654). Engish jurist/scholar and Orientalist. Wrote *De Diis Syris (The Gods of Syria)* (1617); *History of Tithes* (1618), which put him in conflict with clergy, who suppressed the book; *Mare Clausum* (1635); and *Table Talk* (published posthumously in 1689).

136. Jean François La Harpe (1739–1803). Wrote *Letters on Ancient and Modern Literature* as well as *Melanie ou la religieus*, an attack on religious vows. He is said to have recanted his views late in life, writing a work on Reason in 1796.

137. Francis Adrian Van der Kemp (1752–1829). Dutch minister and friend to John Adams, Thomas Jefferson, and George Washington. He planned the Erie Canal.

cius and Arrian on Epictetus,[138] and them I hope to get from a library in Philadelphia. Lest, however, I should fail there, I wish you or Mr. Belsham would procure and send them from London. While I am capable of anything I cannot be idle, and I do not know that I can do anything better. This, too, is an undertaking that Mr. Jefferson recommends to me."

In another letter, dated Northumberland, January 16th, 1804, Dr. Priestley says to Mr. Lindsay:

"I have now finished and transcribed for the press, my comparison of the Grecian philosophers with those of revelation, and with more ease and more to my own satisfaction than I expected. They who liked my pamphlet entitled, 'Socrates and Jesus compared,' will not, I flatter myself, dislike this work. It has the same object and completes the scheme. . . . It has increased my own sense of the unspeakable value of revelation, and must, I think, that of every person who will give due attention to the subject."

I have now given you all that relates to yourself in Priestley's letters. This was possibly, and not improbably, the last letter this great, this learned, indefatigable, most excellent and extraordinary man ever wrote, for on the 4th of February, 1804, he was released from his labors and sufferings. Peace, rest, joy and glory to his soul! For I believe he had one, and one of the greatest. I regret, oh how I lament that he did not live to publish this work! It must exist in manuscript. Cooper must know something of it. Can you learn from him where it is, and get it printed?

I hope you will still perform your promise to Doctor Rush.

If Priestley had lived, I should certainly have corresponded with him. His friend Cooper,[139] who, unfortunately for him and me and

138. Simplicius. Early sixth-century Neoplatonist who wrote a commentary on Epictetus's *Enchiridon* (Manual). Flavius Arrian (c. 87–after 145 CE) compiled the *Works of Epictetus* and wrote his biography.

139. Thomas Cooper (1759–1839). British-born American educator sent to prison and fined four hundred dollars for writing pamphlets attacking Alien and Sedition Acts of 1798. Author of *Tracts, Ethical, Theological, and Political* (1789–1790) and *An English Version of the Institutes of Justinian* (1812).

you, had as fatal an influence over him as Hamilton had over Washington, and whose rash hot head led Priestley into all his misfortunes and most [of] his errors in conduct, could not have prevented explanations between Priestley and me.

I should propose to him a thousand, a million questions. And no man was more capable or better disposed to answer them candidly than Dr. Priestley.

Scarcely anything that has happened to me in my curious life, has made a deeper impression upon me than that such a learned, ingenious, scientific and talented madcap as Cooper, could have influence enough to make Priestley my enemy.

I will not yet communicate to you more than a specimen of the questions I would have asked Priestley.

One is: "Learned and scientific, Sir, you have written largely about matter and spirit, and have concluded there is no human soul. Will you please to inform me what matter is and what spirit is? Unless we know the meaning of words, we cannot reason in or about words."

I shall never send you all my questions that I would put to Priestley, because they are innumerable. But I may hereafter send you two or three.

I am, in perfect charity, your old friend.

John Adams

25. JOHN ADAMS TO THOMAS JEFFERSON
QUINCY, August 9, 1813

I believe I told you in my last that I had given you all in Lindsay's memorial that interested you, but I was mistaken. In Priestley's letter to Lindsay December 19, 1803, I find this paragraph:

"With the work I am now composing, I go on much faster and better than I expected, so that in two or three months, if, my health continues as it now is, I hope to have it ready for the press, though I shall hardly proceed to print it till we have dispatched the notes.

It is upon the same plan with that of Socrates and Jesus compared, considering all the more distinguished of the Grecian sects of philosophy, till the establishment of Christianity in the Roman Empire. If you liked that pamphlet, I flatter myself you will like this.

I hope it is calculated to show, in a peculiarly striking light, the great advantage of revelation, and that it will make an impression on candid unbelievers if they will read.

But I find few that will trouble themselves to read anything on the subject, which, considering the great magnitude and interesting nature of the subject, is a proof of a very improper state of mind, unworthy of a rational being."

I send you this extract for several reasons: First, because you set him upon this work; Secondly, because I wish you to endeavor to bring it to light and get it printed; Thirdly, because I wish it may stimulate you to pursue your own plan which you promised to Dr. Rush.

I have not seen any work which expressly compares the morality of the Old Testament with that of the New, in all their branches, nor either with that of the ancient philosophers. Comparisons with the Chinese, the East Indians, the Africans, the West Indians, etc., would be more difficult; with more ancient nations impossible. The documents are destroyed.

John Adams

26. JOHN ADAMS TO THOMAS JEFFERSON
   August (14?) 1813

Theoginis[140] lived five hundred and forty years before Jesus Christ. Has Science, Moral, Philosophy, Criticism, or Christianity, advanced, improved, or enlightened Mankind upon this subject (the Well-born), and, shown them that the idea of the "Well-born" is a prejudice, a phantasm, a point no point, a gape fly away, a dream?

I say it is an ordinance of God Almighty in the constitution of

---

140. Theognis (540 BCE?). Wrote poems to Apollo and moral maxims.

human nature, wrought into the fabric of the universe. Philosophers and politicians may nibble and quibble, but they will never get rid of it. Their only resource is to control it. Wealth is another monster to be subdued.

John Adams

27. THOMAS JEFFERSON TO JOHN ADAMS
MONTICELLO, August 22, 1813

DEAR SIR,

Since my letter of June the 27th, I am in your debt for many, all of which I have read with infinite delight. They open a wide field for reflection, and offer subjects enough to occupy the mind and the pen indefinitely. I must follow the good example you have set, and when I have not time to take up every subject, take up a single one.

Your approbation of my outline to Dr. Priestley is a great gratification to me. I very much suspect that if thinking men would have the courage to think for themselves, and to speak what they think, it would be found they do not differ in religious opinions as much as is supposed. I remember to have heard Dr. Priestley say, that if all England would candidly examine itself and confess, it would find that Unitarianism was really the religion of all.

I observe a bill is now depending in parliament for the relief of Anti-Trinitarians. It is too late in the day for men of sincerity to pretend they believe in the Platonic mysticisms that three are one, and one is three; and yet that the one is not three, and the three are not one; to divide mankind by a single letter into Consubstantialists[141] and Like-substantialists.[142] But this constitutes the craft, the power and the profit of the priests. Sweep away their gossamer fabrics of factitious religion, and they would catch no more flies. We should all then, like the Quakers, live without an order of priests, moralize for ourselves,

141. *Homoousios*—Jesus is same substance/essence as the Father.
142. *Homoiious*—Jesus not of same substance/essence as Father, but of like or similar substance.

follow the oracle of conscience, and say nothing about what no man can understand, nor therefore believe; for I suppose belief to be the assent of the mind to an intelligible proposition.

It is with great pleasure I can inform you, that Priestley finished the comparative view of the doctrines of the philosophers of antiquity, and of Jesus, before his death; and that it was printed soon after.

And, with still greater pleasure, that I can have a copy of his work forwarded from Philadelphia, by a correspondent there, and presented for your acceptance, by the same mail which carries, you this, or very soon after. The branch of the work which the title announces is executed with learning and candor, as was everything Priestley wrote, but perhaps a little hastily; for he felt himself pressed by the hand of death.

The Abbe Batteux had, in fact, laid the foundation of this part in his Causes Premieres,[143] with which he has given us the originals of Ocellus and Timaeus, who first committed the doctrines of Pythagoras to writing,[144] and Enfield,[145] to whom the Doctor refers, had done it more copiously. But he has omitted the important branch, which, in your letter of August the 9th, you say you have never seen executed, a comparison of the morality of the Old Testament with that of the New. And yet, no two things were ever more unlike. I ought not to have asked him to give it. He dared not. He would have been eaten alive by his intolerant brethren, the Cannibal priests. And yet, this was really the most interesting branch of the work.

Very soon after my letter to Doctor Priestley, the subject being still in my mind, I had leisure during an abstraction from business for a day or two, while on the road, to think a little more on it, and to sketch more fully than I had done to him, a syllabus of the matter which I thought should enter into the work. I wrote it to Doctor Rush, and

---

143. Charles Batteux (1713–1780). Paris professor who wrote on Epicurus. Author of *History of First Causes*.

144. Pythagoreans. Lucanus Ocellus (fifth century BCE) wrote *On the Nature of the Universe* and Locrius Timaeus wrote *The Soul and the World*.

145. William Enfield (1741–1791). Dissenting theologian. Author of *The History of Philosophy from the Earliest Times*, drawn from Jakob Brucker's *Historia Critica Philosophiae*.

there ended all my labor on the subject; himself and Doctor Priestley being the only two depositories of my secret.

The fate of my letter to Priestley, after his death, was a warning to me on that of Doctor Rush. At my request, his family was so kind as to quiet me by returning my original letter and syllabus. By this, you will be sensible how much interest I take in keeping myself clear of religious disputes before the public, and especially of seeing my syllabus disemboweled by the Auspices of the modern Paganism. Yet I enclose it to you with entire confidence, free to be perused by yourself and Mrs. Adams, but by no one else, and to be returned to me.

You are right in supposing, in one of yours, that I had not read much of Priestley's Predestination, his no-soul system, or his controversy with Horsley. But I have read his Corruptions of Christianity, and Early Opinions of Jesus, over and over again. I rest on them, and on Middleton's writings,[146] especially his letters from Rome, and to Waterland, as the basis of my own faith. These writings have never been answered, nor can be answered by quoting historical proofs, as they have done. For these facts, therefore, I cling to their learning, so much superior to my own.

Thomas Jefferson

28. JOHN ADAMS TO THOMAS JEFFERSON
QUINCY, September 14, 1813

DEAR SIR,

I owe you a thousand thanks for your favor of August 22d and its enclosures, and for Dr. Priestley's doctrines of Heathen Philosophy compared with those of Revelation. Your letter to Dr. Rush and the syllabus, I return enclosed with this according to your injunctions, though with great reluctance. May I beg a copy of both?

---

146. Conyers Middleton. Author of *A Free Inquiry into the Miraculous Powers (which are supposed to have existed in the Christian Church through Successive Ages)* (1748–1749).

They will do you no harm; me and others much good.

I hope you will pursue your plan, for I am confident you will produce a work much more valuable than Priestley's, though that is curious, and considering the expiring powers with which it was written, admirable.

The bill in Parliament for the relief of Anti-Trinitarians, is a great event, and will form an epoch in ecclesiastical history. The motion was made by my friend Smith, of Clapham, a friend of the Belshams.

I should be very happy to hear that the bill is passed.

The human understanding is a revelation from its Maker which can never be disputed or doubted. There can be no skepticism, Pyrrhonism,[147] or incredulity, or infidelity, here. No prophecies, no miracles are necessary to prove the celestial communication.

This revelation has made it certain that two and one make three, and that one is not three nor can three be one. We can never be so certain of any prophecy, or the fulfillment of any prophecy, or of any miracle, or the design of any miracle, as we are from the revelation of nature, i.e., Nature's God, that two and two are equal to four. Miracles or prophecies might frighten us out of our wits; might scare us to death; might induce us to lie, to say that we believe that two and two make five. But we should not believe it. We should know the contrary.

Had you and I been forty days with Moses on Mount Sinai, and been admitted to behold the divine Shekinah,[148] and there told that one was three and three one, we might not have had courage to deny it, but we could not have believed it. The thunders, and lightnings, and earthquakes, and the transcendent splendors and glories might have overwhelmed us with terror and amazement, but we could not have believed the doctrine. We should be more likely to say in our hearts whatever we might say with our lips, "This is chance. There is no God, no truth. This is all delusion, fiction, and a lie, or it is all chance." But what is chance? It is motion. It is action. It is event. It is phenomenon without cause. Chance is no cause at all, it is nothing.

---

147. Pyrrho (360–270 BCE). Greek philosopher of skeptical school of thought. He believed "We can be certain of nothing" and judgment should be suspended on every proposition.

148. Face, Countenance, presence of God.

And nothing has produced all this pomp and splendor. And nothing may produce our eternal damnation in the flames of hell-fire and brimstone, for what we know, as well as this tremendous exhibition of terror and falsehood.

God has infinite wisdom, goodness and power. He created the universe. His duration is eternal, a parts ante and a parts post. His presence is as extensive as space. What is space? An infinite spherical vacuum? He created this speck of dirt and the human species for his glory, and with the deliberate design of making nine-tenths of our species miserable forever, for his glory.

This is the doctrine of Christian Theologians in general, ten to one.

Now, my friend, can prophecies or miracles convince you or me, that infinite benevolence, wisdom and power, created and preserves for a time, innumerable millions, to make them miserable forever for his own glory?

Wretch! What is his glory? Is he ambitious? Does he want promotion? Is he vain, tickled with adulation? Exulting and triumphing in his power and the sweetness of his vengeance?

Pardon me, my Maker, for these awful questions. My answer to them is always ready. I believe no such things! My adoration of the Author of the Universe is too profound and too sincere.

The love of God and his creation, delight, joy, triumph, exultation in my own existence, though but an atom, a molecule organique in the universe, are my religion. Howl, snarl, bite, ye Calvinistic, ye Athanasian divines, if you will. Ye will say I am no Christian! I say ye are no Christians, and there the account is balanced! Yet I believe all the honest men among you are Christians, in my sense of the word.

When I was at college, I was a metaphysician, at least I thought myself such. And such men as Locke, Hemmenway and West,[149] thought me so too; for we were forever disputing though in great good humor.

When I was sworn as an attorney, in 1758, in Boston, though I lived in Braintree, I was in a low state of health, thought in great danger of a consumption; living on milk, vegetable pudding and water.

---

149. Samuel Locke, Moses Hemmenway, and Samuel West—Harvard classmates of Adams.

Not an atom of meat, or a drop of spirit. My next neighbor, my cousin, my friend Dr. Savil,[150] was my physician. He was anxious about me, and did not like to take the sole responsibility of my recovery. He invited me to a ride. I mounted my horse and rode with him to Hingham, on a visit to Dr. Ezekiel Hersey, a physician of great fame, who felt my pulse, looked in my eyes, heard Savil describe my regimen and course of medicine, and then pronounced his oracle: "Persevere, and as sure as there is a God in Heaven you will recover."

He was an everlasting talker, and ran out into history, philosophy, metaphysics, etc., and frequently put questions to me as if he wanted to sound me, and see if there was anything in me besides hectic fever. I was young, and then very bashful, however saucy I may have sometimes been since. I gave him very modest and very diffident answers. But when I got upon metaphysics, I seemed to feel a little bolder, and ventured into something like argument with him.

I drove him up, as I thought, into a corner, from which he could not escape. "Sir, it will follow from what you have now advanced, that the universe, as distinct from God, is both infinite and eternal."

"Very true," said Dr. Hersey, "your inference is just, the consequence is inevitable, and I believe the universe to be both eternal and infinite."

Here I was brought up! I was defeated. I was not prepared for this answer. This was fifty-five years ago.

When I was in England, from 1785 to 1788, I may say I was intimate with Dr. Price. I had much conversation with him at his own house, at my house, and at the houses and tables of my friends. In some of our most unreserved conversations when we have been alone, he has repeatedly said to me:

> "I am inclined to believe that the universe is eternal and infinite. It seems to me that an eternal and infinite effect must necessarily flow from an eternal and infinite cause; and an infinite wisdom, goodness and power, that could have been induced to produce a universe in time, must have produced it from eternity. It seems to me the effect must flow from the cause."

---

150. Dr. Elisha Savil.

Now, my friend Jefferson, suppose an eternal, self-existent being, existing from eternity, possessed of infinite wisdom, goodness and power, in absolute, total solitude, six thousand years ago, conceiving the benevolent project of creating a universe! I have no more to say at present. It has been long, very long, a settled opinion in my mind, that there is now, never will be, and never was but one being who can understand the universe. And that it is not only vain, but wicked, for insects to pretend to comprehend it.

John Adams

29. JOHN ADAMS TO THOMAS JEFFERSON
   September 15, 1813

Dr. Price was "inclined to think" that infinite Wisdom and Goodness could not permit infinite Power to be inactive from Eternity: but that, an infinite and eternal universe must have necessarily flowed from these attributes.

Plato's system was "good" was eternal, self-existent, etc. His Ideas, his Word, his Reason, his Wisdom, his Goodness, or in one word, his "Logos," was omnipotent and produced the universe from all eternity.

Now! As far as you and I can understand Hersey, Price, and Plato, are they not one theory, of one mind? What is the difference? I own an eternal solitude of a self-existent Being, infinitely wise, powerful, and good is too altogether incomprehensible and incredible. I could as soon believe the Athanasian Creed.

You will ask me what conclusions I draw from all this. I answer: I drop into myself and acknowledge myself to be a fool. No mind but One can see through the immeasurable system. It would be presumption and impiety in me to dogmatize on such subjects. My duties in my little infinitesimal circle I can understand and feel. The duties of a son, brother, a father, a neighbor, a citizen, I can see and feel. But, I trust the Ruler with the skies.

John Adams

30. JOHN ADAMS TO THOMAS JEFFERSON
September 22, 1813

DEAR SIR,

Considering all things, I admire Dr. Priestley's last effort, for which I am entirely indebted to you. But as I think it is extremely imperfect, I beg of you to pursue the investigation according to your promise to Dr. Rush and according to your syllabus.

It may be presumptuous in me to denominate anything of Dr. Priestley's imperfect, but I avow that, among all the vast exertions of genius, I have never found one that is not imperfect. And, this last is egregiously so.

I will instance at present in one article: I found no notice of Cleanthes,[151] one of whose sayings alone ought to have commanded his attention. He compared philosophers to instruments of music which made a noise without understanding it, or themselves.

He was ridiculed by his brother philosophers and called "an ass." He owned he was the "Ass of Zeno" and the only one whose back and shoulders were stout enough to carry his burdens.

Why has not Priestley quoted more from Zeno and his disciples? Were they too Christian, though he (Zeno) lived two centuries and a half before Christ?

If I did not know it would be sending coal to Newcastle, I would, with all my dimness of eyes and trembling of fingers, copy in Greek the Hymn of Cleanthes,[152] and, request you compare it with anything of Moses, David, or Solomon.

Instead of those ardent figures which are so difficult to understand, we find that divine simplicity which constitutes the charm of Grecian eloquence in prose and verse. Pope had read if Priestley had not: "Most glorious and immortal beings, though denominated by innumerable names and titles, always omnipotent, Beginning and end of Nature, governing the universe by fixed laws, blessed be thy name!"

---

151. Stoic philosopher of Assus in Lydia and disciple of Zeno. Poor and a slow learner (but persevering), his fellow disciples called him an "ass."

152. *Hymn to Jupiter.*

What think you of this translation? Is it too Jewish, or too Christian? Pope did not think it was either. For, the first sentence in his universal prayer is more Jewish and more Christian still. If it is not a literal translation, it is a close paraphrase of this simple verse of Cleanthes:

"Father of all, in every age,
in every clime adored
by saint and by sage,
Jehovah, Jove, or Lord."

But, it may be said, for it has been said, that Pope was a Deist and Swift[153] too, as well as Bolingbroke. What will not men say? But is the Existence, the Omnipotence, the Eternity, the Alpha and Omega, and the Universal Providence of one Supreme Being, governing by fixed Laws, asserted by St. John in his Gospel, or in the Apocalypse, whether his or not, in clearer or more precise terms?

Can you conjecture a reason why Grotius[154] has not translated this Hymn?

Were Grotius and Priestley both afraid that the Stoics would appear too much like Unitarian Jews and Christians?

. . . It appears to me that the Great Principle of the Hebrews was the fear of God; that of the Gentiles, Honor the Gods; that of Christians, the Love of God. Could the quiveration of my nerves and the inflammation of my eyes be cured and my age diminished by 20 or 30 years, I would attend you in these researches with infinitely more pleasure than I would be George the 4th, Napoleon, Alexander, or Madison. But, only a few hours, a few moments remain for your old friend.

John Adams

---

153. Jonathan Swift (1667–1745). Minister. Author of *Letters Concerning the Sacramental Test* and *An Argument against Abolishing Christianity* (both 1708), and *The Sentiments of a Church of England Man with Respect to Church and Government*.

154. Hugo Grotius (1583–1645). Dutch legal scholar, playwright, and poet. He was an Anti-Calvinist, Arminian Free Will advocate. Wrote *True Religion Explained and Defended against the Archenemies Thereof in the Times* (1632) and *Mare Liberum* (Freedom of the Seas) (1609).

31. JOHN ADAMS TO THOMAS JEFFERSON
September (or October 4) 1813

"It is not only permitted but enjoined upon all mortals to address you."

Why should not our Divines translate it: "It is our duty and our privilege to address the Throne of thy grace and pray for all needed and lawful blessings, temporal and spiritual?"

Hera was the Goddess of honesty, justice, decency, and right; the wife of Jove, another name for Juno. She presided over all oracles, deliberations, and counsels. She commanded all mortals to pray to Jupiter for all lawful benefits and blessings. Now, is not this the essence of Christian devotion? Is not this Christian piety? Is it not an acknowledgement of the essence of a Supreme Being? of his universal providence? of a righteous administration of the government of the universe? And, what can Jews and Christians do more?

Priestley, the heroic Priestley, would not have dared answer or to ask these questions, though he might have answered them consistently enough with the spirit of his system.

I regret that Grotius has not translated this hymn. I cannot account for his omission of it.

. . . In this manner are the most ancient Greek theologians rendered and transmitted to our Youth by the Christians: "For we are of your race, being only a copy of your voice, however many a mortal lives or creeps on the earth."

I presume this is the phrase quoted by Saint Paul when he says to the Athenians, "One of your own poets has said we are all his offspring." Acts 17th.28: "For in him we live and move and have our being." Certain also of your poets have said: "For we are also all his offspring."

"Forasmuch as then as we are the offspring of God, we ought not to think that the Godhead is like unto silver or gold, or stone graven by man's device."

This reasoning is irresistible. For, what can be more mad than to represent the eternal, almighty, omnipresent Cause and Principle of the universe by statues, pictures, coins, and medals?

Moses says, Genesis 1:27: "God created man in his own image." What then is the difference between Moses and Cleanthes? Are not the being and attributes of the Supreme Being, the resemblance, the image, the shadow of God in the intelligence and moral qualities of man, and the lawfulness and duty of prayer, as clearly asserted by Cleanthes as by Moses? And, did not the Chaldeans, the Egyptians, the Persians, the Indians, and the Chinese, believe all this as well as the Jews and the Greeks?

Alexander appears to have behaved to the Jews as Napoleon did to the Mahometans in the pyramid of Grand Cairo. Ptolemy, the greatest of his generals, and a greater man than himself, was so impressed with what he learned in Judea, that he employed 70 learned men to translate the Hebrew Scriptures into Greek nearly 300 years before Christ. He sent learned men to collect books from all nations and deposited them in the Alexandrian Library.

Will any man make me believe that Caesar, that Pompey, that Cicero, that Seneca,[155] that Tacitus, that Dionysius Hallicarnassensis,[156] that Plutarch,[157] had never heard of the Septuagint?[158] The curiosity of Pompey to see the interior of the temple shows that the system of the Jews was become an object of speculation. It is impossible to believe that the Septuagint was unknown and unheard of by the Greeks or Romans at that time, at least by the great generals, orators, historians, philosophers, and statesmen, who looked through the then known world for information of everything.

On the other hand, how do we know how much Moses, Samuel, Joshua, David, Solomon, Esdras, Daniel, Ezekiel, Isaiah, and Jeremiah learned in Babylon, Egypt, and Persia? The destruction of the Library at Alexandria is all the answer we can obtain to these questions. I

---

155. Lucius Annaeus Seneca. See note 115.

156. Dionysius Halicarnassensis. Greek historian during the reign of Augustus. Wrote *Roman Antiquities*.

157. (c. 46–c. 120 CE). Greek Historian, Priest of Apollo. Wrote on moral matters, including *On the Worship of Isis and Osiris*, *On the Decline of Oracles*, and *On the Delays of Divine Vengeance*. Also wrote *Lives of Noble Greeks and Romans*.

158. The Greek translation of the Old Testament.

believe the Jews, Grecians, Romans, and Christians all conspired or connived at that savage catastrophe.

I believe Cleanthes to be as good a Christian as Priestley. But, enough of my school-boy criticisms, crude philosophy, problematical history, and heretical divinity for the present.

John Adams

32. THOMAS JEFFERSON TO JOHN ADAMS
   October 12, 1813

DEAR SIR,

I now send you, according to your request, a copy of the Syllabus. To fill up this skeleton with arteries, with veins, with nerves, muscles, and flesh, is really beyond my time and information. Whoever would undertake it would find great aid in Enfield's judicious abridgement of Brucker's history of philosophy.[159]

To compare the morals of the old with the new testament would require an attentive study of the former, a search through all its books for its precepts, and through all its history for its practices and the principles they prove.

As commentaries too on these, the philosophy of the Hebrews must be inquired into, their Mishna, their Gemara, Cabala, Jezirah, Sohar, Cosri, and their Talmud must be examined and understood in order to do them full justice. Brucker, it should seem, has gone deeply into these repositories or their ethics. Enfield, his epitomizer, concludes in these words:

> "Ethics were so little studied among the Jews, that, in their whole compilation called the Talmud, there is only one treatise on moral subjects. Their books of Morals chiefly consisted in a minute enumeration of duties. From the Law of Moses were deducted 613 precepts, which were divided into two classes, affirmative and negative, 248 in the former, 365 in the latter.

---

159. See footnote 145.

It may serve to give the reader some idea of the low state of moral philosophy among the Jews in the Middle age to add that of the 248 affirmative precepts, only 3 were considered obligatory upon women. In order to obtain salvation, it was judged sufficient to fulfill any one single law in the hour of death; the observance of the rest being deemed necessary only to increase the felicity of the future life. What a wretched depravity of sentiment and manners must have prevailed before such corrupt maxims could have obtained credit! It is impossible to collect from these writings a consistent series of moral doctrine." (Enfield, B. 4, chap. 3)

It was the reformation of this "wretched depravity" that Jesus undertook. In extracting the pure principles which he taught, we should strip off the artificial vestments in which they have been muffled by priests, who have travestied them into various forms as instruments of riches and power to them.

We must dismiss the Platonist, Plotinists, Stagyrites,[160] Gamalielites, Eclectics, Gnostics, Scholastics, their essences and emanations, their Logos and Demiurges,[161] Aeons, Daemons, male and female, with a long train of etc., etc. etc., or shall I say at once, of Nonsense.[162]

We must reduce our volume to the simple evangelists, select even from them the very words of Jesus, paring off the Amphibologisms[163] into which they have been led by forgetting often, or not understanding, what had fallen from him, by giving their own misconceptions as his dicta, and expressing unintelligibly for others what they had not understood themselves. There will be found remaining the most sublime and benevolent code of morals which has ever been offered to man.

---

160. Followers of Aristotle (of Stagira, Macedonia). Aristotle wrote *Metaphysics, On the Soul,* and *On the Heavens.*

161. Platonic Creator of Worlds.

162. Philosophic/theological groups and their various terms to explain God/Creators/Spirits.

163. Using two sides/both sides of words, or giving another meaning to someone's spoken or written words than what was intended. Substituting or mistranslating words.

I have performed this operation for my own use by cutting verse by verse out of the printed book, and arranging the matter which is evidently his, and which is as easily distinguishable as diamonds in a dunghill. The result is 8 vo. [octavo][164] of 46 pages of pure and sophisticated doctrines, such as were professed and acted on by the unlettered apostles, the apostolic fathers, and the Christians of the first century. Their Platonizing successors, indeed in after times, in order to legitimize the corruptions which they had incorporated into the doctrines of Jesus, found it necessary to disavow the primitive Christians, who had taken their principles from the mouth of Jesus himself, or his apostles, and the Fathers contemporary with them. They excommunicated their followers as heretics, branding them with the opprobrious name of Ebionites[165] or Beggers.

For a comparison of the Grecian philosophy with that of Jesus, materials might be largely drawn from the same source. Enfield gives a history and detailed account of the opinions and principles of the different sects. These relate to:

> the gods, their natures, grades, places and powers;
> the demi-gods and daemons, and their agency with man;
> the universe, its structure, extent, production and duration;
> the origin of things from the elements of fire, water, air, earth;
> the human soul, its essence and derivation;

the summum bonum and finis bonorum; with a thousand idle dreams and fancies on these and other subjects, the knowledge of which is withheld from Man, leaving but a short chapter for his moral duties, and the principal section of that given to what he owes himself, to precepts for rendering him impassible and unassailable by the evils of life, and for preserving his mind in a state of constant serenity.

Such a canvas is too broad for the age of seventy, and especially of one whose chief occupations have been in the practical business of life. We

---

164. Book made from one large page cut into eighths.

165. From the Hebrew word for "the poor." Jewish Christian sect that held to the Torah and rejected Paul and the virgin birth, though Origen apparently denies the latter.

must leave therefore to others, younger and more learned than we are, to prepare this euthanasia for Platonic Christianity, and its restoration to the primitive simplicity of its founder. I think you give it a just outline of theism of the three religions when you say that the principle of the Hebrew was the fear, of the Gentile the honor, and of the Christian the love of God.

An expression in your letter of September 14 that "the human understanding is a revelation from its maker" gives the best solution that I believe can be given of the question: What did Socrates mean by his Daemon? He was too wise to believe, and too honest to pretend, that he had real and familiar converse with a superior and invisible being. He probably considered the suggestions of his conscience or reason as revelations or inspirations from the Supreme mind, bestowed on important occasions by a special superintending providence.

I acknowledge all the merits of the hymn of Cleanthes to Jupiter, which you ascribe to it. It is as highly sublime as a chaste and correct imagination can permit itself to go. Yet in contemplation of a being so superlative, the hyperbolic flights of the Psalmist may often be followed with approbation, even with rapture; and I have no hesitation in giving him the palm over all the Hymnists of every language, and of every time.

Thomas Jefferson

33. THOMAS JEFFERSON TO JOHN ADAMS
MONTICELLO, October 28, 1813

DEAR SIR,

According to the reservation between us, of taking up one of the subjects of our correspondence at a time, I turn to your letters of August the 16th and September the 2d.

The passage you quote from Theognis, I think has an ethical rather than a political object. The whole piece is a moral exhortation and this passage particularly seems to be a reproof to man; who, while with his domestic animals he is curious to improve the race, by employing always the finest male, pays no attention to the improvement of his own race, but intermarries with the vicious, the ugly, or the old, for considerations of wealth or ambition. It is in conformity with the principle adopted afterwards by the Pythagoreans, and expressed by Ocellus in another form, which, as literally as intelligibility will admit, may be thus translated:

"Concerning the interprocreation of men, how, and of whom it shall be, in a perfect manner, and according to the laws of modesty and sanctity, conjointly, this is what I think right. First, to lay it down that we do not commix for the sake of pleasure, but of the procreation of children. For the powers, the organs and desires for coition have not been given by God to man for the sake of pleasure, but for the procreation of the race. For, as it were incongruous, for a mortal born to partake of divine life, the immortality of the race being taken away, God fulfilled the purpose by making the generations uninterrupted and continuous. This, therefore, we are especially to lay down as a principle, that coition is not for the sake of pleasure."

But nature, not trusting to this moral and abstract motive, seems to have provided more securely for the perpetuation of the species, by making it the effect of the oestrum implanted in the constitution of both sexes. And not only has the commerce of love been indulged on this unhallowed impulse, but made subservient also to wealth and ambition by marriage, without regard to the beauty, the healthiness, the understanding, or virtue of the subject from which we are to breed. The selecting the best male for a harem of well-chosen females also, which Theognis seems to recommend from the example of our sheep and asses, would doubtless improve the human, as it does the brute animal, and produce a race of veritable aristocrats.

For, experience proves that the moral and physical qualities of man, whether good or evil, are transmissible in a certain degree from father to son. But I suspect that the equal rights of men will rise up against this privileged Solomon and his harem, and oblige us to continue acquiescence under the degeneration of the race of men which

Theognis complains of, and to content ourselves with the accidental aristoi produced by the fortuitous concourse of breeders.

For, I agree with you that there is a natural aristocracy among men. The grounds of this are virtue and talents. Formerly, bodily powers gave place among the aristoi. But since the invention of gunpowder has armed the weak as well as the strong with missile death, bodily strength, like beauty, good humor, politeness and other accomplishments, has become but an auxiliary ground of distinction. There is also an artificial aristocracy, founded on wealth and birth, without either virtue or talents; for with these it would belong to the first class. The natural aristocracy I consider as the most precious gift of nature, for the instruction, the trusts, and government of society: And indeed, it would have been inconsistent in creation to have formed man for the social state, and not to have provided virtue and wisdom enough to manage the concerns of the society.

May we not even say that that form of government is the best, which provides the most effectually for a pure selection of these natural aristoi into the offices of government? The artificial aristocracy is a mischievous ingredient in government, and provision should be made to prevent its ascendancy.

On the question, what is the best provision, you and I differ; but we differ as rational friends, using the free exercise of our own reason, and mutually indulging its errors. You think it best to put the pseudo-aristoi into a separate chamber of legislation, where they may be hindered from doing mischief by their coordinate branches, and where, also, they may be a protection to wealth against the agrarian and plundering enterprises of the majority of the people. I think that to give them power in order to prevent them from doing mischief, is arming them for it, and increasing instead of remedying the evil.

For, if the co-ordinate branches can arrest their action, so may they that of the co-ordinates. Mischief may be done negatively as well as positively. Of this, a cabal in the Senate of the United States has furnished many proofs. Nor do I believe them necessary to protect the wealthy; because enough of these will find their way into every branch of the legislation to protect themselves. Fifteen to twenty legislatures of our own, in action for thirty years past, have proved that no fears of an equalization of property are to be apprehended from them.

I think the best remedy is exactly that provided by all our constitutions, to leave to the citizens the free election and separation of the aristoi from the pseudo-aristoi, of the wheat from the chaff. In general they will elect the really good and wise. In some instances, wealth may corrupt, and birth blind them; but not in sufficient degree to endanger the society.

It is probable that our difference of opinion may, in some measure, be produced by a difference of character in those among whom we live. From what I have seen of Massachusetts and Connecticut myself, and still more from what I have heard, and the character given of the former by yourself, who know them so much better, there seems to be in those two States a traditional reverence for certain families, which has rendered the offices of the government nearly hereditary in those families. I presume that from an early period of your history, members of those families happening to possess virtue and talents, have honestly exercised them for the good of the people, and by their services have endeared their names to them. In coupling Connecticut with you, I mean it politically only, not morally. For having made the Bible the common law of their land, they seem to have modeled their morality on the story of Jacob and Laban.[166]

But although this hereditary succession to office with you, may, in some degree, be founded in real family merit, yet in a much higher degree, it has proceeded from your strict alliance of Church and State.[167] These families are canonized in the eyes of the people on common principles, "you tickle me, and I will tickle you."

In Virginia we have nothing of this. Our clergy, before the revolution, having been secured against rivalry by fixed salaries, did not give themselves the trouble of acquiring influence over the people. Of wealth, there were great accumulations in particular families, handed

---

166. Jacob contracts to work seven years in exchange for Laban's daughter Rachel. But, after the specified time, Jacob is forced to marry Leah, Laban's firstborn daughter. Jacob then contracts to work seven more years for Rachel.

167. Massachusetts (1834) and Connecticut (1818) were the two last colonial states to do away with church-state alliances/establishments in their constitutions.

down from generation to generation, under the English law of entails. But the only object of ambition for the wealthy was a seat in the King's Council. All their court then was paid to the crown and its creatures; and they Philipized in all collisions between the King and the people. Hence they were unpopular; and that unpopularity continues attached to their names. A Randolph, a Carter, or a Burwell must have great personal superiority over a common competitor to be elected by the people even at this day.

At the first session of our legislature after the Declaration of Independence, we passed a law abolishing entails. And this was followed by one abolishing the privilege of primogeniture, and dividing the lands of intestates equally among all their children, or other representatives. These laws, drawn by myself, laid the axe to the foot of pseudo-aristocracy.

And had another which I prepared been adopted by the legislature, our work would have been complete. It was a bill for the more general diffusion of learning. This proposed to divide every county into wards of five or six miles square, like your townships; to establish in each ward a free school for reading, writing and common arithmetic; to provide for the annual selection of the best subjects from these schools, who might receive, at the public expense, a higher degree of education at a district school; and from these district schools to select a certain number of the most promising subjects, to be completed at an university, where all the useful sciences should be taught.

Worth and genius would thus have been sought out from every condition of life, and completely prepared by education for defeating the competition of wealth and birth for public trusts. My proposition had, for a further object, to impart to these wards those portions of self-government for which they are best qualified, by confiding to them the care of their poor, their roads, police, elections, the nomination of jurors, administration of justice in small cases, elementary exercises of militia; in short, to have made them little republics, with a warden at the head of each, for all those concerns which, being under their eye, they would better manage than the larger republics of the county or State.

A general call of ward meetings by their wardens on the same day through the State would at any time produce the genuine sense of the people on any required point and would enable the State to act in mass, as your people have so often done with so much effect by their town meetings.

The law for religious freedom, which made a part of this system, having put down the aristocracy of the clergy, and restored to the citizen the freedom of the mind, and those of entails and descents nurturing an equality of condition among them, this on education would have raised the mass of the people to the high ground of moral respectability necessary to their own safety, and to orderly government; and would have completed the great object of qualifying them to select the veritable aristoi, for the trusts of government, to the exclusion of the pseudalists; and the same Theognis who has furnished the epigraphs of your two letters, assures us that, "Curnis, good men have never hurt any city." Although this law has not yet been acted on but in a small and inefficient degree, it is still considered as before the legislature, with other bills of the revised code, not yet taken up, and I have great hope that some patriotic spirit will, at a favorable moment, call it up, and make it the keystone of the arch of our government.

With respect to aristocracy, we should further consider, that before the establishment of the American States, nothing was known to history but the man of the old world, crowded within limits either small or overcharged, and steeped in the vices which that situation generates. A government adapted to such men would be one thing; but a very different one, that for the man of these States. Here every one may have land to labor for himself if he chooses; or, preferring the exercise of any other industry, may exact for it such compensation as not only to afford a comfortable subsistence, but wherewith to provide for a cessation from labor in old age.

Every one, by his property, or by his satisfactory situation, is interested in the support of law and order. And such men may safely and advantageously reserve to themselves a wholesome control over their public affairs, and a degree of freedom, which, in the hands of the canaille[168] of the cities of Europe, would be instantly perverted to the

---

168. Rabble, riff-raff.

demolition and destruction of everything public and private. The history of the last twenty-five years of France, and of the last forty years in America, nay of its last two hundred years, proves the truth of both parts of this observation.

But even in Europe a change has sensibly taken place in the mind of man. Science had liberated the ideas of those who read and reflect, and the American example had kindled feelings of right in the people. An insurrection has consequently begun, of science, talents, and courage, against rank and birth, which have fallen into contempt. It has failed in its first effort, because the mobs of the cities, the instrument used for its accomplishment, debased by ignorance, poverty, and vice, could not be restrained to rational action.

But the world will recover from the panic of this first catastrophe. Science is progressive, and talents and enterprise on the alert. Resort may be had to the people of the country, a more governable power from their principles and subordination; and rank, and birth, and tinsel-aristocracy will finally shrink into insignificance, even there. This, however, we have no right to meddle with. It suffices for us, if the moral and physical condition of our own citizens qualifies them to select the able and good for the direction of their government, with a recurrence of elections at such short periods as will enable them to displace an unfaithful servant, before the mischief he meditates may be irremediable.

I have thus stated my opinion on a point on which we differ, not with a view to controversy, for we are both too old to change opinions which are the result of a long life of inquiry and reflection; but on the suggestions of a former letter of yours, that we ought not to die before we have explained ourselves to each other. We acted in perfect harmony, through a long and perilous contest for our liberty and independence. A constitution has been acquired, which, though neither of us thinks perfect, yet both consider as competent to render our fellow citizens the happiest and the securest on whom the sun has ever shone. If we do not think exactly alike as to its imperfections, it matters little to our country, which, after devoting to it long lives of disinterested labor, we have delivered over to our successors in life, who will be able to take care of it and of themselves.

Of the pamphlet on aristocracy which has been sent to you, or who may be its author, I have heard nothing but through your letter. If the person you suspect, it may be known from the quaint, mystical, and hyperbolical ideas, involved in affected, new-fangled and pedantic terms which stamp his writings. Whatever it is, I hope your quiet is not to be affected at this day by the rudeness or intemperance of scribblers; but that you may continue in tranquility to live and to rejoice in the prosperity of our country, until it shall be your own wish to take your seat among the aristoi who have gone before you.

Ever and affectionately yours.

Thomas Jefferson

34. JOHN ADAMS TO THOMAS JEFFERSON
QUINCY, November 14, 1813

DEAR SIR,

Accept my thanks for the comprehensive syllabus in your favor of October 12th.

The Psalms of David, in sublimity, beauty, pathos and originality, or, in one word, in poetry, are superior to all the odes, hymns and songs in our language. But I had rather read them in our prose translation, than in any version I have seen. His morality, however, often shocks me, like Tristram Shandy's execrations.[169]

Blacklock's[170] translation of Horace's "Justum"[171] is admirable; superior to Addison's.[172] Could David be translated as well, his superiority would be universally acknowledged. We cannot compare the

---

169. Laurence Sterne's comic novel *The Life and Opinions of Tristram Shandy, Gentleman* appeared between 1759 and 1767.

170. Thomas Blacklock (1721–1791). Blind Scot poet. Author of *Parclesis: or Consolations Deduced from Natural and Revealed Religion* (1767), *Two Discourses on the Spirit and Evidences of Christianity* (1768), and *Treatise on Morals*.

171. Horace (65–8 BCE). Roman poet. Wrote maxims/epistles on love and morals.

172. Joseph Addison (1672–1719). Collaborated with Sir Richard Steele on *The Spectator*, a collection of 555 essays on morals and manners.

sublime poetry. By Virgil's "Pollio,"[173] we may conjecture there was prophecy as well as sublimity. Why have those verses been annihilated? I suspect Platonic Christianity, Pharisaical Judaism or Machiavellian politics, in this case, as in all other cases, of the destruction of records and literary monuments. The auri sacra fames, et dominandi saeva cupido. [The horrible hunger for gold and the savage lust of power. Vergil's *Aeniad* III, 59. Cappon translation.]

Among all your researches in Hebrew history and controversy, have you ever met a book the design of which is to prove that the ten commandments, as we have them in our Catechisms and hung up in our churches, were not the ten commandments written by the finger of God upon tables delivered to Moses on Mount Sinai, and broken by him in a passion with Aaron for his golden calf, nor those afterwards engraved by him on tables of stone; but a very different set of commandments?

There is such a book, by J. W. Goethe; Schriften, Berlin, 1775–1779.[174] I wish to see this book. You will perceive the question in Exodus, 20:1, 17, 22, 28; chapter 24:3, etc.; chapter 24:12; chapter 25:31; chapter 31:18; chapter 31:19 ; chapter 34:1; chapter 34:10, etc.[175]

I will make a covenant with this people. Observe that which I command this day:

1. Thou shalt not adore any other God. Therefore take heed not to enter into covenant with the inhabitants of the country; neither take for your sons their daughters in marriage. They would allure thee to the worship of false gods. Much less shall you in any place erect images.
2. The feast of unleavened bread shalt thou keep. Seven days shalt thou eat unleavened bread, at the time of the month Abib; to remember that about that time, I delivered thee from Egypt.
3. Every first born of the mother is mine; the male of thine herd,

---

173. Vergil or Virgil (70–19 BCE). Roman poet. Some early Christians thought his *Pollio* forecast the birth of Jesus. Constantine was impressed.

174. Johann Wolfgang von Goethe (1749–1832). German poet, novelist, and playwright. Author of *Faust*.

175. Exodus 20 has a different set of "Ten Commandments" than does Exodus 34, the "rewrite" after the first set of commandments is broken by Moses.

be it stock or flock. But you shall replace the first born of an ass with a sheep. The first born of your sons shall you redeem. No man shall appear before me with empty hands.

4. Six days shalt thou labor. The seventh day thou shalt rest from ploughing and gathering.
5. The feast of weeks shalt thou keep with the firstlings of the wheat harvest; and the feast of harvesting at the end of the year.
6. Thrice in every year all male persons shall appear before the Lord. Nobody shall invade your country, as long as you obey this command.
7. Thou shalt not sacrifice the blood of a sacrifice of mine, upon leavened bread.
8. The sacrifice of the Passover shall not remain until the next day.
9. The firstlings of the produce of your land, thou shalt bring to the house of the Lord.
10. Thou shalt not boil the kid, while it is yet sucking.

And the Lord spake to Moses: Write these words, as after these words I made with you and with Israel a covenant.

I know not whether Goethe translated or abridged from the Hebrew, or whether he used any translation, Greek, Latin, or German. But he differs in form and words somewhat from our version, Exodus 34:10 to 28. The sense seems to be the same. The tables were the evidence of the covenant, by which the Almighty attached the people of Israel to himself. By these laws they were separated from all other nations, and were reminded of the principal epochs of their history.

When and where originated our ten commandments? The tables and the ark were lost. Authentic copies in few, if any hands; the ten Precepts could not be observed, and were little remembered. If the book of Deuteronomy was compiled, during or after the Babylonian captivity, from traditions, the error or amendment might come in there.

But you must be weary, as I am at present of problems, conjectures, and paradoxes, concerning Hebrew, Grecian and Christian and all other antiquities; but while we believe that the finis bonorum will be happy, we may leave learned men to their disquisitions and criticisms.

I admire your employment in selecting the philosophy and divinity of Jesus, and separating it from all mixtures. If I had eyes and nerves I would go through both Testaments and mark all that I understand. To examine the Mishna, Gemara, Cabbala, Jezirah, Sohar, Cosri and Talmud of the Hebrews would require the life of Methuselah, and after all his 969 years would be wasted to very little purpose.

The daemon of hierarchical despotism has been at work both with the Mishna and Gemara. In 1238 a French Jew made a discovery to the Pope (Gregory Ninth) of the heresies of the Talmud. The Pope sent thirty-five articles of error to the Archbishops of France, requiring them to seize the books of the Jews and burn all that contained any errors. He wrote in the same terms to the kings of France, England, Aragon, Castile, Leon, Navarre and Portugal. In consequence of this order, twenty cartloads of Hebrew books were burnt in France; and how many times twenty cartloads were destroyed in the other kingdoms?[176] The Talmud of Babylon and that of Jerusalem were composed from 120 to 500 years after the destruction of Jerusalem.

If Lightfoot[177] derived light from what escaped from Gregory's fury, in explaining many passages in the New Testament, by comparing the expressions of the Mishna with those of the Apostles and Evangelists, how many proofs of the corruptions of Christianity might we find in the passages burnt?

John Adams

35. JOHN ADAMS TO THOMAS JEFFERSON
QUINCY, November 15, 1813

DEAR SIR,

I cannot appease my melancholy commiseration for our armies in this furious snow storm, in any way so well as by studying your letter of October 8.

---

176. In 1238, Pope Gregory IX sent Inquisitors to Spain.

177. John Lightfoot (1602–1675). Wrote *A Commentary on the New Testament: From the Talmud and Hebraica.*

We are now explicitly agreed upon one important point, viz., that there is a natural aristocracy among men, the grounds of which are virtue and talents. You very justly indulge a little merriment upon this solemn subject of aristocracy. I often laugh at it too, for there is nothing in this laughable world more ridiculous than the management of it by all the nations of the earth; but while we smile, mankind have reason to say to us, as the frogs said to the boys, what is sport to you, are wounds and death to us.

When I consider the weakness, the folly, the pride, the vanity, the selfishness, the artifice, the low craft and mean cunning, the want of principle, the avarice, the unbounded ambition, the unfeeling cruelty of a majority of those (in all nations) who are allowed an aristocratical influence, and, on the other hand, the stupidity with which the more numerous multitude not only become their dupes, but even love to be taken in by their tricks, I feel a stronger disposition to weep at their destiny, than to laugh at their folly.

But though we have agreed in one point, in words, it is not yet certain that we are perfectly agreed in sense. Fashion has introduced an indeterminate use of the word talents. Education, wealth, strength, beauty, stature, birth, marriage, graceful attitudes, motions, gait, air, complexion, physiognomy are talents, as well as genius, science, and learning. Any one of these talents that, in fact, commands or influences two votes in society, gives to the man who possesses it the character of an aristocrat in my sense of the word.

Pick up the first hundred men you meet, and make a republic. Every man will have an equal vote; but when deliberations and discussions are opened, it will be found that twenty-five, by their talents, virtues being equal, will be able to carry fifty votes. Every one of these twenty-five is an aristocrat in my sense of the word; whether he obtains his one vote in addition to his own, by his birth, fortune, figure, eloquence, science, learning, craft, cunning, or even his character for good fellowship, and a bon vivant.

What gave Sir William Wallace[178] his amazing aristocratical supe-

---

178. (1272?–1305). Scottish national hero. After defeat of English at Stirling Bridge, he was appointed Guardian of the Kingdom.

riority? His strength. What gave Mrs. Clark[179] her aristocratical influence to create generals, admirals, and bishops? Her beauty. What gave Pompadour and Du Barry[180] the power of making cardinals and popes? And I have lived for years in the Hotel de Valentinois with Franklin, who had as many virtues as any of them. In the investigation of the meaning of the word "talents," I could write 630 pages as pertinent as John Taylor's of Hazlewood; but I will select a single example; for female aristocrats are nearly as formidable as males:

A daughter of a greengrocer walks the streets in London daily, with a basket of cabbage sprouts, dandelions, and spinach, on her head. She is observed by the painters to have a beautiful face, an elegant figure, a graceful step, and a debonair. They hire her to sit. She complies; and is painted by forty artists in a circle around her. The scientific Dr. William Hamilton outbids the painters, sends her to school for a genteel education, and marries her. This lady not only causes the triumphs of the Nile, Copenhagen, and Trafalgar, but separates Naples from France, and finally banishes the king and queen from Sicily.

Such is the aristocracy of the natural talent of beauty. Millions of examples might be quoted from history, sacred and profane, from Eve, Hannah, Deborah, Susanna, Abigail, Judith, Ruth, down to Helen, Mrs. de Mainbenon,[181] and Mrs. Fitzherbert.[182] For mercy's sake do not compel me to look to our chaste States and territories to find women, one of whom lct go would in the words of Holopherne's guards, deceive the whole earth.

The proverbs of Theognis, like those of Solomon, are observations on human nature, ordinary life, and civil society, with moral reflec-

---

179. British authoress Emily Clark, "grand-daughter of the late Colonel Frederick," descended from Theodore, king of Corsica. Wrote *Ianthe* and *Ermine Montrose*.

180. Jeanne Antoinette Poisson/Marquise de Pompadour (1721–1764) and Marie Jeanne Becu/Comtesse Du Barry (1743?–1793)—mistresses to King Louis XV.

181. François d'Aubigne/Marquise de Maintenon (1635–1719). Second wife of King Louis XIV. Founded Saint-Cyr School for the daughters of poor nobility. Wrote essays/letters on education.

182. Maria Anne Fitzherbert (1756–1837). Illegal wife of George Prince of Wales (later, George IV). It was an illegal marriage because George had been too young and Maria was a Catholic going into her third marriage.

tions on the facts. I quoted him as a witness of the fact, that there was as much difference in the races of men as in the breeds of sheep, and as a sharp reprover and censurer of the sordid, mercenary practice of disgracing birth by preferring gold to it. Surely no authority can be more expressly in point to prove the existence of inequalities, not of rights, but of moral, intellectual, and physical inequalities in families, descents and generations. If a descent from pious, virtuous, wealthy, literary, or scientific ancestors, is a letter of recommendation, or intro-duction in a man's favor, and enables him to influence only one vote in addition to his own, he is an aristocrat; for a democrat can have but one vote. Aaron Burr has 100,000 votes from the single circumstance of his descent from President Burr and President Edwards.

Your commentary on the proverbs of Theognis, reminded me of two solemn characters; the one resembling John Bunyan,[183] the other Scarron.[184] The one John Torrey,[185] the other Ben Franklin. Torrey, a poet, an enthusiast, a superstitious bigot, once very gravely asked my brother, whether it would not be better for mankind if children were always begotten by religious motives only? Would not religion in this sad case have as little efficacy in encouraging procreation, as it has now in discouraging it? I should apprehend a decrease of population, even in our country where it increases so rapidly.

In 1775, Franklin made a morning visit at Mrs. Yard's, to Sam Adams and John. He was unusually loquacious. "Man, a rational creature!" said Franklin. "Come, let us suppose a rational man. Strip him of all his appetites, especially his hunger and thirst. He is in his chamber, engaged in making experiments, or in pursuing some problem. He is highly entertained." At this moment a servant knocks:

"Sir, dinner is on the table."
"Dinner! pox! pough! But what have you for dinner?"
"Ham and chickens."

183. (1628–1688). English author and preacher. While imprisoned for illegal preaching, he wrote *The Pilgrim's Progress*.

184. Paul Scarron (1610–1660). Miserably deformed French poet, dramatist, and playwright. Early husband of Madame Maintenon.

185. Botanist at Middlebury College.

"Ham! And must I break the chain of my thoughts to go down and gnaw a morsel of damned hog's arse? Put aside your ham; I will dine to-morrow."

Take away appetite, and the present generation would not live a month, and no future generation would ever exist; and thus the exalted dignity of human nature would be annihilated and lost, and in my opinion the whole loss would be of no more importance than putting out a candle, quenching a torch, or crushing a firefly, if in this world we only have hope. Your distinction between natural and artificial aristocracy, does not appear to me founded. Birth and wealth are conferred upon some men as imperiously by nature as genius, strength, or beauty. The heir to honors, and riches, and power, has often no more merit in procuring these advantages, than he has in obtaining a handsome face, or an elegant figure.

When aristocracies are established by human laws, and honor, wealth and power are made hereditary by municipal laws and political institutions, then I acknowledge artificial aristocracy to commence; but this never commences till corruption in elections become dominant and uncontrollable. But this artificial aristocracy can never last. The everlasting envies, jealousies, rivalries, and quarrels among them; their cruel rapacity upon the poor ignorant people, their followers, compel them to set up Caesar, a demagogue, to be a monarch, a master to put each in his place.

Here you have the origin of all artificial aristocracy, which is the origin of all monarchies. And both artificial aristocracy and monarchy, and civil, military, political, and hierarchical despotism, have all grown out of the natural aristocracy of virtues and talents. We, to be sure, are far remote from this. Many hundred years must roll away before we shall be corrupted. Our pure, virtuous, public-spirited, federative republic will last forever, govern the globe, and introduce the perfection of man; his perfectibility being already proved by Price, Priestley, Condorcet, Rousseau, Diderot,[186] and Godwin.[187]

---

186. Denis Diderot (1713–1784). French philosopher. Chief editor of the *Encyclopedia*. His *Philosophical Thoughts* (1746) was burned by the Parliament of Paris for its anti-Christian content.

Mischief has been done by the Senate of the United States. I have known and felt more of this mischief than Washington, Jefferson, and Madison all together. But this has been all caused by the constitutional power of the Senate, in executive business, which ought to be immediately, totally, and essentially abolished. Your distinction between the aristoi and the pseudo-aristoi will not help the matter. I would trust one as well as the other with unlimited power. The law wisely refuses an oath as a witness in his own case, to the saint as well as the sinner.

No romance would be more amusing than the history of your Virginian and our New England aristocratical families. Yet even in Rhode Island there has been no clergy, no church, and I had almost said no State, and some people say no religion. There has been a constant respect for certain old families. Fifty-seven or fifty-eight years ago, in company with Colonel, Counsellor, Judge John Chandler, whom I have quoted before, a newspaper was brought in. The old sage asked me to look for the news from Rhode Island, and see how the elections had gone there. I read the list of Wanbous, Watrous, Greens, Whipples, Malboues, etc. "I expected as much," said the aged gentleman. "For, I have always been of opinion that in the most popular governments, the elections will generally go in favor of the most ancient families." To this day, when any of these tribes—and we may add Ellerys, Channings, Champlins, etc., are pleased to fall in with the popular current, they are sure to carry all before them.

You suppose a difference of opinion between you and me on the subject of aristocracy. I can find none. I dislike and detest hereditary honors, offices, emoluments, established by law. So do you. I am for excluding legal, hereditary distinctions from the United States as long as possible. So are you. I only say that mankind has not yet discovered any remedy against irresistible corruption in elections to offices of great power and profit, but making them hereditary.

But will you say our elections are pure? Be it so, upon the whole;

---

187. William Godwin (1756–1836). English political philosopher/novelist. Minister who turned atheist in 1785 and married feminist writer Mary Wollstonecraft in 1797. Godwin wrote *Enquiry Concerning Political Justice and its Influence on General Virtue and Happiness* (1797) and *Enquiry: Reflections on Education, Manners, and Literature*.

but do you recollect in history a more corrupt election than that of Aaron Burr to be President, or that of De Witt Clinton last year? By corruption here, I mean a sacrifice of every national interest and honor to private and party objects.

I see the same spirit in Virginia that you and I see in Rhode Island and the rest of New England. In New York it is a struggle of family feuds—a feudal aristocracy. Pennsylvania is a contest between German, Irish and Old England families. When Germans and Irish unite they give 30,000 majorities. There is virtually a white rose and a red rose, a Caesar and a Pompey, in every State in this Union, and contests and dissensions will be as lasting. The rivalry of Bourbons and Noailleses[188] produced the French Revolution, and a similar competition for consideration and influence exists and prevails in every village in the world. Where will terminate the rabies agri [madness for land]? The continent will be scattered over with manors much larger than Livingston's, Van Rensselaer's or Philips'; even our Deacon Strong will have a principality among you southern folk. What inequality of talents will be produced by these landjobbers?

Where tends the mania of banks? At my table in Philadelphia, I once proposed to you to unite in endeavors to obtain an amendment of the Constitution prohibiting to the separate States the power of creating banks; but giving Congress authority to establish one bank with a branch in each State, the whole limited to ten millions of dollars. Whether this project was wise or unwise, I know not, for I had deliberated little on it then, and have never thought it worth thinking of since. But you spurned the proposition from you with disdain. This system of banks, begotten, brooded and hatched by Duer, Robert and Gouverneur Morris, Hamilton and Washington,[189] I have always considered as a system of national injustice, a sacrifice of public and private interest to a few aristocratical friends and favorites. My scheme could have had no such effect.

---

188. Bourbons controlled the French throne from 1589 to 1792, regaining power after the rule of Napoleon. Noailles were a French peerage noble family created in 1663, that is, *duc de noailles*, which assisted in coronations.

189. Federalists.

Verres[190] plundered temples, and robbed a few rich men, but he never made such ravages among private property in general, nor swindled so much out of the pockets of the poor, and middle class of people, as these banks have done. No people but this would have borne the imposition so long. The people of Ireland would not bear Wood's half-pence.[191] What inequalities of talent have been introduced into this country by these aristocratical banks! Our Winthrops, Winslows, Bradfords, Saltonstalls, Quinceys, Chandlers, Leonards, Hutchinsons, Olivers, Sewalls,[192] etc., are precisely in the situation of your Randolphs, Carters, and Burwells, and Harrisons.[193] Some of them unpopular for the part they took in the late Revolution, but all respected for their names and connections; and whenever they fell in with the popular sentiments are preferred, ceteris paribus,[194] to all others.

Your old friend,
John Adams

36. JOHN ADAMS TO THOMAS JEFFERSON
QUINCY, December 3, 1813

DEAR SIR,

The proverbs of the old Greek poets are as short and pithy as any of Solomon or Franklin. Hesiod[195] has several. His, "Honor the gods established by law." I know not how we can escape martyrdom without a discreet attention to this precept: You have suffered, and I have suffered more than you, for want of a strict observance of this rule.

There is another oracle of this Hesiod, which requires a kind of

---

190. Caius Verres (120–43 BCE). Rapacious Roman governor of Sicily. Tried in 70 BCE, with Cicero's orations against him.

191. Name given to William Wood's coins made for Ireland, but secured with 10,000 pounds bribe to the king of England's mistress, the Duchess of Kendal.

192. Massachusetts families.

193. Virginian families.

194. Other things being equal.

195. Greek epic poet of eighth century BCE. Wrote *Theogony* and *Works and Days*.

dance upon a tight rope and a slack rope too, in philosophy and theology: "Ah, faith and likewise faithlessness have destroyed men." If believing too little or too much is so fatal to mankind, what will become of us all?

In studying the perfectibility of human nature and its progress towards perfection in this world, on this earth, remember that I have met many curious and interesting characters.

About three hundred years ago, there appeared a number of men of letters, who appeared to endeavor to believe neither too little nor too much. They labored to imitate the Hebrew archers, who could shoot to a hair's breadth. The Pope and his church believed too much. Luther and his church believed too little. This little band was headed by three great scholars: Erasmus, Vives[196] and Budaeus.[197] This triumvirate is said to have been at the head of the republic of letters in that age.

Had Condorcet been master of his subject, I fancy he would have taken more notice, in his History of the Progress of Mind, of these characters. Have you their writings? I wish I had. I shall confine myself at present to Vives. He wrote commentaries on the City of God of St. Augustine, some parts of which were censured by the Doctors of the Louvain, as too bold and too free. I know not whether the following passage of the learned Spaniard was among the sentiments condemned or not: "I have been much afflicted," says Vives, "when I have seriously considered how diligently, and with what exact care, the actions of Alexander, Hannibal, Scipio, Pompey, Caesar and other commanders, and the lives of Socrates, Plato, Aristotle and other philosophers, have been written and fixed in an everlasting remembrance, so that there is not the least danger they can ever be lost; but then the acts of the Apostles, and martyrs and saints of our religion, and of the affairs of the rising and established church, being involved in much darkness, are almost totally unknown, though they are of so

---

196. Juan Luis Vives (1492–1540). Spanish humanist and friend of Erasmus. Author of *The Spirit and Life*. Wrote a commentary on St. Augustine's City of God and professed some form of evolution. Though he called for the education of women, he considered Woman inferior to Man.

197. Guillaume Bude (1467–1540). French humanist. Founded the College of France and the National Library.

much greater advantage than the lives of the philosophers or great generals, both as to the improvement of our knowledge and practice. For what is written of these holy men, except a very few things, is very much corrupted and defaced with the mixture of many fables, while the writer, indulging his own humor, doth not tell us what the saint did, but what the historian would have had him do. And the fancy of the writer dictates the life and not the truth of things." And again Vives says: "There have been men who have thought it a great piece of piety, to invent lies for the sake of religion."

The great Cardinal Barronius,[198] too, confesses: "There is nothing which seems so much neglected to this day, as a true and certain account of the affairs of the church, collected with an exact diligence. And that I may speak of the more ancient, it is very difficult to find any of them who have published commentaries on this subject, which have hit the truth in all points."

Canus,[199] too, another Spanish prelate of great name, says: "I speak it with grief and not by way of reproach, Laertius has written the lives of the philosophers with more ease and industry than the Christians have those of the saints. Suetonius[200] has represented the lives of the Caesars with much more truth and sincerity than the Catholics have the affairs (I will not say of the emperors) but even those of the martyrs, holy virgins and confessors. For, they have not concealed the vice or the very suspicions of vice, in good and commendable philosophers or princes, and in the worst of them they discover the very colors or appearances of virtue. But the greatest parts of our writers either follow the conduct of their affections, or industriously feign many things; so that I, for my part, am very often both weary and ashamed of them, because I know that they have thereby brought nothing of advantage to the church of Christ, but very much inconvenience."

---

198. Cesare Baronius (1538–1607). Wrote *Ecclesiastical Annals*.

199. Melchior Cano (1509–1560). Spanish theologian. Sent to Council of Trent in 1551. Fell out of favor with Pope Paul IV for supporting Spanish Court versus Holy See. Wrote *De Locis Theologicus,* on ten loci, or points, on which to base the science of theology, that is, Reason, Scripture, History, Philosophy, and so on.

200. Gaius Suetonius Tranquillus (c. 69–140 CE). Roman biographer. Wrote *The Lives of the Caesars.*

Vives and Canus are moderns, but Arnobius, the converter of Laetantius, was ancient. He says: "But neither could all that was done be written, or arrive at the knowledge of all men? Many of our great actions being done by obscure men and those who had no knowledge of letters. And if some of them are committed to letters and writings, yet even here, by the malice of the devils and men like them, whose great design and study is to intercept and ruin this truth, by interpolating or adding some things to them, or by changing or taking out words, syllables or letters, they have put a stop to the faith of wise men, and corrupted the truth of things."

Indeed, Mr. Jefferson, what could be invented to debase the ancient Christianism, which Greeks, Romans, Hebrews and Christian factions, above all the Catholics, have not fraudulently imposed upon the public? Miracles after miracles have rolled down in torrents, wave succeeding wave in the Catholic Church, from the Council of Nice,[201] and long before, to this day.

Aristotle, no doubt, thought his "neither trusting all things nor distrusting all" very wise and very profound; but what is its worth? What man, woman or child ever believed everything or nothing? Oh! That Priestley could live again, and have leisure and means! An inquirer after truth, who had neither time nor means, might request him to search and re-search for answers to a few questions:

1. Have we more than two witnesses of the life of Jesus— Matthew and John?
2. Have we one witness to the existence of Matthew's gospel in the first century?
3. Have we one witness of the existence of John's gospel in the first century?
4. Have we one witness of the existence of Mark's gospel in the first century?

---

201. Council of Nicaea held in 325 CE to decide controversy between Arian and Athanasius. Arian held that Jesus was not of the same substance as God, the Father, but rather a similar or like substance. Athanasius held that Jesus and the Father were of the same substance. The council also decided on the date to celebrate Easter, considering moon phases, and so on.

5. Have we one witness of the existence of Luke's gospel in the
first century?
6. Have we any witness of the existence of St. Thomas's gospel,
the gospel of the infancy in the first century?
7. Have we any evidence of the existence of the Acts of the Apostles in the first century?
8. Have we any evidence of the existence of the supplement to the
Acts of the Apostles, Peter and Paul, or Paul and Tecla, in the
first century?

Here I was interrupted by a new book, Chateaubriand's[202] Travels in
Greece, Palestine and Egypt, and by a lung fever with which the amiable companion of my life has been violently and dangerously attacked.

December 13th: I have fifty more questions to put to Priestley, but
must adjourn them to a future opportunity.

I have read Chateaubriand with as much delight as I ever read
Bunyan's Pilgrim's Progress, Robinson Crusoe's Travels or Gul-
liver's, or Whitefield's or Wesley's Life, or the Life of St. Francis, St.
Anthony, or St. Ignatius Loyola. A work of infinite learning, perfectly
well written, a magazine of information, but enthusiastic, bigoted,
superstitious, Roman Catholic throughout. If I were to indulge in
jealous criticism and conjecture, I should suspect that there had been
an Ecumenical council of Popes, Cardinals and Bishops, and that this
traveler has been employed at their expense to make this tour, to lay a
foundation for the resurrection of the Catholic Hierarchy in Europe.

Have you read La Harpe's Cours de Literature, in fifteen volumes?
Have you read St. Pierre's Studies of Nature? I am now reading the
controversy between Voltaire and Monotte.

Our friend Rush has given us for his last legacy, an analysis of
some of the diseases of the mind. Johnson[203] said, "We are all more or
less mad." And who is or has been more mad than Johnson?

---

202. François Auguste Rene, Vicomte de Chateaubriand (1768–1848). French
writer and statesman. Wrote *The Genius of Christianity* (1802).
203. Samuel Johnson (1709–1784). English clergy. Wrote *The Vanity of Human
Wishes* and *The Rambler*. He was a friend to Rev. John Taylor and Dr. Brocklesby.

I know of no philosopher, or theologian, or moralist, ancient or modern, more profound, more infallible than Whitefield, if the anecdote I heard be true.

He began: "Father Abraham," with his hands and eyes gracefully directed to the heavens, as I have more than once seen him; "Father Abraham whom have you there with you? Have you Catholics?"

"No."

"Have you Protestants?"

"No."

"Have you Churchmen?"

"No."

"Have you Dissenters?"

"No."

"Have you Presbyterians?"

"No."

"Quakers?"

"No."

"Anabaptists?"

"No."

"Who have you there? Are you alone?"

"No."

"My brethren, you have the answer to all these questions in the words of my text: 'He who fears God and works righteousness, shall be accepted of Him.'"

Allegiance to the Creator and Governor of the Milky-Way, and the Nebulae, and benevolence to all His creatures, is my Religion.

Si quid novisti rectius istis, candidus imperti. [If you know anything better than these maxims, candidly share them.]

I am as ever,
John Adams

37. JOHN ADAMS TO THOMAS JEFFERSON
QUINCY, December 25, 1813

DEAR SIR,

Answer my letters at your leisure. Give yourself no concern. I write as for a refuge and protection against ennui.

The fundamental principle of all philosophy and all Christianity is "Rejoice always in all things!"

"Be thankful at all times for all good, and all that we call evil."

Will it not follow that I ought to rejoice and be thankful that Priestley has lived? That Gibbon has lived? That Hume has lived though a conceited Scotchman? That Bolingbroke has lived, though a haughty, arrogant, supercilious dogmatist? That Burke[204] and Johnson have lived, though superstitious slaves, or self-deceiving hypocrites, both?

Is it not laughable to hear Burke call Bolingbroke a superficial writer? To hear him ask: "Who ever read him through?" Had I been present, I would have answered him, "I, I myself, I have read him through more than fifty years ago, and more than five times in my life, and once within five years past. And in my opinion, the epithet 'superficial,' belongs to you and your friend Johnson more than to him!"

I might say much more. But I believe Burke and Johnson to have been as political Christians as Leo Tenth.[205]

I return to Priestley, though I have great complaints against him for personal injuries and persecution, at the same time that I forgive it all, and hope and pray that he may be pardoned for it all above.

Dr. Brocklesby, an intimate friend and convivial companion of Johnson, told me that Johnson died in agonies of horror of annihilation; and all the accounts we have of his death, corroborate this account of Brocklesby. Dread of annihilation! Dread of nothing! A

---

204. Edmond Burke (1729–1797). Irish-born English writer and statesman. Attacked Bolingbroke's religious skepticism in *Vindication of Natural Society* (1756).

205. Born Giovanni di Lorenzo de Medici (1475–1521). Issued *Bull of Indulgences* to authorize the sell of indulgences. Escaped assassination plot of other Cardinals. Excommunicated Martin Luther in 1521. "It has served us well this myth of Christ"—quote to his brother often attributed to Leo.

dread of nothing, I should think, would be no dread at all. Can there be any real, substantial, rational fear of nothing?

Were you on your death-bed and in your last moments informed by demonstration of revelation, that you would cease to think and to feel, at your dissolution, should you be terrified? You might be ashamed of yourself for having lived so long to bear the proud man's contumely. You might be ashamed of your Maker, and compare Him to a little girl, amusing herself, her brothers and sisters, by blowing bubbles in soap-suds. You might compare Him to boys sporting with crackers and rockets, or to men employed in making mere artificial fire-works, or to men and women at fairs and operas, or Sadlers Wells[206] exploits, or to politicians in their intrigues, or to heroes in their butcheries, or to Popes in their devilisms. But what should you fear? Nothing. Emori nolo, sed me mortuum esse nihil estimo. ["I have no wish to die, but that I be dead and considered as nothing."]

To return to Priestley, you could make a more luminous book than his, upon the doctrines of heathen philosophers compared with those of revelation. Why has he not given us a more satisfactory account of the Pythagorean Philosophy and Theology? He barely names Eileus,[207] who lived long before Plato. His treatise of kings and monarchy has been destroyed, I conjecture, by Platonic Philosophers, Platonic Jews or Christians, or by fraudulent republicans or despots.

His treatise of the universe has been preserved. He labors to prove the eternity of the world. The Marquis D'Argens[208] translated it, in all its noble simplicity. The Abbe Batteaux has since given another translation. D'Argens not only explains the text, but sheds more light upon the ancient systems. His remarks are so many treatises, which develop the concatenation of ancient opinions. The most essential ideas of the theology, of the physics, and of the morality of the ancients are clearly

---

206. Sadler's Wells, London theater opened originally in 1683 as a "Musick House" by Thomas (or some say Dick) Sadler. Home to juggling acts, animal acts, and so on in the early eighteenth century.

207. Adams must mean Ocellus Lucanus, whose work *On the Universe* was translated by both D'Argens and Batteux.

208. Jean-Baptiste de Boyer (1703–1771). French Writer. Wrote *New Memoirs Establishing a True Knowledge for Mankind* (1747).

explained, and their different doctrines compared with one another and with the modern discoveries. I wish I owned this book and one hundred thousand more that I want every day, now when I am almost incapable of making any use of them.

No doubt he informs us that Pythagoras was a great traveler. Priestley barely mentions Timaeus, but it does not appear that he had read him. Why has he not given us an account of him and his book? He was before Plato, and gave him the idea of his Timaeus, and much more of his philosophy.

After his master, he maintained the existence of matter; that matter was capable of receiving all sorts of forms; that a moving power agitated all the parts of it, and that an Intelligence produced a regular and harmonious world. This intelligence had seen a plan, an idea (Logos) in conformity to which it wrought, and without which it would not have known what it was about, or what it wanted to do.

This plan was the idea, image or model which had represented to the Supreme Intelligence the world before it existed, which had directed it in its action upon the moving power, and which it contemplated in forming the elements, the bodies and the world. This model was distinguished from the intelligence which produced the world, as the architect is from his plans. He divided the productive cause of the world into a spirit which directed the moving force, and into an image which determined it in the choice of the directions which it gave to the moving force, and the forms which it gave to matter.

I wonder that Priestley has overlooked this, because it is the same philosophy with Plato's, and would have shown that the Pythagorean as well as the Platonic philosophers probably concurred in the fabrication of the Christian Trinity. Priestley mentions the name of Achylas,[209] but does not appear to have read him, though he was a successor of Pythagoras, and a great mathematician, a great statesman and a great general. John Gram, a learned and honorable Dane, has

---

209. Archytas of Tarentum (now part of Italy) (c. 428–c. 347 BCE). Scientist and philosopher. Close friend of Plato. Believed there was "No absolute difference between organic and inorganic world." Wrote *On Harmony, On Agriculture, On Studies*, and *On the Number 10*.

given a handsome edition of his works, with a Latin translation and an ample account of his life and writings. Zaleucus,[210] the Legislator of Locris, and Charondas of Sybaris, were disciples of Pythagoras, and both celebrated to immortality for the wisdom of their laws, five hundred years before Christ. Why are those laws lost? I say the spirit of party has destroyed them; civil, political and ecclesiastical bigotry.

Despotical, monarchical, aristocratical and democratical fury have all been employed in this work of destruction of everything that could give us true light, and a clear insight of antiquity. For every one of these parties, when possessed of power, or when they have been undermost, and struggling to get uppermost, has been equally prone to every species of fraud and violence and usurpation.

Why has not Priestley mentioned these Legislators? The preamble to the laws of Zaleucus, which is all that remains, is as orthodox Christian theology as Priestley's, and Christian benevolence and forgiveness of injuries almost as clearly expressed.

Priestley ought to have done impartial justice to philosophy and philosophers. Philosophy, which is the result of reason, is the first, the original revelation of the Creator to his creature, man. When this revelation is clear and certain by intuition or necessary induction, no subsequent revelation supported by prophecies or miracles can supersede it. Philosophy is not only the love of wisdom, but the science of the universe and its cause.

There is, there was, and there will be but one master of philosophy in the universe. Portions of it, in different degrees, are revealed to creatures.

Philosophy looks with an impartial eye on all terrestrial religions. I have examined all, as well as my narrow sphere, my straitened means and my busy life would allow me, and the result is, that the Bible is the best book in the world: It contains more of my little philosophy than all the libraries I have seen; and such parts of it as I cannot reconcile to my little philosophy, I postpone for future investigation.

Priestley ought to have given us a sketch of the religion and morals

210. (c. 650, 660 BCE). Greek lawgiver of Locris, Italy. An early codification of *lex talionis*, law of retaliation: "an eye for an eye."

of Zoroaster, of Sanchoniathon, of Confucius, and all the founders of
religions before Christ, whose superiority would, from such a comparison, have appeared the more transcendent.

Priestley ought to have told us that Pythagoras passed twenty
years in his travels in India, in Egypt, in Chaldea, perhaps in Sodom
and Gomorrah, Tyre and Sidon. He ought to have told us that in India
he conversed with the Brahmins, and read the Shasta,[211] five thousand
years old, written in the language of the sacred Sancrists,[212] with the
elegance and sentiments of Plato.

Where is to be found theology more orthodox, or philosophy more
profound, than in the introduction to the Shasta? "God is one creator
of all universal sphere, without beginning, without end. God governs
all the creation by a general providence, resulting from his eternal
designs. Search not the essence and the nature of the eternal, who is
one; your research will be vain and presumptuous. It is enough that,
day by day, and night by night, you adore his power, his wisdom and
his goodness, in his works. The eternal willed in the fullness of time,
to communicate of his essence and of his splendor, to beings capable
of perceiving it. They as yet existed not. The eternal willed and they
were. He created Birma, Vitsnou and Siv[213] [Brahma, Vishnu, and
Shiva?]." These doctrines, sublime, if ever there were any sublime,
Pythagoras learned in India, and taught them to Zaleucus and his other
disciples. He there learned also his metempsychosis, but this never
was popular, never made much progress in Greece or Italy, or any
other country besides India and Tartary, the region of the grand
immortal Lama. And how does this differ from the possessions of
demons in Greece and Rome? From the demon of Socrates? From the
worship of cows and crocodiles in Egypt and elsewhere?

After migrating through various animals, from elephants to serpents, according to their behavior, souls that at last behaved well,

---

211. *Shastra* or *Sasta*. Sacred Vedic texts.

212. Sanskrit (Samskrta). Ancient classical language of India and Hinduism,
which includes older Vedic.

213. Brahma, the Creator; Vishnu, the Preserver; Shiva, the Destroyer—Hindu
Trinity.

became men and women, and then if they were good, they went to heaven. All ended in heaven, if they became virtuous.

Who can wonder at the widow of Malabar? Where is the lady, who, if her faith were without doubt that she should go to heaven with her husband on the one, or migrate into a toad or a wasp on the other, would not lie down on the pile, and set fire to the fuel?

Modifications and disguises of the Metempsychosis,[214] have crept into Egypt, and Greece, and Rome, and other countries. Have you read Farmer on the Daemons and possessions of the New Testament?

According to the Shasta, Moisazor, with his companions, rebelled against the Eternal, and were precipitated down to Ondoro, the region of darkness.

Do you know anything of the Prophecy of Enoch?

Can you give me a comment on the 6th, the 9th, the 14th verses of the epistle of Jude?[215]

If I am not weary of writing, I am sure you must be of reading such incoherent rattle. I will not persecute you so severely in future, if I can help it.

So farewell,
John Adams

38. THOMAS JEFFERSON TO JOHN ADAMS
MONTICELLO, January 24, 1814

DEAR SIR,

I have great need of the indulgence so kindly extended to me in your favor of December 25, of permitting me to answer your friendly let-

---

214. Belief held by Pythagoreans, Orphic, and Bacchus mysteries that the soul transfers from one body to another (reincarnation) after death, as opposed to Epicureans, who believed the soul dissipates after death.

215. Catholic Epistle of St. Jude the Apostle. Verse 6 deals with fallen angels. Verse 9 mentions a dispute between Archangel Michael and the Devil concerning the body of Moses. Verse 14 relates the prophecy of Enoch, seventh from Adam, that the "Lord cometh with thousands of his saints." The epistle called for action against heretics.

ters at my leisure. My frequent and long absences from home are a first cause of tardiness in my correspondence and a second the accumulation of business during my absence, some of which imperiously commands first attentions. I am now in arrear to you for your letters of November 12, 14, 16, December 3, 19, and 25.

You ask me if I have ever seen the work of J. W. Goethe, Schriften? Never; nor did the question ever occur to me before, where get we the Ten Commandments? The book indeed gives them to us verbatim, but where did it get them? For it tells us they were written by the finger of God on tables of stone, which were destroyed by Moses; it specifies those on the second set of tables in different form and substance, but still without saying how the others were recovered.

But the whole history of these books is so defective and doubtful, that it seems vain to attempt minute inquiry into it; and such tricks have been played with their text, and with the texts of other books relating to them, that we have a right from that cause to entertain much doubt what parts of them are genuine: In the New Testament there is internal evidence that parts of it have proceeded from an extraordinary man; and that other parts are of the fabric of very inferior minds. It is as easy to separate those parts, as to pick out diamonds from dunghills.

The matter of the first was such as would be preserved in the memory of the hearers, and handed on by tradition for a long time; the latter such stuff as might be gathered up, for imbedding it, anywhere, and at any time. I have nothing of Vives, or Budaeus, and little of Erasmus. If the familiar histories of the Saints, the want of which they regret, would have given us the histories of those tricks which these writers acknowledge to have been practiced, and of the lies they agree have been invented for the sake of religion, I join them in their regrets. These would be the only parts of their histories worth reading.

It is not only the sacred volumes they have thus interpolated, gutted, and falsified, but the works of others relating to them, and even the laws of the land. We have a curious instance of one of these pious frauds in the laws of Alfred.[216] He composed, you know, from the laws

---

216. King Alfred. Ruled 871–901 CE. Introduced rule based on Mosaic Law. Based his laws on those of predecessors, Ina, Offa, and Aethelbert.

of the Heptarchy,[217] a digest for the government of the United Kingdom, and in his preface to that work he tells us expressly the sources from which he drew it, to wit, the laws of Ina,[218] of Offa[219] and Aethelbert[220] (not naming the Pentateuch).

But his pious interpolator, very awkwardly, premises to his work four chapters of Exodus (from the 20th to the 23d) as a part of the laws of the land; so that Alfred's preface is made to stand in the body of the work. Our judges, too, have lent a ready hand to further these frauds, and have been willing to lay the yoke of their own opinions on the necks of others; to extend the coercions of municipal law to the dogmas of their religion, by declaring that these make a part of the law of the land. In the Year-Book 34, H. 6, p. 38, in Quare impedit [Lester J. Cappon elaborates: "Reports of cases in the Year Book cover the period from Edward I (1292) to Henry VIII (1536). The reference is to a law of the thirty-fourth year of Henry VI's reign, folio 38. Cases in Quare inpedit are actions in English law brought only in the Court of Common Pleas to recover the right of a patron over a church or benefice."], where the question was how far the common law takes notice of the ecclesiastical law, Prisot,[221] Chief Justice, in the course of his argument, says, "A tiels leis que ils de seint eglise ont, en ancien scripture, covient a nous a donner credence; car ces common luy sur quels touts manners leis sont fondes; et auxy, sin, nous sumus obliges de canustre lour esy de saint eglise," etc. Finch begins the business of falsification by mistranslating and misstating the words of Prisot thus: "to such laws of the church as have warrant in Holy Scripture our law gives credence." Citing the above case and the words of Prisot in the margin in Finch's law, B.1, c. 3 [Book 1, chapter 3], here then we find ancien scripture, ancient writing, translated "holy scripture." This, Wingate, in 1658, erects into a maxim of law in the very words of

---

217. Name given to seven Anglo-Saxon kingdoms of the seventh and eighth centuries, prior to ninth-century Dane invasions.

218. Ina, king of West Saxons. Ruled 688–728.

219. Offa, king of Mercia. Ruled 755–794.

220. King Aethelbert. Ruled 560–616.

221. Sir John Prisot, chief justice of the Common Bench in England (1449–1460).

Finch, but citing Prisot and not Finch. And Sheppard, to wit. Religion, in 1675 laying it down in the same words of Finch, quotes the Year-Book, Finch and Wingate. Then, comes Sir Matthew Hale, (in the case of the King v. Taylor, I Ventr. 293, 3 Keb. 607 [I Ventris 293, vol. 3, Keble, p. 607]), who declares that, "Christianity is part and parcel of the laws of England." Citing nobody, and resting it, with his judgment against the witches, on his own authority, which indeed was sound and good in all cases into which no superstition or bigotry could enter.

Thus strengthened, the court in 1728, in the King v. Woolston, would not suffer it to be questioned whether to write against Christianity was punishable at common law, saying it had been so settled by Hale in Taylor's case, 2 Stra. 834 [vol. 2, Strange, p. 834]. Wood, therefore, 409, without scruple, lays down as a principle, that all blaspheming and profaneness are offences at the common law, and cites Strange. Blackstone, in 1763, repeats, in the words of Sir Matthew Hale, that "Christianity is part of the laws of England," citing Ventris and Strange, ubi supra. And Lord Mansfield, in the case of the Chamberlain of London v. Evans, in 1767, qualifying somewhat the position, says that "the essential principles of revealed religion are part of the common law."

Thus we find this string of authorities all hanging by one another on a single hook, a mistranslation by Finch of the words of Prisot, or on nothing. For all quote Prisot, or one another, or nobody. Thus Finch misquotes Prisot; Wingate also, but using Finch's words; Sheppard quotes Prisot, Finch and Wingate; Hale cites nobody; the court in Woolston's case cites Hale; Wood cites Woolston's case; Blackstone that and Hale, and Lord Mansfield volunteers his own ipse dixit.

And who now can question but that the whole Bible and Testament are a part of the common law? And, who can now question that Connecticut, in her blue laws,[222] laying it down as a principle that the laws of God should be the laws of their land, except where their own con-

---

222. Laws originally written on blue paper. Laws tied rights, such as voting, to church membership. "No one shall kiss his or her children on the Sabbath or feast days." Heretics were not to be fed or housed. Traveling, cooking victuals, cutting hair, shaving, crossing rivers—all were prohibited on the Sabbath.

tradicted them, did anything more than express, with a salvo, what the English judges had less cautiously declared without any restriction?

And what, I dare say, our cunning Chief Justice would swear to, and find as many sophisms to twist it out of the general terms of our declarations of rights, and even the stricter text of the Virginia "act for the freedom of religion," as he did to twist Burr's neck out of the halter of treason. May we not say then with Him who was all candor and benevolence, "Woe unto you, ye lawyers, for ye laden men with burdens grievous to bear."

I think with you, that Priestley, in his comparison of the doctrines of philosophy and revelation, did not do justice to the undertaking. But he felt himself pressed by the hand of death. Enfield has given us a more distinct account of the ethics of the ancient philosophers; but the great work of which Enfield's is an abridgment, Brucker's History of Philosophy, is the treasure which I would wish to possess, as a book of reference or of special research only, for who could read six volumes quarto, of one thousand pages each, closely printed, of modern Latin? Your account of D'Argens' Aeileus makes me wish for him also. Aeileus furnishes a fruitful text for a sensible and learned commentator. The Abbe Batteaux, which I have, is a meager thing.

You surprise me with the account you give of the strength of family distinction still existing in your State. With us it is so totally extinguished, that not a spark of it is to be found but lurking in the hearts of some of our old Tories; but all bigotries hang to one another, and this in the Eastern States hangs, as I suspect, to that of the priesthood. Here youth, beauty, mind and manners, are more valued than a pedigree.

Thomas Jefferson

39. JOHN ADAMS TO THOMAS JEFFERSON
QUINCY, February 1814

Your researches in the laws of England establishing Christianity as the law of the land, and part of the common law, are curious and very important. Questions without number will arise in this country. Religious controversies, and ecclesiastical contests, are as common, and will be as sharp as any in civil politics, foreign and domestic. In what sense, and to what extent the Bible is law, may give rise to as many doubts and quarrels as any of our civil, political, military, or maritime laws, and will intermix with them all, to irritate factions of every sort.

I dare not look beyond my nose into futurity. Our money, our commerce, our religion, our National and State Constitutions, even our arts and sciences, are so many seed plots, of division, faction, sedition and rebellion. Everything is transmuted into an instrument of electioneering. Election is the grand Brahma, the immortal Lama, I had almost said, the Juggernaut; for wives are almost ready to burn upon the pile, and children to be thrown under the wheel.

You will perceive, by these figures that I have been looking into Oriental history and Hindoo religion. I have read voyages, and travels, and everything I could collect, and the last is Priestley's "Comparison of the Institutions of Moses with those of the Hindoos and other Ancient Nations," a work of great labor, and not less haste. I thank him for the labor, and forgive, though I lament the hurry. You would be fatigued to read, and I, just recruiting from a little longer confinement and indisposition than I have had for thirty years, have not strength to write many observations. But I have been disappointed in the principal points of my curiosity:

1st. I am disappointed by finding that no just comparison can be made, because the original Shasta and the original Vedams[223] are not obtained, or if obtained, not yet translated into any European language.

2d. In not finding such morsels of the sacred books as have been translated and published, which are more honorable to the original Hindoo religion than anything he has quoted.

3d. In not finding a full development of the history of the doctrine of the Metempsychosis which originated . . .

4th. In the history of the rebellion of innumerable hosts of angels in Heaven against the Supreme Being, who after some thousands of years of war, conquered them, and hurled them down to the regions of total darkness, where they have suffered a part of the punishment of their

---

223. Vedas. Sacred Hindu scripture.

crime, and then were mercifully released from prison, permitted to ascend to earth, and migrate into all sorts of animals, reptiles, birds, beasts, and men, according to their rank and character, and even into vegetables, and minerals, there to serve on probation. If they passed without reproach their several gradations, they were permitted to become cows and men. If as men they behaved well, i.e., to the satisfaction of the priests, they were restored to their original rank and bliss in Heaven.

5th. In not finding the Trinity of Pythagoras and Plato, their contempt of matter, flesh, and blood, their almost adoration of fire and water, their metempsychosis, and even the prohibition of beans, so evidently derived from India.

6th. In not finding the prophecy of Enoch deduced from India, in which the fallen angels make such a figure. But you are weary. Priestley has proved the superiority of the Hebrews to the Hindoos, as they appear in the Gentoo laws and institutes of Menu;[224] but the comparison remains to be made with the Shasta.

In his remarks on Mr. Dupuis,[225] page 342, Priestley says: "The History of the fallen angels is another circumstance, on which Mr. Dupuis lays much stress. According to the Christians, he says, Vol. I, page 336, there was from the beginning a division among the angels; some remaining faithful to the light, and others taking the part of darkness, etc.; but this supposed history is not found in the Scriptures. It has only been inferred, from a wrong interpretation of one passage in the 2nd epistle of Peter, and a corresponding one in that of Jude, as has been shown by judicious writers.

That there is such a person as the Devil, is not a part of my faith, nor that of many other Christians; nor am I sure that it was the belief of any of the Christian writers. Neither do I believe the doctrine of demoniacal possessions, whether it was believed by the sacred writers or not; and yet my unbelief in these articles does not affect my faith in the great facts of which the Evangelists were eye and ear witnesses.

---

224. Laws of Manu (Man). Ancient Hindu codes of the Dharmasastras. Manu survives flood.

225. Charles François Dupuis (1742–1809). Wrote *Origin of all Cults* and *Memoir Explaining the Zodiac and Mythology.*

They might not be competent judges in the one case, though perfectly so with respect to the other."

I will ask Priestley, when I see him, do you believe those passages in Peter and Jude to be interpolations? If so, by whom made? And when? And where? And for what end? Was it to support, or found, the doctrine of the fall of man, original sin, the universal corruption, depravation, and guilt of human nature and mankind; and the subsequent incarnation of God to make atonement and redemption? Or do you think that Peter and Jude believed the book of Enoch to have been written by the seventh from Adam, and one of the sacred canonical books of the Hebrew Prophets? Peter, 2d epistle, c.2d, v. 4th [chapter 2, verse 4], says, "For, if God spared not the angels that sinned but cast them down to hell, and delivered them into chains of darkness to be reserved unto Judgment."

Jude, v. 6th [verse 6], says, "And the angels, who kept not their first estate, but left their own habitations, he hath reserved in everlasting chains under darkness, unto the judgment of the great day." Verse 14th, "And Enoch, also, the seventh from Adam, prophesied of these sayings, behold the Lord cometh with ten thousands of his saints, to execute judgment upon all," etc. Priestley says that "a wrong interpretation" has been given to these texts. I wish he had favored us with his right interpretation of them.

In another place, page 326, Priestley says, "There is no circumstance of which Mr. Dupuis avails himself so much, or repeats so often, both with respect to the Jewish and Christian religions, as the history of the Fall of Man, in the book of Genesis. I believe with him and have maintained in my writings, that this history is either an allegory, or founded on uncertain tradition, that it is an hypothesis to account for the origin of evil, adopted by Moses, which by no means accounts for the facts."

March 3d. So far was written almost a month ago; but sickness has prevented progress. I had much more to say about this work. I shall never be a disciple of Priestley. He is as absurd, inconsistent, credulous and incomprehensible, as Athanasius. Read his letter to the Jews in this volume. Could a rational creature write it? Aye! Such rational creatures as Rochefoucauld, and Condorcet, and John Taylor in politics, and Towers' Juricus [Jurieu?] and French Prophets in Theology. Priestley's account of the philosophy and religion of India, appears to me to be such a work as a man of busy research would produce, who should undertake to describe Christianity from the sixth to the twelfth century, when a deluge of wonders overflowed the world; when miracles were performed and proclaimed from every convent, and monastery, hospital, churchyard, mountain, valley, cave and cupola.

There is a book which I wish I possessed. It has never crossed the Atlantic. It is entitled Acta Sanctorum,[226] in forty-seven volumes in folio. It contains the lives of the Saints. It was compiled in the beginning of the sixteenth century by Bollandus, Henschenius, and Papebrock. What would I give to possess in one immense mass, one stupendous draught, all the legends, true, doubtful and false!

These Bollandists dared to discuss some of the facts, and hint that some of them were doubtful. E. G. Papebrock doubted the antiquity of the Carmelites from Elias; and whether the face of Jesus Christ was painted on the handkerchief of St. Veronique; and whether the prepuce of the Savior of the world, which was shown in the church of Antwerp, could be proved to be genuine? For these bold skepticisms he was libeled in pamphlets, and denounced by the Pope, and the Inquisition in Spain. The Inquisition condemned him; but the Pope not daring to acquit or condemn him, prohibited all writings pro and con. But as the physicians cure one disease by exciting another, as a fever by a salivation, this Bull was produced by a new claim. The brothers of the Order of Charity asserted a descent from Abraham, nine hundred years anterior to the Carmelites.

A philosopher who should write a description of Christianism from the Bollandistic Saints of the sixth and tenth century would probably produce a work tolerably parallel to Priestley's upon the Hindoos.

John Adams

---

226. *Acts of the Saints* produced by Jesuits, that is, Bollandus and so on, beginning in 1643. Contained accounts of court proceedings and death accounts of martyrs/saints.

40. THOMAS JEFFERSON TO JOHN ADAMS
MONTICELLO, July 5, 1814

I am just returned from one of my long absences, having been at my other home for five weeks past. Having more leisure there than here for reading, I amused myself with reading seriously Plato's Republic. I am wrong, however, in calling it amusement, for it was the heaviest task-work I ever went through. I had occasionally before taken up some of his other works, but scarcely ever had patience to go through a whole dialogue. While wading through the whimsies, the puerilities and unintelligible jargon of this work, I laid it down often to ask myself how it could have been that the world should have so long consented to give reputation to such nonsense as this.

How the soi-disant [so-called] Christian world, indeed, should have done it, is a piece of historical curiosity. But how could the Roman good sense do it? And particularly, how could Cicero bestow such eulogies on Plato? Although Cicero did not wield the dense logic of Demosthenes,[227] yet he was able, learned, laborious, practiced in the business of the world, and honest. He could not be the dupe of mere style, of which he was himself the first master in the world. With the moderns, I think, it is rather a matter of fashion and authority. Education is chiefly in the hands of persons who, from their profession, have an interest in the reputation and the dreams of Plato. They give the tone while at school, and few in their after years have occasion to revise their college opinions.

But fashion and authority apart, and bringing Plato to the test of reason, take from him his sophisms, futilities and incomprehensibilities, and what remains? In truth, he is one of the race of genuine sophists, who has escaped the oblivion of his brethren, first, by the elegance of his diction, but chiefly, by the adoption and incorporation of his whimsies into the body of artificial Christianity.

His foggy mind is forever presenting the semblances of objects which, half seen through a mist, can be defined neither in form nor

---

227. Athenian orator and statesman (384–322 BCE). Wrote *Philippics*, speeches against King Philip II of Macedonia, and *On the Crown*.

dimensions. Yet this, which should have consigned him to early oblivion, really procured him immortality of fame and reverence. The Christian priesthood, finding the doctrines of Christ leveled to every understanding, and too plain to need explanation, saw in the mysticism of Plato materials with which they might build up an artificial system, which might, from its indistinctness, admit everlasting controversy, give employment for their order, and introduce it to profit, power and preeminence.

The doctrines which flowed from the lips of Jesus himself are within the comprehension of a child; but thousands of volumes have not yet explained the Platonisms engrafted on them; and for this obvious reason, that nonsense can never be explained. Their purposes, however, are answered. Plato is canonized, and, it is now deemed as impious to question his merits as those of an Apostle of Jesus. He is peculiarly appealed to as an advocate of the immortality of the soul. And yet, I will venture to say that were there no better arguments than his in proof of it, not a man in the world would believe it.

It is fortunate for us, that Platonic republicanism has not obtained the same favor as Platonic Christianity; or we should now have been all living, men, women, and children, pell mell together, like beasts of the field or forest. Yet "Plato is a great philosopher," said La Fontaine.[228]

But, says Fontenelle,[229] "Do you find his ideas very clear?"

"Oh, no, he is of an obscurity impenetrable." "Do you not find him full of contradictions?"

"Certainly," replied La Fontaine, "he is but a sophist." Yet immediately after, he exclaims again, "Oh, Plato was a great philosopher."

Socrates had reason, indeed, to complain of the misrepresentations of Plato; for in truth, his dialogues are libels on Socrates.

Thomas Jefferson

---

228. Jean de La Fontaine (1621–1692). French Poet noted for his *La Fontaine Fables*. Also wrote *Love between Cupid and Psyche* and *Contes and Nouvelles en Vers*, borrowing Italian tales about marital infidelities and love affairs. Latter book banned.

229. Bernard De Fontanelle (1657–1757). French writer. Author of *Conversations on the Plurality of Worlds* (1686).

41. JOHN ADAMS TO THOMAS JEFFERSON
QUINCY, July 16, 1814

I am bold to say, that neither you nor I will live to see the course which the "wonders of the times" will take. Many years and perhaps centuries must pass, before the current will acquire a settled direction. If the Christian religion, as I understand it, or as you understand it, should maintain its ground, as I believe it will, yet Platonic, Pythagonic, Hindoo, Cabalistic Christianity,[230] which is Catholic Christianity, and which has prevailed for 1,500 years, has received a mortal wound of which the monster must finally die; yet so strong is his constitution, that he may endure for centuries before he expires.

Government has never been much studied by mankind, but their attention has been drawn to it in the latter part of the last century, and the beginning of this, more than at any former period; and the vast variety of experiments that have been made of constitutions in America, in France, in Holland, in Geneva, in Switzerland, and even in Spain and South America, can never be forgotten.

There will be catastrophes noted. The result, in time, will be improvements; and I have no doubt that the horrors we have experienced for the last forty years, will ultimately terminate in the advancement of civil and religious liberty, and ameliorations in the condition of mankind; for I am a believer in the probable improvability and improvement, the ameliorability and amelioration in human affairs; though I never could understand the doctrine of the perfectibility of the human mind. This has always appeared to me like the philosophy, or theology of the Gentoos, viz., that a Brahman, by certain studies, for a certain time pursued, and by certain ceremonies, a certain number of times repeated, becomes omniscient and almighty.

Our hopes, however, of sudden tranquility, ought not to be too sanguine. Fanaticism and superstition will still be selfish, subtle, intriguing, and at times furious. Despotism will still struggle for dom-

---

230. Small, often secret, groups meeting, planning, and controlling changes to, or overthrows of, current systems and beliefs in Christianity.

ination; monarchy will still study to rival nobility in popularity; aristocracy will continue to envy all above it, and despise and oppress all below it; democracy will envy all, contend with all, endeavor to pull down all; and when by chance it happens to get the upper hand for a short time, it will be revengeful, bloody, and cruel. These and other elements of fanaticism and anarchy, will yet, for a long time, continue a fermentation, which will excite alarms and require vigilance.

Napoleon is a military fanatic like Achilles, Alexander, Caesar, Mahomet, Zingis Kouli, Charles XII, etc. The maxim and principle of all of them was the same: "Jura negat sibi lata (i.e., nata) nihil non arrogat armis." ["He denies that laws were made for him; he arrogates everything to himself by force of arms."]

"The man who first pronounced the barbarous word 'Dieu' ought to have been immediately destroyed," says Diderot. In short, philosophers, ancient and modern, appear to me as mad as Hindoos, Mahometans, and Christians. No doubt they would all think me mad, and, for anything I know, this globe may be the Bedlam, Le Bicatre (i.e., Bicetre) of the universe.[231]

Cicero was educated in the Groves of Academus, where the name and memory of Plato were idolized to such a degree, that if he had wholly renounced the prejudices of his education, his reputation would have been lessened, if not injured and ruined. In his two volumes of Discourses on Government, we may presume that he fully examined Plato's laws and republic, as well as Aristotle's writings on government. But these have been carefully destroyed, not improbably with the general consent of philosophers, politicians and priests. The loss is as much to be regretted as that of any production of antiquity.

Nothing seizes the attention of the staring animal so surely as paradox, riddle, mystery, invention, discovery, wonder, temerity. Plato and his disciples, from the fourth-century Christians to Rousseau and Tom Paine, have been fully sensible of this weakness in mankind, and have too successfully grounded upon it their pretensions to fame.

---

231. Madhouse of the universe. Alluding to London's Bedlam (St. Mary of Bethlehem), priory turned into hospital for the insane in 1547.

Theology I would leave to Ray,[232] Derham,[233] Nicuentent,[234] and Paley,[235] rather than to Luther, Zinzindorf,[236] Swedenborg,[237] Wesley or Whitefield, or Thomas Aquinas or Wollebius. Metaphysics I would leave in the clouds with the materialists and spiritualists, with Leibnitz,[238] Berkley, Priestley and Edwards, and I might add Hume and Reed, or if permitted to be read, it should be with romances and novels.

John Adams

42. JOHN ADAMS TO THOMAS JEFFERSON
JUNE 19, 1815

DEAR SIR,

Education, which you brought into View in one of your Letters, is a Subject so vast, and the Systems of Writers are so various and so con-

---

232. John Ray (1628–1705). Anglican priest, naturalist, and philosopher. Wrote *The Wisdom of God Manisfested in the Works of Creation* (1691) and *Three Physico-Theological Discourses* (1692).

233. William Derham (1657–1735). Anglican clergyman and Isaac Newton devotee. Wrote *Astrotheology: or, A Demonstration of the Being and Attributes of God* (1715) and *Pluralist*, which posited the possibility of created life on planets beyond earth, per God's plan.

234. Probably meaning Nicholas of Cusa/Nikolaus Krebs (1401–1464). Pluralist who wrote *De Docta Ignorantia*.

235. William Paley (1743–1805). Anglican priest. Wrote *Evidences of Christianity*, *Moral Philosophy*, and *Natural Theology*. Introduced concept of *Watchmaker* creator.

236. Count Nikolaus Ludwig von Zinzendorf (1700–1760). German leader of Moravian (John Hus founder, fifteenth century) Church/Unitas Fratrum, "Heart Religion." Believed personal salvation was based on individual relationship with Christ. Addressed Holy Spirit as "Mother." Allowed female ordinations. Converted John and Charles Wesley, who later split off to form Methodist Church.

237. Emanuel Swedenborg (1688–1772). Wrote scientific and theological works on cosmology and soul, including *Outlines of a Philosophical Argument on the Infinite and the Final Cause of Creation*, *Heaven and Hell*, *The Last Judgement*, and *Principles of Natural Things*.

238. Gottfried Wilhelm Leibnitz (1646–1716). German mathematician and philosopher. Wrote *Theodicy* and *Monadology*.

tradictory that human Life is too short to examine it; and a Man must die before he can learn to bring up his Children.

The Phylosophers, Divines, Politicians and Paedagogues, who have published their Theories and Practices in this department, are without number. Your present Inquiries, I presume, are not confined to early Education, perhaps do not comprehend it. The Constitution of a University is your Object, as I understand you. Here also the Subject is infinite. The Science has so long laboured with a Dropsy, that it is a wonder the Patient has not long since expired. Sciences of all kinds have need of Reform, as much as Religion and Government.

The War of the Reformation still continues. The struggle between different and opposite systems of religion and government has lasted from Huss and Wickliff [239] to Lindsey and Priestley. How many powder Plots,[240] Bartholomew's Days,[241] Irish massacres,[242] Paris guillotines, how many Charles' and Maurice's, Louis's, and William Georges and Napoleons, have intervened? And the Philosophers, if we believe Condorcet, have been as errant hypocrites as any of them.

I am as ever,
John Adams

---

239. John Wycliffe (c. 1320–1384). English minister and Bible translater. Attacked the papacy and the institutional church, including an attack on transubstantiation. After translating the Bible into English, he sent the book out into the countryside with missionaries known as Lollards.

240. In 1605, the plot of persecuted English Catholics, including Guy Fawkes, to seize and use gunpowder to blow up the House of Lords and overthrow the government of King James was thwarted. Fawkes and others were hanged. Rebellions in the north and Ireland were quelled.

241. Catherine de Medici persuades her son, Charles IX, to begin a slaughter of French Protestants (Huguenots) on August 24, 1572. The slaughters continued into October. Over seventy thousand were killed in France, which led to resumption of religious civil wars.

242. Catholics killed an estimated two hundred thousand Protestants in Northern Ireland massacre (River Dam painting) in 1641.

43. JOHN ADAMS TO THOMAS JEFFERSON
QUINCY, June 20, 1815

DEAR SIR,

The fit of recollection came upon both of us so nearly at the same time, that I may, some time or other, begin to think there is something in Priestley's and Hartley's vibrations.[243] The day before yesterday I sent to the post office a letter to you, and last night I received your kind favor of the 10th.

The question before the human race is, whether the God of Nature shall govern the world by His own laws, or whether priests and kings shall rule it by fictitious miracles?

Or, in other words, whether authority is originally in the people? Or, whether it has descended for 1800 years in a succession of popes and bishops, or brought down from heaven by the Holy Ghost in the form of a dove, in a phial of holy oil?

Who shall take the side of God and Nature? Brahmans? Mandarins? Druids? Or Tecumseh and his brother the prophet? Or shall we become disciples of the Philosophers? And who are the philosophers? Frederic? Voltaire? Rousseau? Buffon?[244] Diderot? Condorcet?

These philosophers have shown themselves as incapable of governing mankind, as the Bourbons or the Guelphs.[245] Condorcet has let the cat out of the bag. He has made precious confessions. I regret that I have only an English translation of his "Outlines of a Historical View of the Progress of the Human Mind." But in pages 247, 248, and 249, you will find it frankly acknowledged, that the philosophers of the eighteenth century, adopted all the maxims, and practiced all the arts

---

243. David Hartley (1705–1757). English physician/philosopher. Wrote *Observations on Man*. Believed that white substance in brain and spinal cord caused sensations leading to mental phenomena.

244. Georges Louis Leclerc, Comte de Buffon (1707–1788). French naturalist and taxonomist. Wrote *Natural History*.

245. The Guelph faction arose in thirteenth- and fourteenth-century Italy. The Guelphs supported the pope versus the Ghibellines, who supported Germany. The factions had first bloomed in Germany over territorial disputes.

of the Pharisees, the ancient priests of all countries, the Jesuits, the Machiavellians, etc., etc., to overthrow the institutions that such arts had established.

This new philosophy was, by his own account, as insidious, fraudulent, hypocritical, and cruel, as the old policy of the priests, nobles, and kings. When and where were ever found, or will be found, sincerity, honesty, or veracity, in any sect or party in religion, government, or philosophy? Johnson and Burke were more of Catholics than Protestants at heart, and Gibbon became an advocate for the Inquisition.

There is no act of uniformity in the Church, or State, philosophic. There are as many sects and systems among them, as among Quakers and Baptists. Bonaparte will not revive Inquisitions, Jesuits or slave trade, for which habitudes the Bourbons have been driven again into exile.

We shall get along, with or without war. I have at last procured the Marquis D'Argens' Occellus, Timaeus, and Julian. Three such volumes I never read. They are a most perfect exemplification of Condorcet's previous confessions. It is astonishing they have not made more noise in the world.

Our Athanasians have printed in a pamphlet in Boston, your letters and Priestley's from Belsham's Lindsey. It will do you no harm. Our correspondence shall not again be so long interrupted.

Affectionately,
John Adams

P. S. Have you read Carnot?[246] Is it not afflicting to see a Man of such large Views so many noble Sentiments and such exalted integrity, groping in the dark for a Remedy? a balance or a mediator between Independence and Despotism? How shall his "Love of Country," his "Honor" and his "national Spirit" be produced.

I cannot write a hundreth part of what I wish to say to you.

J. A.

---

246. Lazare Nicolas Marguerite Carnot (1753–1823). French statesmen, general, and military engineer. Wrote numerous works on military strategy, politics, science, and poetry.

44. JOHN ADAMS TO THOMAS JEFFERSON
QUINCY, June 22, 1815

DEAR SIR,

Can you give me any information concerning A. G. Camus?[247] Is he a Chateaubriand[248] or a Marquis D'Argens? Does he mean to abolish Christianity or to restore the Inquisition, the Jesuits, the Pope and the Devil?

Within a few days I have received a thing as unexpected to me as an apparition from the dead: Rapport "a L'Institut National [Speech at the National Institute], Par A. G. Camus, imprime par ordre de L'Institut, Pluviose An XI." (1803]

In page 55 of this report, he says, "Certain pieces which I found in the chamber of accounts in Brussels, gave me useful indications concerning the grand collection of the Bollandists; and conducted me to make researches into the state of that work, unfortunately interrupted at this day. It would add to the Institute to propose to government the means of completing it as it has done with success for the collection of the historians of France, of diplomas and ordinances." [Here Adams interjected a note not included here.]

". . . Almost all the history of Europe, and a part of that of the east, from the seventh century to the thirteenth, is in the lives of personages to whom have been given the title of Saints. Every one may have remarked, that in reading history, there is no event of any importance, in civil order, in which some Bishop, some Abbe, some Monk, or some Saint, did not take a part. It is, therefore, a great service, rendered by the Jesuits (known under the name of the Bollandists) to those who would write history, to have formed the immense collection, extended to fifty-two volumes in folio, known under the title of the Acts of the Saints.

---

247. Armand-Gaston Camus (1740–1804). French revolutionary and archivist after the Revolution. Translated Aristotle's *History of Animals* (including the "fanciful and primitive") from Greek to French in 1783. Jefferson had a copy in his library.

248. French novelists, who left France and returned. François Rene Vicomte de Chateaubriand (1768–1848) wrote *Atala* based on his travels in North America. He also wrote *Genie de Christianisme* (1802), a five-volume work on the beauty of Christianity.

The service they have rendered to literature is considerably augmented by the insertion, in their Acts of the Saints, of a great number of diplomas and dissertations, the greatest part of which are models of criticism. There is no man, among the learned, who does not interest himself in this great collection. My intention is not to recall to your recollection the original authors, or their first labors. We may easily know them by turning over the leaves of the collection, or if we would find the result already written, it is in the Historical Library of Mensel, T. 1 [Tome 1], part 1, p. 306, or in the Manual of Literary History, by Bougine, T. 2, p. 641. I shall date what I have to say to you only from the epoch of the suppression of the society, of which the Bollandists were members.

At that time, three Jesuits were employed in the collection of the Acts of the Saints; to wit, the Fathers De Bie, De Bue, and Hubens. The Father Gesquiere, who had also labored at the Acts of the Saints, reduced a particular collection entitled Select Fragments from Belgical Writers, and extracts or references to matters contained in a collection entitled Museum of Bellarmine. These four monks inhabited the house of the Jesuits at Antwerp. Independently of the use of the library of the convent, the Bollandists had their particular library, the most important portion of which was a state of the Lives of the Saints for every day of the month, with indications of the books in which were found those which were already printed, and the original manuscripts, or the copies of manuscripts, which were not yet printed. They frequently quote this particular collection in their general collection.

The greatest part of the copies they had assembled, were the fruit of a journey of the Fathers Papebroch and Henshen, made to Rome in 1660. They remained there till 1662. Papebroch and his associate brought from Rome copies of seven hundred Lives of Saints, in Greek or in Latin. The citizen La Serna has in his library a copy, taken by himself, from the originals, of the relation of the journey of Papebroch to Rome, and of the correspondence of Henshen with his colleagues. The relation and the correspondence are in Latin. See Catalogue de la Serna, T. 3, N. 3903 [Note 3903].

After the suppression of the Jesuits, the commissioners apposed their seals upon the library of the Bollandists, as well as on that of the Jesuits of Antwerp. But Mr. Girard, then Secretary of the Academy at Brussels, who is still living, and who furnished me a part of the documents I use, charged with the inventory and sale of the books, withdrew those of the Bollandists, and transported them to Brussels.

The Academy of Brussels proposed to continue the Acts of the Saints under its own name, and for this purpose to admit the four Jesuits into the number of its members. The Father Gesquiere alone consented to this arrangement. The other Jesuits obtained of government, through the intervention of the Bishop of Newstadt, the assurance, that they might continue their collection. In effect, the Empress Maria Theresa approved, by a decree of the 19th of June, 1778, a plan which was presented to her, for the continuation of the works, both by the Bollandists and of Gesquiere.

This plan is in ample detail. It contains twenty articles, and would be useful to consult, if any persons should resume the Acts of the Saints. The establishment of the Jesuits was fixed in the Abbey of Candenberg, at Brussels; the library of the Bollandists was transported to that place; one of the monks of the Abbey was associated with them; and the Father Hubens being dead, was replaced by the Father Berthod, a Benedictine, who died in 1789. The Abbey of Candenberg having been suppressed, the government assigned to the Bollandists a place in the ancient College of the Jesuits, at Brussels. They there placed their library, and went there to live.

There they published the fifty-first volume of their collection in 1786, the fifth tome of the month of October, printed at Brussels, at the printing press Imperial and Royal, (in Typis Caesario regiis [in types Imperial and Royal].) They had then two associates, and they flattered themselves that the Emperor would continue to furnish the expense of their labors. Nevertheless, in 1788, the establishment of the Bollandists was suppressed, and they even proposed to sell the stock of the printed volumes; but, by an instruction (Avis) of the 6th of December, 1788, the ecclesiastical commission superseded the sale, till the result could be known of a negotiation which the Father De Bie had commenced with the Abbe of St. Blaise, to establish the authors, and transport the stock of the work, as well as the materials for its continuation at St. Blaise.

In the meantime, the Abby of Tongerloo[249] offered the government to purchase the library and stock of the Bollandists, and to cause the work to be continued by the ancient Bollandists, with the monks of Tongerloo associated with them. These propositions were accepted. The Fathers De Bie, De Bue, and Gesqueire, removed to Tongerloo; the monks of Candenberg refused to follow them, though they had been associated with them. On the entry of the French troops into Belgium, the monks of Tongerloo quitted their Abby; the Fathers De Bie, and Gesquiere, retired to Germany, where they died; the Father De Bue retired to the City Hall, heretofore Province of Hainault, his native country. He lives, but is very aged. One of the monks of Tongerloo, who had been associated with them, is the Father Heylen; they were not able to inform me of the place of his residence. Another monk associated with the Bollandists of 1780, is the Father Fonson, who resides at Brussels.

In the midst of these troubles, the Bollandists have caused to be printed the fifty-second volume of the Acts of the Saints, the sixth volume of the month of October. The fifty-first volume is not common in commerce, because the sale of it has been interrupted by the continual changes of the residence of the Bollandists. The fifty-second volume, or the sixth of the same month of October, is much rarer. Few persons know its existence.

The citizen La Serna has given me the two hundred and ninety-six first pages of the volume, which he believes were printed at Tongerloo. He is persuaded that the rest of the volume exists, and he thinks it was at Rome that it was finished.

The citizen D'Herbonville, Prefect of the two Neths at Antwerp, has made, for about eighteen months, attempts with the ancient Bollandists, to engage them to resume their labors. They have not had success. Perhaps the present moment would be the most critical, (opportune,) especially if the government should consent to give to the Bollandists assurance of their safety.

---

249. Tougerloo, a Belgian abbey near Antwerp.

The essential point would be to make sure of the existence of the manuscripts which I have indicated; and which, by the relation of the citizen La Serna, filled a body of a library of about three toises [a toise is a unit of length equal to 1.949 meters] in length, and two in breadth. If these manuscripts still exist, it is easy to terminate the Acts of the Saints; because we shall have all the necessary materials. If these manuscripts are lost, we must despair to see this collection completed.

I have enlarged a little on this digression on the Acts of the Saints, because it's a work of great importance; and because these documents, which cannot be obtained with any exactitude but upon the spots, seem to me to be among the principal objects which your travelers have to collect, and of which they ought to give you an account."

Now, my friend Jefferson! I await your observations on this morsel. You may think I waste my time and yours. I do not think so. If you will look into the "Nouveau Dictionnaire Historique," under the words "Bollandus, Heinshemius, and Papebrock," you will find more particulars of the rise and progress of this great work, "The Acts of the Saints."

I shall make only an observation of two:

1. The Pope never suppressed the work, and Maria Theresa established it. It therefore must be Catholic.

2. Notwithstanding the professions of the Bollandists, to discriminate the true from the false miracles, and the dubious from both, I suspect that the false will be found the fewest, the dubious the next, and the true the most numerous of all.

3. From all that I have read, of the legends, of the lives, and writings of the Saints, and even of the Fathers, and of ecclesiastical history in general, I have no doubt that the Acta Sanctorum is the most enormous mass of lies, frauds, hypocrisy, and imposture that ever was heaped together on this globe. If it were impartially consulted, it would do more to open the eyes of mankind, than all the philosophers of the 18th century, who were as great hypocrites as any of the philosophers or theologians of antiquity.

John Adams

45. THOMAS JEFFERSON TO JOHN ADAMS
MONTICELLO, August 10, 1815

DEAR SIR,

The simultaneous movements in our correspondence have been remarkable on several occasions. It would seem as if the state of the air, or state of the times, or some other unknown cause, produced a sympathetic effect on our mutual recollections. I had sat down to answer your letters of June the 19th, 20th and 22d, with pen, ink and paper before me, when I received from our mail that of July the 30th.

You ask information on the subject of Camus. All I recollect of him is that he was one of the deputies sent to arrest Dumourier at the head of his army, who were, however, themselves arrested by Dumourier, and long detained as prisoners. I presume, therefore, he was a Jacobin. You will find his character in the most excellent revolutionary history of Toulongeon. I believe, also, he may be the same person who has given us a translation of Aristotle's Natural History, from the Greek into French.

Of his report to the National Institute on the subject of the Bollandists, your letter gives me the first information. I had supposed them defunct with the Society of Jesuits, of which they were; and that their works, although above ground, were, from their bulk and insignificance, as effectually entombed on their shelves as if in the graves of their authors.

Fifty-two volumes in folio, of the Acta Sanctorum in dog-Latin, would be a formidable enterprise to the most laborious German. I expect, with you, they are the most enormous mass of lies, frauds, hypocrisy and imposture, that was ever heaped together on this globe. By what chemical process M. Camus supposed that an extract of truth could be obtained from such a farrago of falsehood, I must leave to the chemists and moralists of the age to divine.

Thomas Jefferson

46. JOHN ADAMS TO THOMAS JEFFERSON
QUINCY, August 24, 1815

DEAR SIR,

If I am neither deceived by the little information I have, or by my wishes for its truth, I should say that France is the most Protestant country of Europe at this time, though I cannot think it the most reformed. In consequence of these reveries, I have imagined that Camus and the Institute meant, by the revival and continuance of the Acta Sanctorum, to destroy the Pope, and the Catholic Church and Hierarchies, de fonde en comble [from top to bottom], or in the language of Frederick, Voltaire, D'Alembert, etc., "Ecraser le miserable [Crush the Wretch]." This great work must contain the most complete history of the corruptions of Christianity that has ever appeared, Priestley's not excepted; and his history of ancient opinions not excepted.

The Congress of 1774 resembled in some respects, though I hope not many, the Council of Nice in Ecclesiastical History. It assembled the Priests from the East and the West, the North and the South, who compared notes, engaged in discussions and debates, and formed results by one vote or two votes, which went out to the World as unanimous.

John Adams

47. JOHN ADAMS TO THOMAS JEFFERSON
QUINCY, November 13, 1815

DEAR SIR,

The fundamental article of my political creed is, that despotism, or unlimited sovereignty, or absolute power, is the same in a majority of a popular assembly, an aristocratical council, an oligarchical junto, and a single emperor; equally arbitrary, cruel, bloody, and in every respect diabolical.

Accordingly, arbitrary power, wherever it has resided, has never failed to destroy all the records, memorials, and histories of former times which it did not like, and to corrupt and interpolate such as it was cunning enough to preserve or tolerate. We cannot therefore say with much confidence, what knowledge or what virtues may have prevailed in some former ages in some quarters of the world.

Nevertheless, according to the few lights that remain to us, we may say that the eighteenth century, notwithstanding all its errors and vices, has been, of all that are past, the most honorable to human nature. Knowledge and virtues were increased and diffused. Arts, sciences useful to men, ameliorating their condition, were improved more than in any former equal period.

But what are we to say now? Is the nineteenth century to be a contrast to the eighteenth? Is it to extinguish all the lights of its predecessors? Are the Sorbonne, the Inquisition, the Index Expurgatorius, and the knights-errant of St. Ignatius Loyola[250] to be revived and restored to all their salutary powers of supporting and propagating the mild spirit of Christianity? The proceedings of the allies and their Congress at Vienna, the accounts from Spain, France, etc., the Chateaubriands and the Genlis,[251] indicate which way the wind blows. The priests are at their old work again. The Protestants are denounced, and another St. Bartholomew's day threatened.

This, however, will probably, twenty-five years hence, be honored with the character of "the effusions of a splenetic mind, rather than as the sober reflections of an unbiased understanding." I have received Memoirs of the Life of Dr. Price, by William Morgan, F.R.S. In pages 151 and 155 Mr. Morgan says:

> "So well assured was Dr. Price of the establishment of a free Constitution in France, and of the subsequent overthrow of despotism throughout Europe, as the consequence of it, that he never failed to

---

250. Also called *Index Liborum Prohibitorum* (Index of prohibited/forbidden books). Initiated in 1559 by the Sacred Congregation of the Inquisition and enforced by the Jesuits, who were founded by Loyola.

251. Stefanie Felicite, Comtesse de Genlis, left France during the French Revolution but came back under Napoleon. She became governess to future king of France Louis Philippe and produced at least ninety volumes of moral tales and comedies.

express his gratitude to heaven for having extended his life to the present happy period, in which after sharing the benefits of one revolution, he has been spared to be a witness to two other revolutions, both glorious.

But some of his correspondents were not quite so sanguine in their expectations from the last of the revolutions; and among these, the late American Ambassador, Mr. John Adams. In a long letter which he wrote to Dr. Price at this time, so far from congratulating him on the occasion, he expresses himself in terms of contempt, in regard to the French Revolution; and after asking rather too severely what good was to be expected from a nation of Atheists, he concluded with foretelling the destruction of a million of human beings as the probable consequence of it. These harsh censures and gloomy predictions were particularly ungrateful to Dr. Price. Nor, can it be denied that they must have then appeared as the effusions of a splenetic mind, rather than as the sober reflections of an unbiased understanding."

John Adams

48. THOMAS JEFFERSON TO JOHN ADAMS
MONTICELLO, January 11, 1816

DEAR SIR,

Of the last five months I have passed four at my other domicile, for such it is in a considerable degree. No letters are forwarded to me there because the cross post to that place is circuitous and uncertain. During my absence, therefore, they are accumulating here, and awaiting acknowledgments. This has been the fate of your favor of November 13th.

I agree with you in all its eulogies on the eighteenth century. It certainly witnessed the sciences and arts, manners and morals, advanced to a higher degree than the world had ever before seen. And might we not go back to the era of the Borgias, by which time the barbarous ages had reduced national morality to its lowest point of depravity, and observe that the arts and sciences, rising from that point, advanced gradually through all the sixteenth, seventeenth and eighteenth centuries, softening and correcting the manners and morals of man?

I think, too, we may add to the great honor of science and the arts that their natural effect is, by illuminating public opinion, to erect it into a censor, before which the most exalted tremble for their future, as well as present fame. With some exceptions only, through the seventeenth and eighteenth centuries, morality occupied an honorable chapter in the political code of nations.

You must have observed while in Europe, as I thought I did, that those who administered the governments of the greater powers at least, had a respect to faith, and considered the dignity of their government as involved in its integrity. A wound indeed was inflicted on this character of honor in the eighteenth century by the partition of Poland. But this was the atrocity of a barbarous government chiefly, in conjunction with a smaller one still scrambling to become great, while one only of those already great and having character to lose, descended to the baseness of an accomplice in the crime. France, England, Spain, shared in it only inasmuch as they stood aloof and permitted its perpetration.

How then has it happened that these nations, France especially and England, so great, so dignified, so distinguished by science and the arts, plunged all at once into all the depths of human enormity, threw off suddenly and openly all the restraints of morality, all sensation to character, and unblushingly avowed and acted on the principle that power was right?

Can this sudden apostasy from national rectitude be accounted for?

The treaty of Pillnitz seems to have begun it,[252] suggested perhaps by the baneful precedent of Poland.[253] Was it from the terror of monarchs, alarmed at the light returning on them from the west, and kindling a volcano under their thrones? Was it a combination to extin-

---

252. Declaration of Pillnitz (August 27, 1791). King Leopold of the Holy Roman Empire/Germany and King Frederick William II of Prussia signed a statement calling on European powers to intervene if French revolutionaries harmed the French king or his family. Leopold worded the statement so that he would not have to go to war unless *all* European nations intervened. He did not expect England's William Pitt to support war with France.

253. On May 3, 1791, Poland restored the hereditary monarchy and reformed government.

guish that light, and to bring back, as their best auxiliaries, those enumerated by you, the Sorbonne, the Inquisition, the Index Expurgatorius, and the knights of Loyola?

Whatever it was, the close of the century saw the moral world thrown back again to the age of the Borgias,[254] to the point from which it had departed three hundred years before. France, after crushing and punishing the conspiracy of Pilnitz, went herself deeper and deeper into the crimes she had been chastising. I say France and not Bonaparte. For, although he was the head and mouth, the nation furnished the hands which executed his enormities. England, although in opposition, kept full pace with France, not indeed by the manly force of her own arms, but by oppressing the weak and bribing the strong. At length the whole choir joined and divided the weaker nations among them.

Your prophecies to Dr. Price proved truer than mine; and yet fell short of the fact, for instead of a million, the destruction of eight or ten millions of human beings has probably been the effect of these convulsions. I did not, in '89, believe they would have lasted so long, nor have cost so much blood. But although your prophecy has proved true so far, I hope it does not preclude a better final result. That same light from our west seems to have spread and illuminated the very engines employed to extinguish it. It has given them a glimmering of their rights and their power.

Thomas Jefferson

49. JOHN ADAMS TO THOMAS JEFFERSON
QUINCY, February 2, 1816

DEAR SIR,

I know not what to think of your letter of the 11th of January, but that it is one of the most consolatory I ever received.

To trace the commencement of the Reformation, I suspect we must

---

254. Descended from the Borjas of Spain, this family acquired political power and wealth in Italy, securing the papacy twice in the process.

go farther back than Borgia, or even Huss or Wickliffe, and I want the Acta Sanctorum to assist me in this research. That stupendous monument of human hypocrisy and fanaticism, the church of St. Peter at Rome, which was a century and a half in building, excited the ambition of Leo the Xth, who believed no more of the Christian religion than Diderot, to finish it; and finding St. Peter's pence insufficient, he deluged all Europe with indulgences for sale, and excited Luther to controvert his authority to grant them. Luther, and his associates and followers, went less than half way in detecting the corruptions of Christianity, but they acquired reverence and authority among their followers almost as absolute as that of the Popes had been.

To enter into details would be endless; but I agree with you, that the natural effect of science and arts is to erect public opinion into a censor, which must in some degree be respected by all.

There is no difference of opinion or feeling between us, concerning the partition of Poland, the intended partitions of Pilnitz, or the more daring partitions of Vienna.

Your question "How the apostasy from national rectitude can be accounted for?" is too deep and wide for my capacity to answer. I leave Fisher Ames to dogmatize up the affairs of Europe and mankind. I have done too much in this way. A burned child dreads the fire. I can only say at present, that it should seem that human reason, and human conscience, though I believe there are such things, are not a match for human passions, human imaginations, and human enthusiasm.

You, however, I believe, have hit one mark, "the fires the governments of Europe felt kindling under their seats." And, I will hazard a shot at another, the priests of all nations imagined they felt approaching such flames, as they had so often kindled about the bodies of honest men. Priests and politicians, never before, so suddenly and so unanimously concurred in reestablishing darkness and ignorance, superstition and despotism.

The morality of Tacitus is the morality of patriotism, and Britain and France have adopted his creed; i.e., that all things were made for Rome. "Jura negat sibi Cata (i.e, nata) nihil non arrogat armis," ["He denies that laws were made for him; he arrogates everything to himself by force of arms."] said Achilles. "Laws were not made for me," said the Regent of France, and his cardinal minister Du Bois. The universe was made for me, says man. Jesus despised and condemned such patriotism; but what nation, or what Christian, has adopted His system? He was, as you say, "the most benevolent Being that ever appeared on earth." France and England Bourbons and Bonaparte, and all the sovereigns at Vienna, have acted on the same principle. "All things were made for my use. So man for mine," replies a pampered goose.

The philosophers of the eighteenth century have acted on the same principle: "When it is to combat evil, 'tis lawful to employ the devil." Bonus populus vult decipi, decipiatur. "The people wish to be deceived. Let them be deceived." (Jacques-Auguste de Thou).[255] They have employed the same falsehood, the same deceit, which philosophers and priests of all ages have employed for their own selfish purposes. We now know how their efforts have succeeded. The old deceivers have triumphed over the new. Truth must be more respected than it has ever been, before any great improvement can be expected in the condition of mankind. As Rochefoucauld, his maxims, drew "from history and from practice," I believe them true. From the whole nature of man, moral, intellectual, and physical, he did not draw them.

We must come to the principles of Jesus. But when will all men and all nations do as they would be done by? Forgive all injuries, and love their enemies as themselves? I leave those profound philosophers, whose sagacity perceives the perfectibility of human nature, and, those illuminated theologians, who expect the Apocalyptic reign to enjoy their transporting hopes, provided always that they will not engage us in Crusades and French Revolutions, nor burn us for doubting. My spirit of prophecy reaches no farther than New England GUESSES.

You ask how it has happened that all Europe has acted on the principle that Power was Right. I know not what answer to give you, but this, that Power always sincerely, conscientiously, believes itself right. Power always thinks it has a great soul, and vast views, beyond the

---

255. De Thou (1553–1617). French historian and poet. Wrote *Histories*. When the Congregation of Index banned his book in 1609, the Parlement of Paris banned Cardinal Bellarmine's book on papal power.

comprehension of the weak; and that it is doing God service, when it is violating all His laws. Our passions, ambition, avarice, love, resentment, etc., possess so much metaphysical subtlety, and so much overpowering eloquence, that they insinuate themselves into the understanding and the conscience, and convert both to their party; and I may be deceived as much as any of them, when I say, that Power must never be trusted without a check.

Morgan has misrepresented my guess. There is not a word in my letter about "a million of human beings." Civil wars, of an hundred years, throughout Europe; were guessed at; and this is broad enough for your ideas; for eighteen or twenty millions would be a moderate computation for a century of civil wars throughout Europe. I still pray that a century of civil wars may not desolate Europe and America too, south and north.

Your speculations into futurity in Europe are so probable, that I can suggest no doubt to their disadvantage. All will depend on the progress of knowledge. But how shall knowledge advance? Independent of temporal and spiritual power, the course of science and literature is obstructed and discouraged by so many causes that it is to be feared their motions will be slow. I have just finished reading four volumes of D'israeli's: two on Calamities; two on the Quarrels of Authors.[256] These would be sufficient to show that slow rises genius by poverty and envy oppressed. Even Newton, and Locke, and Grotius, could not escape. France could furnish four other volumes of the woes and wars of authors.

My compliments to Mrs. Randolph, her daughter Ellen, and all her other children; and believe me, as ever. To which Mrs. Adams adds her affectionate regard and a wish that distance did not separate souls congenial.

John Adams

---

256. Isaac D'israeli (1766–1848). English Jew. Had his children baptized in 1817, while he remained a Jew. His son, Benjamin, thus was able to become British prime minister. Isaac's literary works include *Calamities of Authors* (1812–1813) and *Curiosities of Literature* (4 vols., 1791–1823).

50. JOHN ADAMS TO THOMAS JEFFERSON
QUINCY, March 2, 1816

DEAR SIR,

I cannot be serious! I am about to write you the most frivolous letter you ever read.

Would you go back to your cradle and live over again your seventy years? I believe you would return me a New England answer, by asking me another question: Would you live your eighty years over again?

I am not prepared to give you an explicit answer; the question involves so many considerations of metaphysics and physics, of theology and ethics, of philosophy and history, of experience and romance, of tragedy, comedy and farce, that I would not give my opinion without writing a volume to justify it.

I have lately lived over again, in part, from 1753, when I was junior sophister at college, till 1769, when I was digging in the mines as a barrister at law, for silver and gold, in the town of Boston; and got as much of the shining dross for my labor as my utmost avarice at that time craved.

At the hazard of all the little vision that is left me, I have read the history of that period of sixteen years, in the volumes of the Baron de Grimm.[257] In a late letter to you, I expressed a wish to see a history of quarrels and calamities of authors in France, like that of D'israeli in England. I did not expect it so soon; but now I have it in a manner more masterly than I ever hoped to see it.

It is not only a narration of the incessant great wars between the ecclesiastics and the philosophers, but of the little skirmishes and squabbles of Poets, Musicians, Sculptors, Painters, Architects, Tragedians, Comedians, Opera Singers and Dancers, Chansons, Vaudevilles, Epigrams, Madrigals, Epitaphs, Anagrams, Sonnets, etc. No man is more sensible than I am of the service to science and letters,

---

257. Friedrich Melchior, Baron von Grimm (1723–1807). German-born philosopher, critic, and collaborator with French Encyclopedists. In 1765 Grimm arranged for Empress Catherine of Russia to buy Diderot's library, while letting him continue to use it. Catherine also paid Diderot a yearly salary.

Humanity, Fraternity and Liberty, that would have been rendered by the Encyclopedists and Economists, by Voltaire, D'Alembert, Buffon, Diderot, Rousseau, La Lande,[258] Frederick and Catherine, if they had possessed common sense.

But they were all totally destitute of it. They all seemed to think that all Christendom was convinced as they were, that all religion was "visions Judaicques," and that their effulgent lights had illuminated all the world. They seemed to believe, that whole nations and continents had been changed in their principles, opinions, habits and feelings, by the sovereign grace of their almighty philosophy, almost as suddenly as Catholics and Calvinists believe in instantaneous conversion. They had not considered the force of early education on the millions of minds who had never heard of their philosophy. And what was their philosophy? Atheism, pure, unadulterated Atheism.

Diderot, D'Alembert, Frederick, De La Lande and Grimm, were indubitable Atheists. The universe was matter only, and eternal; spirit was a word without a meaning; liberty was a word without a meaning. There was no liberty in the universe; liberty was a word void of sense. Every thought, word, passion, sentiment, feeling, all motion, and action was necessary. All beings and attributes were of eternal necessity. Conscience and morality were all nothing but fate.

This was their creed and this was to perfect human nature, convert the earth into a paradise of pleasure.

Who and what is this fate? He must be a sensible fellow. He must be a master of science. He must be a master of spherical trigonometry and great circle sailing. He must calculate eclipses in his head by intuition. He must be master of the science infinitesimal. He must involve and extract all the roots by intuition, and be familiar with all possible or imaginable sections of the cone. He must be a master of arts, mechanical and imitative. He must have more eloquence than Demosthenes, more wit than Swift or Voltaire, more humor than Butler or Trumbull, and what is more comfortable than all the rest, he must be

258. Michel Richard de la Lande (1657–1726). French composer and organist to Parisian churches. He was director of sacred music for the court of Louis XIV and was noted for his motets for chorus and orchestra.

good natured; for this is upon the whole a good world. There is ten times as much pleasure as pain in it.

Why then should we abhor the word God, and fall in love with the word Fate? We know there exists energy and intellect enough to produce such a world as this, which is a sublime and beautiful one, and a very benevolent one, notwithstanding all our snarling; and a happy one, if it is not made otherwise by our own fault. Ask a mite, in the centre of your mammoth cheese, what he thinks of "the all."

I should prefer the philosophy of Timaeus of Locris, before that of Grimm and Diderot, Frederick and D'Alembert. I should even prefer the Shasta of Hindostan, or the Chaldean, Egyptian, Indian, Greek, Christian, Mahometan, Tubonic, or Celtic theology.

Timaeus and Ocellus taught that three principles were eternal: God, Matter, and Form. God was good, and had ideas. Matter was necessity. Fate, dead without ideas, without form, without feeling, perverse, intractable; capable, however, of being cut into forms, spheres, circles, triangles, squares, cubes, cones, etc. The ideas of the good God labored upon matter to bring it into form; but matter was fate, necessity, dullness, obstinacy, and would not always conform to the ideas of the good God who desired to make the best of all possible worlds; but Matter, Fate, Necessity, resisted, and would not let Him complete His idea. Hence, all the evil and disorder, pain, misery and imperfection of the universe.

We all curse Robespierre and Bonaparte, but were they not both such restless, vain, extravagant animals as Diderot and Voltaire? Voltaire was the greatest literary character, and Bonaparte the greatest military character of the eighteenth century. There is all the difference between them. Both, equally heroes and equally cowards.

When you ask my opinion of a University—it would have been easy to advise Mathematics, experimental Philosophy, Natural History, Chemistry and Astronomy, Geography and the Fine Arts to the exclusion of Metaphysics and Theology. But knowing the eager impatience of the human mind to search into eternity and infinity, the first cause and last end of all things, I thought best to leave it its liberty to inquire till it is convinced, as I have been these fifty years, that there is but one Being in the universe who comprehends it; and our last resource is resignation.

John Adams

51. THOMAS JEFFERSON TO JOHN ADAMS
MONTICELLO, April 8, 1816

DEAR SIR,

I have to acknowledge your two favors of February the 16th and March the 2d, and to join sincerely in the sentiment of Mrs. Adams, and regret that distance separates us so widely. An hour of conversation would be worth a volume of letters. But we must take things as they come.

You ask, if I would agree to live my seventy or rather seventy-three years over again? To which I say, yea. I think with you, that it is a good world on the whole; that it has been framed on a principle of benevolence, and more pleasure than pain dealt out to us. There are, indeed, (who might say nay) gloomy and hypochondriac minds, inhabitants of diseased bodies, disgusted with the present, and despairing of the future; always counting that the worst will happen, because it may happen. To these I say, "How much pains have cost us the evils which have never happened!" My temperament is sanguine. I steer my bark with Hope in the head, leaving Fear astern.

My hopes, indeed, sometimes fail; but not oftener than the forebodings of the gloomy. There are, I acknowledge, even in the happiest life, some terrible convulsions, heavy set-offs against the opposite page of the account. I have often wondered for what good end the sensations of grief could be intended. All our other passions, within proper bounds, have a useful object. And the perfection of the moral character is, not in a stoical apathy, so hypocritically vaunted, and so untruly too, because impossible, but in a just equilibrium of all the passions. I wish the pathologists then would tell us what is the use of grief in the economy, and of what good it is the cause, proximate or remote.

Did I know Baron Grimm while at Paris? Yes, most intimately. He was the pleasantest and most conversable member of the diplomatic corps while I was there; a man of good fancy, acuteness, irony, cunning and egoism. No heart, not much of any science, yet enough of every one to speak its language; his forte was belles-lettres, painting and sculpture. In these he was the oracle of society, and as such, was the Empress Catharine's private correspondent and factor, in all things not diplomatic.

Although I never heard Grimm express the opinion directly, yet I always supposed him to be of the school of Diderot, D'Alembert, D'Holbach,[259] the first of whom committed his system of atheism to writing in "Le bon sens," and the last in his "Systeme de la Nature." It was a numerous school in the Catholic countries, while the infidelity of the Protestant took generally the form of theism. The former always insisted that it was a mere question of definition between them, the hypostasis of which, on both sides, was "Nature," or "the Universe"; that both agreed in the order of the existing system, but the one supposed it from eternity, the other as having begun in time.

And when the atheist descanted on the unceasing motion and circulation of matter through the animal, vegetable and mineral kingdoms, never resting, never annihilated, always changing form, and under all forms gifted with the power of reproduction; the theist pointing "to the heavens above, and to the earth beneath, and to the waters under the earth," asked, if these did not proclaim a first cause, possessing intelligence and power; power in the production, and intelligence in the design and constant preservation of the system; urged the palpable existence of final causes; that the eye was made to see, and the ear to hear, and not that we see because we have eyes, and hear because we have ears; an answer obvious to the senses, as that of walking across the room, was to the philosopher demonstrating the non-existence of motion.

It was in D'Holbach's conventicles that Rousseau imagined all the machinations against him were contrived; and he left, in his Confes-

259. Paul Henri Thiry, Baron D'Holbach (1723–1789). Philosopher and contributor to Diderot's *Encyclopedia*. Wrote *Christianity Unveiled* (1761), *System of Nature* (1770), *Good Sense* (1772), and *The Moral Universe* (1776).

sions, the most biting anecdotes of Grimm. These appeared after I left France; but I have heard that poor Grimm was so much afflicted by them, that he kept his bed several weeks. I have never seen the Memoirs of Grimm. Their volume has kept them out of our market.

I have lately been amusing myself with Levi's book,[260] in answer to Dr. Priestley. It is a curious and tough work. His style is inelegant and incorrect, harsh and petulant to his adversary, and his reasoning flimsy enough. Some of his doctrines were new to me, particularly that of his two resurrections; the first, a particular one of all the dead, in body as well as soul, who are to live over again, the Jews in a state of perfect obedience to God, the other nations in a state of corporeal punishment for the sufferings they have inflicted on the Jews.

And he explains this resurrection of the bodies to be only of the original stamen of Leibnitz, or the homunculus in semine masculino,[261] considering that as a mathematical point, insusceptible of separation or division. The second resurrection is a general one of souls and bodies, eternally to enjoy divine glory in the presence of the Supreme Being. He alleges that the Jews alone preserve the doctrine of the unity of God.

Yet their God would be deemed a very indifferent man with us; and it was to correct their anamorphosis of the Deity, that Jesus preached, as well as to establish the doctrine of a future state. However, Levi insists, that that was taught in the Old Testament, and even by Moses himself and the prophets. He agrees that an anointed prince was prophesied and promised; but denies that the character and history of Jesus had any analogy with that of the person promised.

He must be fearfully embarrassing to the Hierophants of fabricated Christianity because it is their own armor in which he clothes himself for the attack. For example, he takes passages of Scripture from their context, (which would give them a very different meaning,) strings

---

260. David Levi (1742–1801). English-born Jew. Wrote *Letters to Priestley* (1787–1789), *Letters to Thomas Paine, in answer to his Age of Reason* (1797), and *Dissertations on Prophecies* (1793).

261. Homunculus, Latin for "little man," is a reference to an imaginary tiny man living within a person or in masculine semen. Monads are small essences that make up life and the world.

them together, and makes them point towards what object he pleases; he interprets them figuratively, typically, analogically, hyperbolically.

He calls in the aid of emendation, transposition, ellipse, metonymy, and every other figure of rhetoric; the name of one man is taken for another, one place for another, days and weeks for months and years; and finally, he avails himself of all his advantage over his adversaries by his superior knowledge of the Hebrew, speaking in the very language of the divine communication, while they can only fumble on with conflicting and disputed translations.

Such is this war of giants. And how can such pigmies as you and I decide between them? For myself, I confess that my head is not formed tantas componere lites [to settle such great disputes]. And as you began yours of March the 2d, with a declaration that you were about to write me the most frivolous letter I had ever read, so I will close mine by saying, I have written you a full match for it, and by adding my affectionate respects to Mrs. Adams, and the assurance of my constant attachment and consideration for yourself.

Thomas Jefferson

52. JOHN ADAMS TO THOMAS JEFFERSON
QUINCY, May 3, 1816

DEAR SIR,

Yours of April 8th has long since been received.

Jefferson: "Would you agree to live your eighty years over again?"
Adams: "Ay, sans Phrases."
Jefferson: "Would you agree to live your eighty years over again forever?'"
Adams: "I once heard our acquaintance, Chew,[262] of Philadelphia,

262. Benjamin Chew (1722–1810). Chief justice of Pennsylvania and often adversary of Benjamin Franklin. Chew's choice not to support the Declaration of Independence initially cost him positions.

say, 'he should like to go back to twenty-five, to all eternity'; But, I own my soul would start and shrink back on itself at the prospect of an endless succession of balls of soap, almost as much as at the certainty of annihilation. For what is human life? I can speak only for one. I have had more comfort than distress, more pleasure than pain ten to one, nay, if you please, an hundred to one. A pretty large dose, however, of distress and pain. But after all, what is human life? A vapor, a fog, a dew, a cloud, a blossom, a flower, a rose, a blade of grass, a glass bubble, a tale told by an idiot, a ball of soap, vanity of vanities, an eternal succession of which would terrify me almost as much as annihilation."

Jefferson: "Would you prefer to live over again, rather than accept the offer of a better life in a future state?"

Adams: "Certainly not."

Jefferson: "Would you live again rather than change for the worse in a future state, for the sake of trying something new?"

Adams: "Certainly yes."

Jefferson: "Would you live over again once or forever rather than run the risk of annihilation, or of a better or a worse state at or after death?"

Adams: "Most certainly I would not."

Jefferson: "How valiant you are!"

Adams: "Aye, at this moment, and at all other moments of my life that I can recollect. But who can tell what will become of his bravery when his flesh and his heart shall fail him? Bolingbroke said his philosophy was not sufficient to support him in his last hours. D'Alembert said: 'Happy are they who have courage, but I have none.'

Voltaire, the greatest genius of them all, behaved like the greatest coward of them all at his death, as he had like the wisest fool of them all in his lifetime. Hume awkwardly affected to sport away all sober thoughts. Who can answer for his last feelings and reflections, especially as the priests are in possession of the custom of making them the greatest engines of their craft? 'Back, ye unhallowed!'

Jefferson: "How shall we, how can we estimate the real value of human life?"

Adams: "I know not; I cannot weigh sensations and reflections, pleasures and pains, hopes and fears, in money-scales. But I can tell you how I have heard it estimated by philosophers. One of my old friends and clients, a mandamus counselor against his will, a man of letters and virtues, without one vice that I ever knew or suspected, except garrulity, William Vassall,[263] asserted to me, and strenuously maintained, that "pleasure is no compensation for pain." A hundred years of the keenest delights of human life could not atone for one hour of bilious colic that he had felt. The sublimity of this philosophy my dull genius could not reach. I was willing to state a fair account between pleasure and pain, and give credit for the balance, which I found very great in my favor.

Another philosopher, who, as we say, believed nothing, ridiculed the notion of a future state. One of the company asked, "Why are you an enemy to a future state? Are you weary of life? Do you detest existence?"

"Weary of life? Detest existence?" said the philosopher.

"No! I love life so well and am so attached to existence that, to be sure of immortality, I would consent to be pitched about with forks by the devils, among flames of fire and brimstone to all eternity."

Adams: "I find no resources in my courage for this exalted philosophy. I had rather be blotted out."

Jefferson: "One must speak out! What is there in life to attach us to it but the hope of a future and a better? It is a cracker, a rocket, a firework at best. I admire your navigation, and should like to sail with you, either in your bark, or in my own alongside of yours. Hope with her gay ensigns displayed at the prow, fear with her hobgoblins behind the stern. Hope springs eternal, and hope is all that endures. Take away hope and what remains? What pleasure, I mean? Take away fear, and what pain remains? Ninety-nine one-hundredths of the pleasures and pains of life are nothing but hopes and fears."

Adams: "All nations known in history or in travels, have hoped, believed and expected a future and a better state. The Maker of the

---

263. William Vassall's name appeared in the 1778 Massachusetts Banishment Act listing Tories ordered to leave the state and not return subject to "the pain of death without benefit of clergy."

universe, the cause of all things, whether we call it fate, or chance, or GOD, has inspired this hope. If it is a fraud, we shall never know it. We shall never resent the imposition, be grateful for the illusion, nor grieve for the disappointment. We shall be no more. Credit Grimm, Diderot, Buffon, La Lande, Condorcet, D'Holbach, Frederick, Catherine, not I. Arrogant as it may be, I shall take the liberty to pronounce them all Idiologians.[264] Yet, I would not persecute a hair of their heads. The world is wide enough for them and me.

Suppose the cause of the universe should reveal to all mankind at once a certainty that they must all die within a century, and that death is an eternal extinction of all living powers, of all sensation and reflection. What would be the effect? Would there be one man, woman or child existing on this globe, twenty years hence? Would not every human being be a Madame Deffand,[265] Voltaire's 'blind clairvoyant' all her lifetime regretting her existence, bewailing that she had ever been born, grieving that she had ever been dragged, without her consent, into being? Who would bear the gout, the stone, the colic, for the sake of a Ball of Soap, when a pistol, a cord, a pond, or a phial of laudanum was at hand? What would men say to their Maker? Would they thank Him? No; they would reproach Him; they would curse Him to His face."

Voila! A sillier letter than my last. For a wonder, I have filled a sheet, and a greater wonder, I have read fifteen volumes of Grimm. Hold your tongue. I hope to write you more upon this and other topics of your letter. I have read also a History of the Jesuits, in four volumes. Can you tell me the author, or anything of this work?

John Adams

264. Ideologians believed that philosophy's main emphasis should be on the study of mental conceptions produced by sensations from the material world.

265. Marie de Vichy-Chamrond, Marquise du Deffand (1697–1780). Her Paris salon dinner parties hosted the powerful and talented, such as Voltaire, Diderot, D'Alembert, and Montesquieu.

53. JOHN ADAMS TO THOMAS JEFFERSON
QUINCY, May 6, 1816

DEAR SIR,

Neither eyes, or fingers, or paper, held out to dispatch all the trifles I wished to write in my last letter.

In your favor of April 8th you "wonder for what good end the sensations of grief could be intended?" You wish the pathologists would tell us, what is the use of grief in our economy, and of what good it is the cause proximate or remote. When I approach such questions as this, I consider myself, like one of those little eels in Vinegar, or one of those animalcules in black or red pepper, or in the horse-radish root, that bite our tongues so cruelly, reasoning upon the totality. Of what use is this sting upon the tongue? Why might we not have the benefit of these stimulants, without the sting? Why might we not have the fragrance and beauty of the rose without the thorn?

In the first place, however, we know not the connection between pleasure and pain. They seem to be mechanical and inseparable. How can we conceive a strong passion, a sanguine hope suddenly disappointed, without producing pain, or grief? Swift, at 70, recollected the fish he had angled out of water when a boy, which broke loose from his hook; and said, I feel the disappointment at this moment.

A merchant places all his fortune and all his credit in a single India or China ship. She arrives at the Vineyard with a cargo worth a million, in order. Sailing round a cape for Boston, a sudden storm wrecks her—ship, cargo and crew, all lost. Is it possible that the merchant ruined, bankrupt, sent to prison by his creditors—his wife and children starving—should not grieve?

Suppose a young couple, with every advantage of persons, fortunes and connections, on the point of indissoluble union. A flash of lightning, or any one of those millions of accidents which are allotted to humanity, proves fatal to one of the lovers. Is it possible that the other, and all the friends of both, should not grieve?

It seems that grief, as a mere passion; must be in proportion to sensibility. Did you ever see a portrait, or a statue of a great man, without perceiving strong traits of pain and anxiety? These furrows were all ploughed in the countenance, by grief. Our juridical oracle, Sir Edward Coke, thought that none were fit for legislators and magistrates, but "sad men." And who were these sad men? They were aged men, who had been tossed and buffeted in the vicissitudes of life forced upon profound reflection by grief and disappointments and taught to command their passions and prejudices.

But all this you will say is nothing to the purpose. It is only repeating and exemplifying a fact, which my question supposed to be well known, viz., the existence of grief; and is no answer to my question, "What are the uses of grief?"

This is very true, and you are very right; but may not the uses of grief be inferred, or at least suggested by such exemplifications of known facts? Grief compels the India merchant to think; to reflect upon the plans of his voyage: Have I not been rash, to trust my fortune, my family, my liberty, to the caprices of winds and waves in a single ship? I will never again give a loose to my imagination and avarice. It had been wiser and more honest to have traded on a smaller scale upon my own capital.

The desolated lover, and disappointed connections, are compelled by their grief to reflect on the vanity of human wishes and expectations; to learn the essential lesson of resignation; to review their own conduct towards the deceased; to correct any errors or faults in their future conduct towards their remaining friends, and towards all men; to recollect the virtues of the lost friend, and resolve to imitate them; his follies and vices if he had any, and resolve to avoid them.

Grief drives men into habits of serious refection, sharpens the understanding, and softens the heart; it compels them to arouse their reason, to assert its empire over their passions, propensities and prejudices; to elevate them to a superiority over all human events; to give them the imperturbable tranquility of a happy heart; in short, to make them stoics and Christians.

After all, as grief is a pain, it stands in the predicament of all other evil, and the great question occurs, what is the origin, and what the final cause of evil? This perhaps is known only to Omniscience. We poor mortals have nothing to do with it, but to fabricate all the good we can out of all inevitable evils, and, to avoid all that are avoidable, and many such there are, among which are our own unnecessary apprehensions and imaginary fears. Though stoical apathy is impossible, yet patience, and resignation, and tranquility may be acquired by consideration, in a great degree, very much for the happiness of life.

I have read Grimm, in fifteen volumes, of more than five hundred pages each. I will not say like Uncle Toby, "You shall not die till you have read him." But you ought to read him, if possible. It is the most entertaining work I ever read. He appears exactly as you represent him. What is most remarkable of all is his impartiality. He spares no characters but Necker[266] and Diderot. Voltaire, Buffon, D'Alembert, Helvetius, Rousseau, Marmontel,[267] Condorcet, La Harpe, Beaumarchais.[268] All others, are lashed without ceremony, their portraits as faithfully drawn as possible.

It is a complete review of French literature and fine arts from 1753 to 1790: No politics; Criticisms very just; Anecdotes without number,

---

266. Anne-Louise-Germaine Necker, Baroness de Stael-Holstein (1766–1817). French-Swiss woman of letters, opponent of Napoleon, lover of Bishop Talleyrand, and others. Hostess of a Paris salon, exchanging ideas with other great minds of the time. Wrote *Letters on the Works and Character of Jean-Jacques Rousseau* (1788), *The Influence of Passions on the Happiness of Individuals and Nations* (1796), and *On Literature: The Influence of Literature on Society* (1800).

267. Jean François Marmontel (1723–1799). Writer, historian, and contributor to Diderot's *Encyclopedia*. His *Belisaire* (1767) was censured by the Sorbonne and the Archbishop of Paris because of its chapter on tolerance. *The Incas* (1778) linked abuses in Spanish America to religious zeal.

268. Pierre Augustin Caron de Beaumarchais (1732–1799). French dramatist, playwright, King's spy, and pamphleteer. Known for *The Barber of Seville* (1775) and *The Marriage of Figaro* (1778), which was opposed by King Louis XVI. He went to England to physically destroy *Memoirs of a Public Woman*, an attack on Mme. Du Barry by Charles Theveneneau de Morande, and secretly provided money and arms to the American Revolution out of his own pocket and from secret French or Spanish government funds, using the alias Rodrigue Hortalez and Company.

and very merry. One ineffably ridiculous, I wish I could send you, but it is immeasurably long. D'Argens, a little out of health and shivering with the cold in Berlin, asked leave of the King to take a ride to Gascony, his native province. He was absent so long that Frederick concluded the air of the south of France was like to detain his friend; and as he wanted his society and services, he contrived a trick to bring him back. He fabricated a mandement in the name of the Archbishop of Aix, commanding all the faithful to seize the Marquis D'Argens, author of Ocellus, Timaeus and Julian, works atheistical, deistical, heretical and impious in the highest degree. This mandement, composed in a style of ecclesiastical eloquence that never was exceeded by Pope, Jesuit, Inquisitor, or Sorbonite, he sent in print by a courier to D'Argens, who, frightened out of his wit, fled by cross roads out of France, and back to Berlin, to the greater joy of the philosophical court; for the laugh of Europe, which they had raised at the expense of the learned Marquis.

I do not like the late resurrection of the Jesuits. They have a general now in Russia, in correspondence with the Jesuits in the United States, who are more numerous than everybody knows. Shall we not have swarms of them here in as many shapes and disguises as ever a king of the Gypsies, Bamfield More Carew[269] himself assumed in the shape of printers, editors, writers, schoolmasters, etc.?

I have lately read Pascal's letters[270] over again, and four volumes of the history of the Jesuits. If ever any congregation of men could merit eternal perdition on earth and in hell, according to these historians, though like Pascal true Catholics, it is this company Loyola. Our system, however, of religious liberty must afford them an asylum. But if they do not put the purity of our elections to a severe trial, it will be a wonder.

John Adams

---

269. *The Life of Bamfield More Carew*. An eighteenth-century work on English Gypsy life.

270. Blaise Pascal (1623–1662). French scientist, mathematician, and theologian. Wrote *Provincial Letters* (1657) and *Pensees (Thoughts)* (1670). Wrote letters anonymously to defend the Sorbonne's Antoine Arnauld, a Jansenist (men born bad, very few predestined for salvation), against the Jesuits. "Men never do evil so completely and cheerfully as when they do it from religious conviction," is a quote attributed to Pascal.

54. THOMAS JEFFERSON TO JOHN ADAMS
MONTICELLO, August 1, 1816

DEAR SIR,

Your two philosophical letters of May 4th and 6th have been too long in my carton of "letters to be answered." To the question, indeed, on the utility of grief, no answer remains to be given. You have exhausted the subject. I see that, with the other evils of life, it is destined to temper the cup we are to drink.

> Two urns by Jove's high throne have ever stood,
> The source of evil one, and one of good;
> From thence the cup of mortal man he fills,
> Blessings to these, to those distributes ills;
> To most he mingles both.

Putting to myself your question, would I agree to live my seventy-three years over again forever? I hesitate to say. With Chew's limitations from twenty-five to sixty, I would say yes; and I might go further back, but not come lower down. For, at the latter period, with most of us, the powers of life are sensibly on the wane, sight becomes dim, hearing dull, memory constantly enlarging its frightful blank and parting with all we have ever seen or known, spirits evaporate, bodily debility creeps on palsying every limb, and so faculty after faculty quits us, and where then is life ?

If, in its full vigor, of good as well as evil, your friend Vassall could doubt its value, it must be purely a negative quantity when its evils alone remain. Yet I do not go into his opinion entirely. I do not agree that an age of pleasure is no compensation for a moment of pain. I think, with you, that life is a fair matter of account, and the balance often, nay generally, in its favor. It is not indeed easy, by calculation of intensity and time, to apply a common measure, or to fix the par between pleasure and pain; yet it exists, and is measurable on the question, for example, whether to be cut for the stone.

The young, with a longer prospect of years, think these overbalance the pain of the operation. Dr. Franklin, at the age of eighty, thought his residuum of life not worth that price. I should have thought with him, even taking the stone out of the scale. There is a ripeness of time for death, regarding others as well as ourselves, when it is reasonable we should drop off, and make room for another growth. When we have lived our generation out, we should not wish to encroach on another.

I enjoy good health; I am happy in what is around me, yet I assure you I am ripe for leaving all, this year, this day, this hour. If it could be doubted whether we would go back to twenty-five, how can it be whether we would go forward from seventy-three? Bodily decay is gloomy in prospect, but of all human contemplations the most abhorrent is body without mind.

Perhaps, however, I might accept of time to read Grimm before I go. Fifteen volumes of anecdotes and incidents, within the compass of my own time and cognizance, written by a man of genius; of taste, of point, an acquaintance, the measure and traverses of whose mind I know, could not fail to turn the scale in favor of life during their perusal. I must write to Ticknor[271] to add it to my catalogue, and hold on till it comes.

There is a Mr. Van der Kemp of New York, a correspondent, I believe, of yours, with whom I have exchanged some letters without knowing who he is. Will you tell me? I know nothing of the history of the Jesuits you mention in four volumes. Is it a good one? I dislike, with you, their restoration, because it marks a retrograde step from light towards darkness.

We shall have our follies without doubt. Some one or more of them will always be afloat. But ours will be the follies of enthusiasm, not of bigotry, not of Jesuitism. Bigotry is the disease of ignorance, of morbid minds; enthusiasm of the free and buoyant. Education and free discussion are the antidotes of both. We are destined to be a barrier against the returns of ignorance and barbarism. Old Europe will have

---

271. George Ticknor (1791–1871). Author and educator who met Jefferson prior to going to Europe to study. Ticknor was motivated to go to Germany by Mme. de Stael's book, *Germany*. While in Europe, Ticknor met the aged Stael in Paris, and he became Jefferson's book procurer and shipper.

to lean on our shoulders, and to hobble along by our side, under the monkish trammels of priests and kings, as she can.

What a colossus shall we be when the southern continent comes up to our mark! What a stand will it secure as a ralliance for the reason and freedom of the globe! I like the dreams of the future better than the history of the past. So good night! I will dream on, always fancying that Mrs. Adams and you are by my side marking the progress and the obliquities of ages and countries.

Thomas Jefferson

55. JOHN ADAMS TO THOMAS JEFFERSON
QUINCY, August 9, 1816

DEAR SIR,

The biography of Mr. Van der Kemp would require a volume which I could not write if a million were offered me as a reward for the work. After a learned and scientific education he entered the army in Holland, and served as captain, with reputation; but loving books more than arms, he resigned his commission and became a preacher.

My acquaintance with him commenced at Leyden in 1790. He was then minister of the Menonist congregation, the richest in Europe; in that city, where he was celebrated as the most elegant writer in the Dutch language, he was the intimate friend of Luzac[272] and De Gysecaar. In 1788, when the King of Prussia threatened Holland with invasion, his party insisted on his taking a command in the army of defense, and he was appointed to the command of the most exposed and most important post in the seven provinces.

He was soon surrounded by the Prussian forces; but he defended his fortress with a prudence, fortitude, patience, and perseverance, which were admired by all Europe until abandoned by his nation, destitute of provisions and ammunition, still refusing to surrender, he was

---

272. Jean Luzac (1746–1807). Dutch lawyer, editor of *Leyden Gazette*, supporter of American Revolution, and friend to John Adams.

offered the most honorable capitulation. He accepted it; was offered very advantageous proposals; but despairing of the liberties of his country, he retired to Antwerp, determined to emigrate to New York.

He wrote to me in London requesting letters of introduction. I sent him letters to Governor Clinton, and several others of our little great men. His history in this country is equally curious and affecting. He left property in Holland, which the revolutions there have annihilated; and I fear is now pinched with poverty. His head is deeply learned and his heart is pure. I scarcely know a more amiable character.

He has written to me occasionally, and I have answered his letters in great haste. You may well suppose that such a man has not always been able to understand our American politics. Nor have I. Had he been as great a master of our language as he was of his own, he would have been at this day one of the most conspicuous characters in the United States.

So much for Van der Kemp. Now, for your letter of August 1st. Your poet, the Ionian I suppose, ought to have told us whether Jove, in the distribution of good and evil from his two urns, observes any rule of equity or not; whether he thunders out flames of eternal fire on the many, and power, and glory, and felicity on the few, without any consideration of justice?

Let us state a few questions sub rosa [in confidence]:

1. Would you accept a life, if offered you, of equal pleasure and pain? For example, one million of moments of pleasure, and one million of moments of pain! (1,000,000 moments of pleasure = 1,000,000 moments of pain.) Suppose the pleasure as exquisite as any in life and the pain as exquisite as any. For example, stone-gravel, gout, headache, earache, toothache, colic, etc. I would not. I would rather be blotted out.

2. Would you accept a life of one year of incessant gout, headache, etc., for seventy-two years of such life as you have enjoyed? I would not. (One year of colic = seventy-two of Boules de Savon [balls of soap]; pretty, but unsubstantial.) I had rather be extinguished.

You may vary these algebraical equations at pleasure and without end. All this ratiocination, calculation, call it what you will, is founded on the supposition of no future state. Promise me eternal life free from pain, although in all other respects no better than our present terrestrial existence, I know not how many thousand years of Smithfield fevers I would not endure to obtain it. In fine, without the supposition of a future state, mankind and this globe appear to me the most sublime and beautiful bubble and bauble that imagination can conceive.

Let us then wish for immortality at all hazards, and trust the Ruler with His skies. I do; and earnestly wish for His commands, which to the utmost of my power shall be implicitly and piously obeyed.

It is worth while to live to read Grimm, whom I have read; and La Harpe and Mademoiselle D'Espinasse[273] the fair friend of D'Alembert, both of whom Grimm characterizes very distinguished, and are, I am told, in print. I have not seen them, but hope soon to have them.

My history of the Jesuits is not elegantly written, but is supported by unquestionable authorities, is very particular and very horrible. Their restoration is indeed a "step towards darkness, cruelty, perfidy, despotism, death and . . . !" I wish we were out of "danger of bigotry and Jesuitism!"

May we be "a barrier against the returns of ignorance and barbarism!" "What a colossus shall we be!" But will it not be of brass, iron and clay? Your taste is judicious in liking better the dreams of the future, than the history of the past. Upon this principle I prophesy that you and I shall soon meet, and be better friends than ever. So wishes,

John Adams

56. JOHN ADAMS TO THOMAS JEFFERSON
QUINCY, September 3, 1816

DEAR SIR,

Dr. James Freeman[274] is a learned, ingenious, honest and benevolent man, who wishes to see President Jefferson, and requests me to intro-

---

273. Julie de Lespinasse (1732–1776). Niece of Mme. du Deffand. Opened her own Paris salon, where she fostered a love of music and ideas. Wrote volumes of letters.

274. Dr. Freeman (1759–1835). Massachusetts clergyman and the first United States minister to declare himself a Unitarian.

duce him. If you would introduce some of your friends to me, I could, with more confidence, introduce mine to you. He is a Christian, but not a Pythagorian, a Platonic, or a Philonic Christian. You will ken [know, recognize, understand] him, and he will ken you; but you may depend he will never betray, deceive, or injure you.

Without hinting to him anything which had passed between you and me, I asked him your question, "What are the uses of grief?"

He stared and said, "The question was new to him."

All he could say at present was, that he had known in his own parish more than one instance of ladies, who had been thoughtless, modish, extravagant in a high degree, who, upon the death of a child, had become thoughtful, modest, humble, and as prudent, amiable women as any he had known. Upon this I read to him your letters and mine upon this subject of grief, with which he seemed to be pleased. You see I was not afraid to trust him, and you need not be.

Since I am, accidentally, invited to write to you, I may add a few words upon pleasures and pains of life. Vassall thought, a hundred years, nay, an eternity of pleasure, was no compensation for one hour of bilious colic. Read again Moliere's[275] Psyche act 2d, scene 1st, on the subject of grief. And read in another place, "One happy moment compensates for a thousand ills." Thus, differently do men speak of pleasures and pains.

Now, Sir, I will tease you with another question. What have been the abuses of grief?

In answer to this question, I doubt not you might write an hundred volumes. A few hints may convince you that the subject is ample.

1st. The death of Socrates excited a general sensibility of grief at Athens, in Attica, and in all Greece. Plato and Xenophon; two of his disciples, took advantage of that sentiment, by employing their enchanting style to represent their master to be greater and better than

---

275. Molière was the stage name of Jean-Baptiste Poquelin (1622–1673). He was a French comic dramatist famous for his satires on hypocrisy and vices. Wrote *The Precious Ridicules* (1659) and *Tartuffe* (1664), which was banned by Roulles, the Cure of St. Bartholomew, and by the Bishop of Autun. Salons competed to have *Tartuffe* read during the ban. He is most known for *The Misanthrope* (1666).

he probably was; and what have been the effects of Socratic, Platonic, which were Pythagorian, which was Indian philosophy, in the world?

2d. The death of Caesar, tyrant as he was, spread a general compassion, which always includes grief, among the Romans. The scoundrel Mark Anthony availed himself of this momentary grief to destroy the republic, to establish the empire, and to proscribe Cicero.

3d. But to skip over all ages and nations for the present, and descend to our own times. The death of Washington diffused a general grief. The old Tories, the Hyperfederalists, the speculators, set up a general howl. Orations, prayers, sermons, mock funerals, were all employed, not that they loved Washington, but to keep in countenance the funding and banking system; and to cast into the background and the shade, all others who had been concerned in the service of their country in the Revolution.

4th. The death of Hamilton, under all its circumstances, produced a general grief. His most determined enemies did not like to get rid of him in that way. They pitied, too, his widow and children. His party seized the moment of public feeling to come forward with funeral orations, and printed panegyrics, reinforced with mock funerals and solemn grimaces, and all this by people who have buried Otis, Sam Adams, Hancock, and Gerry,[276] in comparative obscurity. Why? Merely to disgrace the old Whigs, and keep the funds and banks in countenance.

5th. The death of Mr. Ames[277] excited a general regret. His long consumption, his amiable character, and reputable talents, had attracted a general interest, and his death a general mourning. His party made the most of it, by processions, orations, and a mock funeral. Why? To glorify the Tories, to abash the Whigs, and maintain the reputation of funds, banks, and speculation. And all this was done in honor of that insignificant boy,[278] by people who have let a Dana, a Gerry, and a Dexter,[279] go to their graves without notice.

---

276. James Otis, Samuel Adams, John Hancock, and Elbridge Gerry.

277. Fisher Ames of Massachusetts, who supported Alexander Hamilton.

278. Alexander Hamilton.

279. Francis Dana, Elbridge Gerry, and Samuel Dexter—supporters of the American Revolution.

6th. I almost shudder at the thought of alluding to the most fatal example of the abuses of grief which the history of mankind has preserved—the Cross.[280] Consider what calamities that engine of grief has produced! With the rational respect which is due to it, knavish priests have added prostitutions of it that fill, or might fill, the blackest and bloodiest pages of human history.

I am with ancient friendly sentiments,
John Adams

57. JOHN ADAMS TO THOMAS JEFFERSON
QUINCY, September 30, 1816

DEAR SIR,

When I read Dr. Priestley's remarks upon "Du Puis," I felt a curiosity to know more about him. . . . If you know anything of this "Monsieur Du Puis" or his "Origine de tous les Cultes" [Origin of all the Religions], candidly impart it. I have read only the first volume. It is learned and curious. The whole work will afford me business, study, and amusement for the winter.

Dr. Priestley pronounced him an Atheist, and, his work "The Ne Plus ultra (none higher) of Infidelity." Priestley agrees with him that the history of the Fall of Adam and Eve is an allegory, a fable, an Arabian Tale, and, so does Dr. Middleton, to account for the origin of Evil, which however it does not.

Priestley says that the Apocalypse, according to Dupuis, is the most learned work ever written. With these brief fletrissures, Priestly seems to have expected to annihilate the influence of Dupuis' Labors as Swift destroyed Blackmore[281] with his:

"Did off Creation[282] with a Jerk and of Redemption made damned

---

280. The Cross of Jesus.
281. William Blackmore (1650–1729). Poet of *The Creation*.
282. Should read, "Undid Creation." Works of Jonathan Swift.

Work." And as he disgraced Men as good at least as himself by his "Wicked Will Whiston[283] and Good Master Ditton."[284]

But, Dupuis is not so easily destroyed. The controversy between Spiritualism and Materialism, between Spiritualists and Materialists, will not be settled by scurrilous epigrams of Swift, or by dogmatic censures of Priestley. You and I have as much authority to settle these disputes as Swift, Priestley, Dupuis, or the Pope.

And, if you will agree with me, we will issue our Bulls. We will enjoin upon all these gentlemen to be silent until they can tell us what Matter is, what Spirit is! And, in the mean time, observe the Commandments and the Sermon on the Mount.

John Adams

58. THOMAS JEFFERSON TO JOHN ADAMS
MONTICELLO, October 14, 1816

Your letter, dear Sir, of May the 6th, had already well explained the uses of grief. That of September the 3d, with equal truth, adduces instances of its abuse; and when we put into the same scale these abuses, with the afflictions of soul which even the uses of grief cost us, we may consider its value in the economy of the human being, as equivocal at least. Those afflictions cloud too great a portion of life to find a counterpoise in any benefits derived from its use. For setting aside its paroxysms on the occasions of special bereavements, all the latter years of aged men are overshadowed with its gloom.

Whither, for instance, can you and I look without seeing the graves

283. William Whiston (1667–1752). English Anglican cleric, later Arian Baptist. Also an astronomer, natural scientist, and navigator. Wrote *A New Theory of Earth* (1696), which posited that a comet caused Mosaic flood, and *Primitive Christianity Revived* (1711–1712).

284. Humphrey Ditton (1675–1715). Master of a mathematics school. Wrote *A Discourse Concerning the Resurrection of Christ* (1712). A proposal by Whiston and Ditton to solve the "longitude problem" led to the Longitude Act of 1714, promising a reward to anyone who did solve the problem. Newton did not believe the Whiston-Ditton solution would work at sea.

of those we have known? And whom can we call up of our early companions who have not left us to regret his loss? This, indeed, may be one of the salutary effects of grief; inasmuch as it prepares us to loose ourselves also without repugnance.

Doctor Freeman's instances of female levity cured by grief are certainly to the point and constitute an item of credit in the account we examine. I was much mortified by the loss of the Doctor's visit, by my absence from home. To have shown how much I feel indebted to you for making good people known to me, would have been one pleasure; and to have enjoyed that of his conversation, and the benefits of his information, so favorably reported by my family, would have been another. I returned home on the third day after his departure. The loss of such visits is among the sacrifices which my divided residence costs me.

Your undertaking the twelve volumes of Dupuis, is a degree of heroism to which I could not have aspired even in my younger days. I have been contented with the humble achievement of reading the analysis of his work by Destutt Tracy,[285] in two hundred pages octavo. I believe I should have ventured on his own abridgment of the work, in one octavo volume, had it ever come to my hands; but the marrow of it in Tracy has satisfied my appetite; and even in that, the preliminary discourse of the analyzer himself, and his conclusion, are worth more in my eye than the body of the work. For the object of that seems to be to smother all history under the mantle of allegory. If histories so unlike as those of Hercules and Jesus, can, by a fertile imagination and allegorical interpretations, be brought to the same tally, no line of distinction remains between fact and fancy.

As this pithy morsel will not overburden the mail in passing and re-passing between Quincy and Monticello, I send it for your perusal. Perhaps it will satisfy you, as it has me; and may save you the labor of reading twenty-four times its volume. I have said to you that it was

---

285. Antoine Louis Claude, Comte Destutt de Tracy (1754–1836). French philosopher and a founder of the Ideologues, who advocated deductive reasoning from sense experience. Wrote *A Treatise on Political Economy* and *A Commentary Review of Montesquieu's "Spirit of Laws."*

written by Tracy; and I had so entered it on the title page, as I usually do on anonymous works whose authors are known to me. But Tracy requested me not to betray his anonym for reasons which may not yet, perhaps, have ceased to weigh. I am bound, then, to make the same reserve with you. Destutt-Tracy is, in my judgment, the ablest writer living on intellectual subjects, or the operations of the understanding.

He has his fourth and last work now in the press at Paris, closing, as he conceives, the circle of metaphysical sciences. This work, which is on Ethics, I have not seen, but suspect I shall differ from it in its foundation, although not in its deductions. I gather from his other works that he adopts the principle of Hobbes that justice is founded in contract solely, and does not result from the construction of man.

I believe, on the contrary, that it is instinct and innate, that the moral sense is as much a part of our constitution as that of feeling, seeing, or hearing; as a wise creator must have seen to be necessary in an animal destined to live in society; that every human mind feels pleasure in doing good to another; that the non-existence of justice is not to be inferred from the fact that the same act is deemed virtuous and right in one society which is held vicious and wrong in another; because, as the circumstances and opinions of different societies vary, so the acts which may do them right or wrong must vary also; for virtue does not consist in the act we do, but in the end it is to effect.

If it is to effect the happiness of him to whom it is directed, it is virtuous, while in a society under different circumstances and opinions, the same act might produce pain, and would be vicious. The essence of virtue is in doing good to others, while what is good may be one thing in one society, and its contrary in another. Yet, however we may differ as to the foundation of morals, (and as many foundations have been assumed as there are writers on the subject nearly,) so correct a thinker as Tracy will give us a sound system of morals. Indeed, it is remarkable that so many writers setting out from so many different premises, yet, meet all in the same conclusions. This looks as if they were guided, unconsciously, by the unerring hand of instinct.

Your history of the Jesuits, by what name of the author or other description is it to be inquired for?

Thomas Jefferson

59. JOHN ADAMS TO THOMAS JEFFERSON
November 4, 1816

Your letter of Oct. 14 has greatly obliged me. Tracy's analysis, I have read once. I have read, not only the Analysis, but Eight volumes out of 12 of the Origin of the Cults, and if life lasts will read the other four. But, my dear Sir, I have often been obliged to stop and talk to myself like the Reverend, Allegorical, Hierogriphical, and Apocaliptical Mr. John Bunyan saying, "John be sober! Be not carried away by sudden blasts of wind, by unexpected flashes of Lightning, nor terrified by the sharpest crashes of Thunder!"

We have now, it seems, a National Bible Society to propagate the King James Bible through all nations. Would it not be better to apply these pious subscriptions to purify Christendom from the Corruptions of Christianity than to propagate those corruptions in Europe, Asia, Africa, and America?

. . . Conclude not from all this that I have renounced the Christian religion or that I agree with Dupuis in all his sentiments. Far from it. I see in every page something to recommend Christianity in its purity, and, something to discredit its corruptions. If I had strength, I would give you my opinion of it in a Fable of the Bees.[286] The Ten Commandments and the Sermon on the Mount contain my religion.

I agree perfectly with you that "the moral sense is as much a part of our constitution as that of feeling," and in all that you say upon this subject.

My History of the Jesuits is in 4 Vol. in twelves under the title, "General History of the Birth and Progress of Company of Jesuits: An

---

286. Bernard Mandeville (1670–1733). Dutch-born English philosopher and satirist. Wrote *Fable of the Bees, or, Private Vices, Public Benefits* (1714), which portrayed virtue as originating from self-interest.

analysis of its constitutions and privileges." It was printed in Amsterdam in 1761. The Work is anonymous because, I suppose, the author was afraid as all the monarchs of Europe were at the time of Jesuitical assassination. The author, however, supports his facts by authentic records and known authorities, which the public may consult.

This Society has been a greater calamity to Mankind than the French Revolution or Napoleon's despotism or Idiology. It has obstructed the progress of reformation and improvement of the human mind in society much longer and more fatally.

. . . I have been disappointed in the review of Sir John Malcolm's "History of Persia."

Those cunning Edinburgh men break off at the point of the only subject that excited my curiosity: the ancient modern religion and government of Persia. . . . I suspect the reviewers evaded the religion of Persia for fear they should be compelled to compare it with Dupuis.

John Adams

60. THOMAS JEFFERSON TO JOHN ADAMS
POPLAR FOREST, November 25, 1816

I receive here, dear Sir, your favor of the 4th, just as I am preparing my return to Monticello for winter quarters, and I hasten to answer to some of your inquiries. The Tracy I mentioned to you is the one connected by marriage with Lafayette's family. The mail which brought your letter brought one also from him. He writes me that he is become blind, and so infirm that he is no longer able to compose anything. So, we are to consider his works as now closed. They are three volumes of Ideology, one on Political Economy, one on Ethics, and one containing his Commentary on Montesquieu, and a little tract on Education. Although his commentary explains his principles of government, he had intended to have substituted for it an elementary and regular treatise on the subject, but he is, prevented by his infirmities. His Analyse de Dupuis he does not avow.

My books are all arrived, some at New York, some at Boston, and

I am glad to hear that those of Harvard are safe also, and the Ura-nologia[287] you mention without telling me what it is. It is something good, I am sure, from the name connected with it; and if you would add to it your fable of the bees, we should receive valuable instruction as to the Uranologia both of the father and son, more valuable than the Chinese will from our Bible Societies.

These incendiaries, finding that the days of fire and fagot are over in the Atlantic hemisphere are now preparing to put the torch to the Asiatic regions. What would they say were the Pope to send annually to this country colonies of Jesuit priests with cargoes of their missal and trans-lations of their Vulgate, to be put gratis into the hands of every one who would accept them and to act thus nationally on us as a nation?

Thomas Jefferson

61. JOHN ADAMS TO THOMAS JEFFERSON
December 12, 1816

DEAR SIR,

I return the Analysis of Dupuis with my thanks for the loan of it. It is but a faint miniature of the original. I have read that original in 12 vol-umes, besides a 13th of plates. I have been a lover and reader of Romances all my life, from Don Quixote and Gil Blas to the Scottish chiefs and a hundred others.

For the last year or two I have devoted myself to this kind of study. I have read 15 volumes of Grim, 7 volumes of Tucker's Neddy Search, 12 volumes of Dupuis besides a 13th of plates, and Tracey's Analysis, and 4 volumes of Jesutical history! Romances all! I have learned nothing of importance to me, for they have made no change in my moral or religious creed, which for 50 or 60 years has been contained in four short words, "Be Just and good." In this result, they agree with me.

---

287. A study of the heavens (skies) with maps, plates, and illustrations on the universe's planetary and star systems. Astronomical and astrological references can be included.

I must acknowledge, however, that I have found in Dupuis more ideas that were new to me than in all the others. My conclusion from all of them is Universal Toleration. Is there any work extant so well calculated to discredit Corruptions and Impostures in Religion as Dupuis?

I am, Sir, with friendship as of old,

John Adams

62. JOHN ADAMS TO THOMAS JEFFERSON
QUINCY, December 16, 1816

Your letter, dear Sir, of November 25th, from Poplar Forest, was sent to me from the post-office the next day after I had sent "The Analysis," with my thanks to you.

"Three vols. of Ideology!'" Pray explain to me this Neological title! What does it mean? When Bonaparte used it, I was delighted with it, upon the common principle of delight in everything we cannot understand. Does it mean Idiotism? The science of non compos mentuism? The science of Lunacy? The theory of delirium? Or, does it mean the science of self-love? Of amour propre? Or the elements of vanity?

The Uranologia, as I am told, is a collection of plates, stamps, charts of the heavens upon a large scale, representing all the constellations. The work of some professor in Sweden. It is said to be the most perfect that ever has appeared. I have not seen it. Why should I ride fifteen miles to see it, when I can see the original every clear evening; and especially as Dupuis has almost made me afraid to inquire after anything more of it than I can see with my naked eye in a star-light night?

That the Pope will send Jesuits to this country, I doubt not; and the Church of England, missionaries too. And the Methodists, and the Quakers, and the Moravians, and the Swedenborgians, and the Menonists, and the Scottish Kirkers, and the Jacobites, and the Jacobins, and the Democrats, and the Aristocrats and the Monarchists, and the Despotists of all denominations; and every emissary of every one of these sects will find a party here already formed, to give him a cordial reception. No power or intelligence less than Raphael's Moderator can reduce this chaos to order.

I am charmed with the fluency and rapidity of your reasoning on the state of Great Britain. . . . If I should write you a volume of observations I made in England, you would pronounce it a satire. Suppose the "Refrain" as the French call it, or the "Burden of the Song," as the English express it, should be, the Religion, the Government, the Commerce, the Manufactures, the Army and Navy of Great Britain, are all reduced to the science of pounds, shillings and pence.

. . . Every one of the fine arts from the earliest times has been enlisted in the service of superstition and despotism. The whole world at this day gazes with astonishment at the grossest fictions, because they have been immortalized by the most exquisite artists—Homer and Milton, Phidias and Raphael. The rabble of the classic skies, and the hosts of Roman Catholic saints and angels, are still adored in paint, and marble, and verse.

Raphael has sketched the actors and scenes in all Apuleius's Amours of Psyche and Cupid. Nothing is too offensive to morals, delicacy, or decency, for this painter. Raphael has painted in one of the most ostentatious churches in Italy—the Creation—and with what genius? God Almighty is represented as leaping into chaos, and boxing it about with His fists, and kicking it about with His feet, till He tumbles it into order! Nothing is too impious or profane for this great master, who has painted so many inimitable Virgins and children.

To help me on in my career of improvement, I have now read four volumes of La Harpe's correspondence with Paul and a Russian minister. Philosophers! Never again think of annulling superstition per Saltum [by a leap]. Testine cente [Hasten Slowly].

John Adams

63. THOMAS JEFFERSON TO JOHN ADAMS
MONTICELLO, January 11, 1817

To advert now to the subjects of those of December the 12th and 16th, Tracy's Commentaries on Montesquieu have never been published in the original. Duane printed a translation from the original manuscript a few years ago. It sold, I believe readily, and, whether a copy can now be had, I doubt. If it can, you will receive it from my bookseller in Philadelphia, to whom I now write for that purpose. Tracy comprehends, under the word "Ideology," all the subjects which the French term Morale, as the correlative to Physique. His works on Logic, Government, Political Economy and Morality, he considers as making up the circle of ideological subjects or of those which are within the scope of the understanding, and not of the senses. His Logic occupies exactly the ground of Locke's work on the Understanding. The translation of that on Political Economy is now printing; but it is no translation of mine. I have only had the correction of it, which was, indeed, very laborious. Le premier jet having been by some one who understood neither French nor English, it was impossible to make it more than faithful. But it is a valuable book.

The result of your fifty or sixty years of religious reading, in the four words, "Be just and good," is that in which all our inquiries must end; as the riddles of all the priesthoods end in four more, "ubi panis, ibi deus [where there is bread, there is God]."

What all agree in, is probably right. What no two agree in, most probably wrong. One of our fan-coloring biographers, who paints small men as very great, inquired of me lately, with real affection too, whether he might consider as authentic, the change in my religion much spoken of in some circles. Now this supposed that they knew what had been my religion before, taking for it the word of their priests, whom I certainly never made the confidants of my creed.

My answer was, "Say nothing of my religion. It is known to my God and myself alone. Its evidence before the world is to be sought in my life; if that has been honest and dutiful to society, the religion which has regulated it cannot be a bad one." Affectionately adieu.

Thomas Jefferson

64. JOHN ADAMS TO THOMAS JEFFERSON
February 2, 1817

DEAR SIR,

In our good old English language of gratitude, I owe you and give you a thousand thanks for Tracy's Review of Montesquieu. . . . I have read a hundred pages and will read the rest. He is a sensible man and is easily understood. He is not an abstruse, mysterious, incomprehensible Condorcet. Though I have banished the subject from my thoughts for many years, yet, if Tracy and I were thirty years younger, I would ask him a hundred or two questions. His book was written when the French Experiment was glowing in the furnace not yet blown out.

He all along supposes that men are rational, conscientious creatures. I say so too, but I say at the same time that their passions and interests generally prevail over their reason and their consciences. If society does not contrive some means of controlling and restraining the former, the world will go on as has done.

I was tolerably informed, fifty years ago, how it had gone on, and how it would go on. Grim, Dupuis, and Eustace[288] have confirmed all my former notions and made immense additions to them. Eustace is a supplement to Dupuis. Both together contain a complete draft of the superstition, credulity, and despotism of our terrestrial universe. They show how Science, Literature, Mechanic Music, and Eloquence, which you love so well and taste so exquisitely, have been subservient to Priests, Kings, Nobles, and common Monarchies and Republics. For they have all used them when they could, but as the Rich had them more often than the Poor, in their power, the latter have always gone to the wall.

Eustace is inestimable to a young scholar and a Classic traveler. But, he is a plausible, insidious Roman Catholic priest and I doubt not Jesuit. He should have read Dupuis before he commenced his travels.

288. Rev. John Chetwode Eustace (1762–1815). Antiquarian who was born in Ireland and died in Italy. Wrote *Classical Tour*, *A Political Catechism Adapted to the Present Moment* (1810), and *The Proofs of Christianity* (1814).

Very little of the religions of nations more ancient than the Greeks and Romans appears to have been known to him.

. . . I forgot one thing I intended to say. I pity our good brother, Mr. Madison. You and I have children and grandchildren, and great-grand-children. Though they have cost us grief, anxiety, often vexation, and sometimes humiliation, yet, it has been cheering to have them hovering about us. And, I verily believe, they have contributed largely to keep us alive. Book cannot always expel ennui.

John Adams

65. JOHN ADAMS TO THOMAS JEFFERSON
QUINCY, April 19, 1817

I verily believe I was as wise and good, seventy years ago, as I am now. At that period Lemuel Bryant was my parish priest, and Joseph Cleverly my Latin schoolmaster. Lemuel was a jolly, jocular, and liberal scholar and divine. Joseph, a scholar and a gentleman, but a bigoted Episcopalian of the school of Bishop Saunders and Dr. Hicks, a downright conscientious, passive, obedience man in Church and State.

The parson and the pedagogue lived much together, but were eternally disputing about government and religion. One day, when the schoolmaster had been more than commonly fanatical and declared [that], "if he were a monarch, he would have but one religion in his dominions." The parson coolly replied, "Cleverly! You would be the best man in the world if you had no religion!"

Twenty times in the course of my late reading have I been on the point of breaking out, "This would be the best of all possible worlds if there were no religion in it!" But, in this exclamation I should have been as fanatical as Bryant or Cleverly. Without religion this world would be something not fit to be mentioned in polite society. I mean hell. So far from believing in the total and universal depravity of human nature, I believe there is no individual totally depraved. The most abandoned scoundrel that ever existed never yet wholly extinguished his conscience. And while conscience remains there is some religion. Popes,

Jesuits, and Sorbonists, and Inquisitors, have some conscience and some religion. So had Marius and Sylla,[289] Caesar, Catiline and Anthony. Augustus had not much more, let Virgil and Horace say what they will.

What shall we think of Virgil and Horace, Sallust, Quintilian, Pliny, and even Tacitus? And even Cicero, Brutus and Seneca? Pompey I leave out of the question, as a mere politician and soldier. Every one of the great creatures has left indelible marks of conscience, and consequently of religion, though every one of them has left abundant proofs of profligate violations of their consciences by their little and great passions and paltry interests.

The vast prospect of mankind, which these books have passed in review before me, from the most ancient records, histories, traditions and fables that remain to us to the present day has sickened my very soul, and almost reconciled me to Swift's travels among the Yahoos; yet I never can be a misanthrope. Homo sum. I must hate myself before I can hate my fellow men; and that I cannot, and will not do. No! I will not hate any of them, base, brutal, and devilish as some of them have been to me.

From the bottom of my soul, I pity my fellow men. Fears and terrors appear to have produced a universal credulity. Fears of calamities of life, and punishments after death, seem to have possessed the souls of all men. But fear of pain and death here do not seem to have been as unconquerable as fear of what is to come hereafter. Priests, Hierophants, Popes, Despots, Emperors, Kings, Princes, and Nobles, have been as credulous as shoeblacks, boots and kitchen scullions. The former seem to have believed in their divine rights as sincerely as the latter.

Autos-da-fe, in Spain and Portugal, have been celebrated with as good faith as excommunications have been practiced in Connecticut, or as baptisms have been refused in Philadelphia.

How is it possible that mankind should submit to be governed, as they have been, is to me an inscrutable mystery. How they could bear to be taxed to build the temple of Diana at Ephesus, the pyramids of Egypt, Saint Peter's at Rome, Notre Dame at Paris, St. Paul's in London, with a million et ceteras, when my navy yards and my quasi

289. Brutal civil war between Marius and Sylla.

army made such a popular clamor, I know not. Yet all my peccadilloes never excited such a rage as the late compensation law!

I congratulate you on the late election in Connecticut. It is a kind of epocha. Several causes have conspired, one which you would not suspect. Some one, no doubt instigated by the devil, has taken it into his head to print a new edition of the "Independent Whig," even in Connecticut, and has scattered the volumes through the State. These volumes, it is said, have produced a burst of indignation against priest-craft, bigotry and intolerance, and in conjunction with other causes, have produced the late election.

John Adams

66. THOMAS JEFFERSON TO JOHN ADAMS
MONTICELLO, May 5, 1817

Your recommendations are always welcome, for indeed, the subjects of them always merit that welcome, and some of them in an extraordinary degree. They make us acquainted with what there is excellent in our ancient sister State of Massachusetts, once venerated and beloved, and still hanging on our hopes, for what need we despair of after the resurrection of Connecticut to light and liberality. I had believed that the last retreat of monkish darkness, bigotry, and abhorrence of those advances of the mind which had carried the other States a century ahead of them.

They seemed still to be exactly where their forefathers were when they schismatized from the covenant of works, and to consider as dangerous heresies all innovations good or bad. I join you, therefore, in sincere congratulations that this den of the priesthood is at length broken up, and that a Protestant Popedom is no longer to disgrace the American history and character.

If by religion we are to understand sectarian dogmas, in which no two of them agree, then your exclamation on that hypothesis is just, "that this would be the best of all possible worlds, if there were no religion in it." But if the moral precepts, innate in man, and made a part of his physical constitution, as necessary for a social being, if the sublime doctrines of philanthropism and deism taught us by Jesus of Nazareth, in which all agree, constitute true religion, then, without it, this would be, as you again say, "something not fit to be named even, indeed, a hell."

You certainly acted wisely in taking no notice of what the malice of Pickering could say of you. Were such things to be answered, our lives would be wasted in the filth of fendings and provings, instead of being employed in promoting the happiness and prosperity of our fellow citizens. The tenor of your life is the proper and sufficient answer.

It is fortunate for those in public trust, that posterity will judge them by their works, and not by the malignant vituperations and invectives of the Pickerings and Gardiners of their age. After all, men of energy of character must have enemies; because there are two sides to every question, and taking one with decision, and acting on it with effect, those who take the other will of course be hostile in proportion as they feel that effect.

Thomas Jefferson

67. JOHN ADAMS TO THOMAS JEFFERSON
QUINCY, May 18, 1817

Oh Lord! Do you think that Protestant Popedom is annihilated in America? Do you recollect, or have you ever attended to the ecclesiastical strifes in Maryland, Pennsylvania, New York, and every part of New England? What a mercy it is that these people cannot whip, and crop, and pillory, and roast, as yet in the United States! If they could, they would.

Do you know the General of the Jesuits, and consequently all his host, have their eyes on this country? Do you know that the Church of England is employing more means and more art, to propagate their demi-popery among us, than ever? Quakers, Anabaptists, Moravians, Swedenborgians, Methodists, Unitarians, Nothingarians in all Europe are employing underhand means to propagate their sectarian system in these States.

The multitude and diversity of them, you will say, is our security against them all. God grant it. But if we consider that the Presbyterians and Methodists are far the most numerous and the most likely to unite, let a George Whitefield arise, with a military cast, like Mahomet or Loyola, and what will become of all the other sects who can never unite?

My friends or enemies continue to overwhelm me with books. Whatever may be their intention, charitable or otherwise, they certainly contribute to continue me to vegetate, much as I have done for the sixteen years last past.

Sir John Malcolm's History of Persia and Sir William Jones' Works are now poured out upon me, and, a little cargo is coming from Europe. What can I do with all this learned lumber? Is it necessary to salvation to investigate all these Cosmogonies and Mythologies? Are Bryant, Gebelin,[290] Dupuis, or Sir William Jones, right?

What a frown upon mankind was the premature death of Sir William Jones! Why could not Jones and Dupuis have conversed or corresponded with each other? Had Jones read Dupuis, or Dupuis Jones, the works of both would be immensely improved, though each would probably have adhered to his system.

I should admire to see a council composed of Gebelin, Bryant, Jones and Dupuis. Let them live together and compare notes. The human race ought to contribute to furnish them with all the books in the universe, and the means of subsistence.

I am not expert enough in Italian to read Botta,[291] and I know not that he has been translated. Indeed, I have been so little satisfied with histories of the American Revolution that I have long since ceased to read them. The truth is lost, in adulatory panegyrics, and in vituperary insolence. I wish you, Mr. Madison, and Mr. Monroe, success in your collegiate institution. And I wish that superstition in religion, exciting superstition in politics, and both united in directing military force,

290. Antoine Court de Gebelin (1728–1784). French scholar who studied languages and mythologies. Wrote *The Primitive World* and *Les Toulousaines*, advocating the right of Protestants. He worked with Ben Franklin to aid the American Revolution and met Mesmer.

291. Carlo Guisseppe Guglielmo (1766–1837). Italian historian. Published *Stories of the American Revolution* (1809), in Italian.

alias glory, may never blow up all your benevolent and philanthropic lucubrations. But the history of all ages is against you.

It is said that no effort in favor of virtue is ever lost. I doubt whether it was ever true; whether it is now true; but hope it will be true. In the moral government of the world, no doubt it was, is, and ever will be true; but it has not yet appeared to be true on this earth.

I am, Sir, sincerely your friend,

John Adams

68. JOHN ADAMS TO THOMAS JEFFERSON
QUINCY, May 26, 1817

DEAR SIR,

Mr. Leslie Combes of Kentucky has sent me "a History of the late War in the Western Country, by Mr. Robert B. McAffee"[292] and "the Philosophy of Human Nature, by Joseph Buchanan."[293] The history I am glad to see, because it will preserve facts to the honor and immortal glory of the Western people. Indeed, I am not sorry that the Philosophy has been published, because it has been a maxim with me for sixty years at least, never to be afraid of a book.

Nevertheless, I cannot foresee much utility in reviewing, in this country, the controversy between the Spiritualists and the Materialists. Why should time be wasted in disputing about two substances, when both parties agree that neither knows anything about either?

If spirit is an abstraction, a conjecture, a chimera, then, matter is an abstraction, a conjecture, a chimera. For, we know as much, or rather as little, about one as the other. We may read Cudworth,[294] Le

---

292. Robert Breckinridge McAfee (1784–1849). US general in the War of 1812.

293. (1785–1829). Buchanan was an educator and physician. His book focused on physiological psychology.

294. Ralph Cudworth (1617–1688). A "Cambridge Platonist." Wrote *The True Intellectual System of the Universe* (1678), an argument against atheism, and *Treatise on Eternal and Immutable Morality*.

Clerc,[295] Leibnitz, Berkley, Hume, Bolingbroke and Priestley, and a million other volumes in all ages, and be obliged at last to confess that we have learned nothing. Spirit and matter still remain riddles. Define the terms, however, and the controversy is soon settled. If spirit is an active something, and matter an inactive something, it is certain that one is not the other. We can no more conceive that extension, or solidity, can think, or feel, or see, or hear, or taste, or smell; than we can conceive that perception, memory, imagination, or reason, can remove a mountain, or blow a rock. This enigma has puzzled mankind from the beginning, and probably will to the end. Economy of time requires that we should waste no more in so idle an amusement.

In the eleventh discourse of Sir William Jones, before the Asiatic Society, vol. 3, page 229, of his works, we find that Materialists and Immaterialists existed in India, and that they accused each other of atheism, before Berkeley, or Priestley, or Dupuis, or Plato, or Pythagoras, was born.

Indeed, Newton himself appears to have discovered nothing that was not known to the ancient Indians. He has only furnished more complete demonstrations of the doctrines they taught. Sir John Malcolm agrees with Jones and Dupuis, in the Astrological origin of heathen mythologies. Vain man! Mind your own business! Do no wrong! Do all the good you can! Eat your canvas-back ducks! Drink your Burgundy! Sleep your siesta when necessary, and TRUST IN GOD!

What a mighty bubble, what a tremendous waterspout, has Napoleon been, according to his life, written by himself! He says he was the creature of the principles and manners of the age; by which, no doubt, he means the age of Reason; the progress of Manilius' Ratio, of Plato's Logos, etc. I believe him. A whirlwind raised him and a whirlwind blew him away to St. Helena. He is very confident that the age of Reason is not past, and so am I; but I hope that Reason will never again rashly and hastily create such creatures as he.

Liberty, equality, fraternity, and humanity, will never again, I hope, blindly surrender themselves to an unbounded ambition for

---

295. Jean Le Clerc (Johannes Clericus) (1657–1736). Swiss theologian, admirer of Ralph Cudworth, and friend to John Locke. Le Clerc was a Copernican.

national conquests, nor implicitly commit themselves to the custody and guardianship of arms and heroes. If they do, they will again end in St. Helena, Inquisitions, Jesuits, and holy leagues.

John Adams

69. JOHN ADAMS TO THOMAS JEFFERSON
July 15, 1817

Is the biography of Democritus and Heraclitus[296] a fable or history? I cannot contemplate human affairs without laughing or crying. I choose to laugh. When people talk of the freedom of writing, speaking, or thinking, I cannot choose but laugh. No such thing ever existed. No such thing now exists. But, I hope it will exist. But it must be hundreds of years after you and I shall write and speak no more.

John Adams

70. JOHN ADAMS TO THOMAS JEFFERSON
QUINCY, October 10, 1817

DEAR SIR,

I thank you for your kind congratulations on the return of my little family from Europe. To receive them all in fine health and good spirits, after so long an absence, was a greater blessing than at my time of life, when they went away, I had any right to hope, or reason to expect.

If the Secretary of State [John Quincy Adams] can give satisfaction to his fellow citizens in his new office, it will be a source of consolation to me while I live; although it is not probable that I shall long be a witness of his good success, or ill success. I shall soon be obliged to say to him, and to you, and to your country and mine, God bless you all! Fare thee well! Indeed, I need not wait a moment. I can say all that

---

296. Heraclitus (c. 540–c. 480 BCE). Greek philosopher from Ephesus. He believed in constant change and impermanence of everything: "All things in flux."

now, with as good a will, and as clear a conscience, as at any time past, or future.

... Can any organization of government secure public and private liberty without a general or universal freedom, without license, or licentiousness of thinking, speaking, and writing. Have the French such freedom? Will their religion, or policy, allow it?

John Adams

71. JOHN ADAMS TO THOMAS JEFFERSON
   January 28, 1818

Permit me to introduce to you Mr. Horace Holley,[297] who is on his way to Kentucky, where he has been invited to undertake the Superintendence of a university. This gentleman was settled very young at Greenfield as successor to Dr. Dwight, but having a mind too inquisitive for Connecticut, he removed to Boston, where he has been settled for nine years and where his fame has erected one of the loftiest temples and assembled the most numerous congregation of auditors in Boston.

You will find him frank enough, candid enough, social enough, learned enough, and eloquent enough. He is indeed an important character. If superstition, bigotry, and fanaticism, and intolerance, will allow him to live in Kentucky, he will contribute somewhat to the illumination of the darkest and most dismal swamps in the wilderness.

I shall regret his removal from Boston, because the city ought always to have one clergyman at least who will compel them to think and inquire. But, if he can be supported in Kentucky, I am convinced he will be more extensively useful. If, upon conversing with him, your conscience will allow you to give him a line to any of your friends in Kentucky, you will do him more service and perhaps more service to

---

297. (1781–1827). Unitarian minister and president of the University of Transylvania in Lexington, Kentucky. When Holley was a student at Yale, Timothy Dwight, an anti-Deist, was president. Holley's graduation speech was on "The Slavery of Free Thinking."

our country and our kind than you or I may be aware. He is one of the few who give me delight.

I am anxious for South America. They will be independent of Spain. But, can they have free governments? Can the Roman religion and a free government exist together?

John Adams

72. THOMAS JEFFERSON TO JOHN ADAMS
MONTICELLO, May 17, 1818

DEAR SIR,

I was so unfortunate as not to receive from Mr. Holly's own hand your favor of January the 28th, being then at my other home. He dined only with my family, and left them with an impression which has filled me with regret that I did not partake of the pleasure his visit gave them. I am glad he is gone to Kentucky. Rational Christianity will thrive more rapidly there than here. They are freer from prejudices than we are, and bolder in grasping at truth. The time is not distant, though neither you nor I shall see it, when we shall be but a secondary people to them. Our greediness for wealth and fantastical expense has degraded, and will degrade, the minds of our maritime citizens. These are the peculiar vices of commerce.

I enter into all your doubts as to the event of the revolution of South America. They will succeed against Spain. But the dangerous enemy is within their own breasts. Ignorance and superstition will chain their minds and bodies under religious and military despotism. I do believe it would be better for them to obtain freedom by degrees only, because that would, by degrees, bring on light and information, and qualify them to take charge of themselves understandingly with more certainty, if in the meantime, under so much control as may keep them at peace with one another.

Surely, it is our duty to wish them independence and self-government, because they wish it themselves, and they have the right, and we none, to choose for themselves. I wish, moreover, that our ideas may be erroneous, and theirs prove well founded. But these are speculations, my friend, which we may as well deliver over to those who are to see their development. We shall only be lookers on, from the clouds above, as now we look down on the labors, the hurry and bustle of the ants and bees. Perhaps in that super mundane region, we may be amused with seeing the fallacy of our own guesses, and even the nothingness of those labors which have filled and agitated our own time here.

Thomas Jefferson

73. JOHN ADAMS TO THOMAS JEFFERSON
May 29, 1818

As Holly is a diamond of superior water, it would be crushed to powder by mountainous oppression in any country. Even in this, he is a light shining in a dark place. His system is founded in the hopes of mankind, but they delight more in fears. When will men have juster notions of the universal eternal Cause? Then will rational Christianity prevail. I regret Holly's misfortune in not finding you.

. . . I agree with you that "it is difficult to say at what moment the Revolution began." In my opinion, it began as early as the first Plantation of the country. Independence of Church and Parliament was a fixed principle or our predecessors in 1620, as it was of Samuel Adams and Christopher Gadsen in 1776. Independence of Church and Parliament were always kept in view in this part of the country, and, I believe in most others. The Hierarchy and Parliamentary Authority were dreaded and detested even by a majority of professed Episcopalians.

John Adams

74. JOHN ADAMS TO THOMAS JEFFERSON
July 18, 1818

Will you accept a curious piece of New England antiquities? It was a tolerable catechism for the education of a boy of 14 years of age, who was destined in the future course of his life to dabble in so many revolutions in America, Holland, and France.

This Doctor Mayhew[298] . . . was intimate with my Parson Bryant and often exchanged with him, which gave me an opportunity to hear him in the pulpit. This discourse was reprinted a year before I entered Harvard College, and, I read it until the substance of it was incorporated into my very nature and indelibly engraved on my memory. It made a greater sensation in New England than Mr. Henry's philippic against the Parsons[299] did in Virginia. It made a noise in Great Britain, where it was reprinted and procured the author a diploma of Doctor of Divinity.

John Adams

75. JOHN ADAMS TO THOMAS JEFFERSON
October 20, 1818

Now, Sir, for my Griefs! The dear partner of my life for fifty-four years as a wife,[300] and, for many more years as lover, now lies in extremis, forbidden to speak or be spoken to.

If human life is a bubble, no matter how soon it breaks, if it is, as I believe, an immortal existence, we ought patiently to wait the instructions of the Great Teacher.

I am, Sir, your deeply afflicted friend,

John Adams

---

298. Jonathan Mayhew (1720–1766). Boston minister. Mayhew opposed Calvinism's five points on Man's total depravity and irresistible grace. He also rejected the Trinity doctrine. Wrote *Discourse Concerning Unlimited Submission and Non-Resistance to the Higher Powers* (1750) and *Observations on the Charter and Conduct of the Society for Propagating the Gospel in Foreign Parts* (1763), wherein he challenged the society's sending missionaries to New England.

299. The Parson's Cause. A legal case argued by Patrick Henry regarding payment to ministers.

300. Abigail Adams died of typhoid fever on October 18, 1818, at the age of seventy-four.

76. THOMAS JEFFERSON TO JOHN ADAMS
MONTICELLO, November 13, 1818

The public papers, my dear friend, announce the fatal event of which your letter of October the 20th had given me ominous foreboding. Tried myself in the school of affliction, by the loss of every form of connection which can rive the human heart, I know well, and feel what you have lost, what you have suffered, are suffering, and have yet to endure. The same trials have taught me that for ills so immeasurable, time and silence are the only medicine. I will not, therefore, by useless condolences, open afresh the sluices of your grief, nor, although mingling sincerely my tears with yours, will I say a word more where words are vain, but that it is of some comfort to us both, that the term is not very distant, at which we are to deposit in the same cerement, our sorrows and suffering bodies, and to ascend in essence to an ecstatic meeting with the friends we have loved and lost, and whom we shall still love and never lose again. God bless you and support you under your heavy affliction.

Thomas Jefferson

77. JOHN ADAMS TO THOMAS JEFFERSON
December 8, 1818

Your letter of November 13 gave me great delight, not only by the divine consolation it afforded me under great affliction, but as it gave me full proof of your restoration to health. While you live, I seem to have a bank at Monticello on which I can draw for a letter of friendship and entertainment when I please.

I know not how to prove physically that we shall meet and know each other in a future state, nor does Revelation, as I can find, give us any positive assurance of such a felicity. My reasons for believing it as I do, most undoubtingly, are all moral and divine.

I believe in God and his wisdom and benevolence. I cannot conceive that such a Being could make such a species as the human merely to live and die on this earth. If I did not believe a future state, I should believe in no God. This universe, this all, this totality, would appear with all its swelling pomp, a boyish firework.

And, if there be a future state, why should the Almighty dissolve forever all tender ties which unite us so delightfully in this world and forbid us to see each other in the next?

John Adams

78. JOHN ADAMS TO THOMAS JEFFERSON
January 29, 1819

How has it happened that religious liberty, fiscal science, coin and commerce, and every branch of political economy should have been better understood and more honestly practiced in that Frog land[301] than any other country in the world?

John Adams

79. JOHN ADAMS TO THOMAS JEFFERSON
February 13, 1819

DEAR SIR,

. . . If these letters [Mademoiselle De Lespinasse's] and the fifteen volumes of De Grimm are to give me an idea of the amelioration of society, government, and manners in France, I should think the age of reason has produced nothing much better than the Mahometans, the Mamalukes,[302] or the Hindoos, or the North American Indians, have produced in different parts of the world.

---

301. Holland.

302. Mamelukes or Mamluks. In 1250 this group of non-Arab slaves in Egypt overthrew the sultanate and remained in power until defeated in 1517 by the Ottomans. In 1811 most were massacred by order of Muhammad Ali.

Hasten slowly, my friend, in all your projects of reformation. Abolish polytheism, however, in every shape if you can. Unfrock every priest who teaches it, if you can.

John Adams

80. THOMAS JEFFERSON TO JOHN ADAMS
MONTICELLO, March 21, 1819

DEAR SIR,

I am indebted to you for Mr. Bowditch's[303] very learned mathematical papers, the calculations of which are not for every reader, although their results are readily enough understood. One of these impairs the confidence I had reposed in La Place's demonstration that the eccentricities of the planets of our system could oscillate only within narrow limits, and therefore could authorize no inference that the system must, by its own laws, come one day to an end. This would have left the question one of infinitude, at both ends of the line of time, clear of physical authority.

Thomas Jefferson

81. JOHN ADAMS TO THOMAS JEFFERSON
May 21, 1819

Though I cannot write, I still enjoy Life. The World is dead. There is nothing to communicate in religion, morals, philosophy, or politics.

John Adams

---

303. Nathaniel Bowditch (1773–1838). Self-taught US mathematician and astronomer. Wrote *New American Practical Navigator* (1802), which was referred to as "the seaman's bible."

82. THOMAS JEFFERSON TO JOHN ADAMS
December 10, 1819

No government can continue good, but under the control of the people. But, their people [Romans] were so demoralized and depraved as to be incapable of exercising a wholesome control. Their reformation then was to be taken up from the beginning. Their minds were to be informed by education as to what is right and what wrong, to be encouraged in habits of virtue and deterred from those of vice by the dread of punishments, proportioned indeed, but irremissible; in all cases, to follow truth as the only guide, and to eschew error which bewilders us in one false consequence after another in endless succession. These are the inculcations necessary to render the people a sure basis for the structure of order and good government.

Thomas Jefferson

83. JOHN ADAMS TO THOMAS JEFFERSON
December 21, 1819

Have you ever found in history one single example of a nation, thoroughly corrupted, that was afterwards restored to virtue? And without virtue there can be no political liberty.

If I were a Calvinist, I might pray that God by a miracle of divine grace would instantaneously convert a whole contaminated nation from turpitude to purity; but even in this I should be inconsistent, for the fatalism of Mahometanism, Materialists, Atheists, Pantheists, and Calvinists, and Church of England articles, appear to me to render all prayer futile and absurd. The French and the Dutch, in our day, have attempted reforms and revolutions. We know the results, and I fear the English reformers will have no better success.

Will you tell me how to prevent riches from becoming the effects of temperance and industry? Will you tell me how to prevent riches from producing luxury? Will you tell me how to prevent luxury from producing effeminacy, intoxication, extravagance, vice and folly? When you will answer me these questions, I hope I may venture to answer yours; yet all these ought not to discourage us from exertion, for with my friend Jeb [Dr. Jebb in England], I believe no effort in favor of virtue is lost, and all good men ought to struggle both by their counsel and example.

To return to the Romans, I never could discover that they possessed much virtue or real liberty there.

John Adams

84. JOHN ADAMS TO THOMAS JEFFERSON
   January 20, 1820

When we say God is Spirit, we know what we mean as well as we do when we say that the pyramids of Egypt are Matter. Let us be content therefore to believe Him to be Spirit, that is, an Essence that we know nothing of, in which originally and necessarily reside all energy, all power, all capacity, all activity, all wisdom, and all goodness.

Behold the Creed and Confession of Faith of your ever affectionate friend,

John Adams

85. THOMAS JEFFERSON TO JOHN ADAMS
   MONTICELLO, March 14, 1820

DEAR SIR,

A continuation of poor health makes me an irregular correspondent. I am, therefore, your debtor for the two letters of January 20th and February 21st. It was after you left Europe that Dugald Stewart,[304] con-

---

304. (1753–1828). Scots philosopher. Wrote *Elements of the Philosophy of the Human Mind* (1792).

cerning whom you inquire, and Lord Dare, second son of the Marquis of Lansdowne, came to Paris. They brought me a letter from Lord Wycombe, whom you knew. I became immediately intimate with Stewart, calling mutually on each other and almost daily, during their stay at Paris, which was of some months.

I consider him and Tracy as the ablest metaphysicians living; by which I mean investigators of the thinking faculty of man. Stewart seems to have given its natural history from facts and observations; Tracy its modes of action and deduction, which he calls Logic and Ideology; and Cabanis,[305] in his Physique et Morale de l'Homme, has investigated anatomically, and most ingeniously, the particular organs in the human structure which may most probably exercise that faculty.

And they ask why may not the mode of action called thought, have been given to a material organ of peculiar structure, as that of magnetism is to the needle, or of elasticity to the spring by a particular manipulation of the steel. They observe that on ignition of the needle or spring, their magnetism and elasticity cease. So on dissolution of the material organ by death, its action of thought may cease also, and that nobody supposes that the magnetism or elasticity retire to hold a substantive and distinct existence. These were qualities only of particular conformations of matter; change the conformation, and its qualities change also.

Mr. Locke, you know, and other materialists, have charged with blasphemy the spiritualists who have denied the Creator the power of endowing certain forms of matter with the faculty of thought. These, however, are speculations and subtleties in which, for my own part, I have little indulged myself.

When I meet with a proposition beyond finite comprehension, I abandon it as I do a weight which human strength cannot lift, and I think ignorance, in these cases, is truly the softest pillow on which I can lay my head. Were it necessary, however, to form an opinion, I confess I should, with Mr. Locke, prefer swallowing one incomprehensibility rather than two.

---

305. Pierre Jean George Cabanis (1757–1808). French philosopher and physiologist. Wrote *Relations of the Physical and Moral in Man* (1802).

It requires one effort only to admit the single incomprehensibility of matter endowed with thought, and two to believe, first that of an existence called spirit, of which we have neither evidence nor idea, and then secondly how that spirit, which has neither extension nor solidity, can put material organs into motion.

These are things which you and I may perhaps know ere long. We have so lived as to fear neither horn of the dilemma. We have, willingly, done injury to no man; and have done for our country the good which has fallen in our way, so far as commensurate with the faculties given us. That we have not done more than we could, cannot be imputed to us as a crime before any tribunal. I look, therefore, to the crisis, as I am sure you also do, as one "who neither fears the final day, nor hopes for it."

In the meantime be our last as cordial as were our first affections,

Thomas Jefferson

86. JOHN ADAMS TO THOMAS JEFFERSON
   May 12, 1820

The question between spirit and matter appears to me nugatory because we have neither evidence nor idea of either. All that we certainly know is that some substance exists which must be the cause of all the qualities and attributes that we perceive.

Sixty years ago at college, I read Berkley.[306] From that time to this, I have been fully persuaded that we know nothing of Essences, that some Essence does exist, which causes our minds with all their ideas, and this visible world with all its wonders. I am certain that this Cause is wise, benevolent, and powerful, beyond all conception. I cannot doubt, but what it is, I cannot conjecture. . . . Oh, delightful ignorance! When I arrive at a certainty that I am ignorant, and that I always must

---

306. George Berkeley (1685–1753). Irish philosopher and bishop opposed to John Locke's views on the nature of material substance. He held that there is no material reality but only ideas belonging to mind and deriving from God. Wrote *Treatise on the Principles of Human Knowledge* (1710).

be ignorant, while I live I am happy. For, I know I can no longer be responsible.

John Adams

87. THOMAS JEFFERSON TO JOHN ADAMS
MONTICELLO, August 15, 1820

Let me turn to your puzzling letter of May the 12th, on matter, spirit, motion, etc. Its crowd of skepticisms kept me from sleep. I read it, and laid it down; read it, and laid it down, again and again; and to give rest to my mind, I was obliged to recur ultimately to my habitual anodyne, I feel, therefore I exist. "I feel bodies which are not myself: there are other existences then. I call them matter. I feel them changing place. This gives me motion. Where there is an absence of matter, I call it void, or nothing, or immaterial space.

On the basis of sensation, of matter and motion, we may erect the fabric of all the certainties we can have or need. I can conceive thought to be an action of a particular organization of matter, formed for that purpose by its Creator, as well as that attraction is an action of matter, or magnetism of loadstone. When he who denies to the Creator the power of endowing matter with the mode of action called thinking, shall show how He could endow the sun with the mode of action called attraction, which reins the planets in the track of their orbits, or how an absence of matter can have a will, and by that will put matter into motion, then the Materialist may be lawfully required to explain the process by which matter exercises the faculty of thinking.

When once we quit the basis of sensation, all is in the wind. To talk of immaterial existences, is to talk of nothings. To say that the human soul, angels, god, are immaterial is to say, they are nothings, or that there is no God, no angels, no soul. I cannot reason otherwise: but I believe I am supported in my creed of materialism by the Lockes, the Tracys and the Stewarts.

At what age of the Christian Church this heresy of immaterialism, or masked atheism, crept in, I do not exactly know. But a heresy it certainly is. Jesus taught nothing of it. He told us, indeed, that "God is a Spirit," but He has not defined what a spirit is, nor said that it is not matter. The ancient fathers generally, of the three first centuries, held it to be matter, light and thin indeed, an ethereal gas; but still matter.

Origen[307] says, "God is in very fact corporeal, but, by reason of so much heavier bodies, incorporeal." Tertullian,[308] "For what is God except body?" And again, "Who will deny that God is body? Although God is spirit, yet spirit is body, of his own nature, in his own image." St. Justin Martyr[309] says, "We say that the divinity is without body, not because it is bodiless, but since the state of not being bounded by anything is a more honorable one than that of being bounded. For this reason, we call him bodiless." And St. Macarius,[310] speaking of angels, says, "For although their bodies are of light texture, nevertheless in substance, form, and figure, their bodies are rare, according to the rarity of nature." And, St. Austin,[311] St. Basil,[312] Lactantius,[313] Tatian,[314] Athenagoras[315] and others,

---

307. (c.185–c. 254). Alexandrian theologian. He tried to reconcile Greek philosophy, that is, Platonism (Ideal, Form, and Logos), with Christian theology. Wrote *De Principiis* and *Contra Celsus*.

308. Quintus Septimius Florens Tertullianus (c.160–c. 225). African (Carthage) convert who used his legal knowledge to denounce paganism and heresies.

309. (c. 100–c. 165). Samaritan Christian theologian who taught in Rome, where he was martyred by Marcus Aurelius. Wrote *Apology* and *Dialogue with Trypho*.

310. St. Macarius the Great (300–390 CE). Egyptian hermit and anti-Arian. He is said to have fought with devils in the desert, healed the sick, and raised the dead.

311. St. Augustine (354–430). Converted by St. Ambrose, bishop of Milan, Augustine was influenced by neo-Platonism. Wrote *Confessions* and *The City of God*.

312. St. Basil the Great (c. 330–379). Father of the Eastern Church and founder of Greek monasticism. Wrote *Longer and Shorter Rules* for monastic life and helped subdue Arianism.

313. Lucius Caecilius Firmianus Lactantius (260–330). African-born Christian apologist; friend to Emperor Constantine; and tutor to Constantine's son, Crispus. Wrote *The Divine Institutions*, a treatise to point out the uselessness of paganism and the truth of Christianity.

314. Tatian, Syrian Christian apologist, beheaded c. 284. Wrote *Address to the Greeks*, a bitter attack on Greek philosophy and manners in comparison to Christianity.

315. Athenian Christian apologist of second half of second century. In *Apology*, he defended Christianity against Roman charges of atheism, citing pagan philosophers who held same views as Christians. Also wrote *Treatise on the Resurrection*.

with whose writings I pretend not a familiarity, are said by those who are better acquainted with them, to deliver the same doctrine. (Enfield X. 3, 1 [Enfield, vol. 10, chap. 3, para. 1].)

Turn to your Ocellus d'Argens, 97, 105 [Ocellus, translated by d'Argens, pp. 97, 105], and to his Timaeus 17 [d'Argen's translation of Timaeus, p. 17] for these quotations. In England, these Immaterialists might have been burnt until the 29 Car .2 [twenty-ninth year of Charles II's reign, 1678], when the writ de haeretico comburendo was abolished; and here until the Revolution, that statute not having extended to us. All heresies, being now done away with us, these schismatists are merely atheists, differing from the material atheist only in their belief, that "nothing made something," and from the material deist, who believes that matter alone can operate on matter.

Rejecting all organs of information, therefore, but my senses, I rid myself of the pyrrhonisms with which an indulgence in speculations hyperphysical and antiphysical, so uselessly occupy and disquiet the mind. A single sense may indeed be sometimes deceived, but rarely, and, never all our senses together, with their faculty of reasoning. They evidence realities, and there are enough of these for all the purposes of life, without plunging into the fathomless abyss of dreams and phantasms.

I am satisfied, and sufficiently occupied with the things which are, without tormenting or troubling myself about those which may indeed be, but of which I have no evidence. I am sure that I really know many, many things, and none more surely than that I love you with all my heart, and pray for the continuance of your life until you shall be tired of it yourself.

Thomas Jefferson

88. THOMAS JEFFERSON TO JOHN ADAMS
MONTICELLO, January 22, 1821

I was quite rejoiced, dear Sir, to see that you had health and spirits enough to take part in the late convention of your State, for revising its Constitution, and to bear your share in its debates and labors. The amendments, of which we have as yet heard, prove the advance of liberalism in the intervening period; and encourage a hope that the human mind will some day get back to the freedom it enjoyed two thousand years ago. This country, which has given to the world the example of physical liberty, owes to it that of moral emancipation also, for as yet it is but nominal with us. The inquisition of public opinion overwhelms in practice, the freedom asserted by the laws in theory.

Our anxieties in this quarter are all concentrated in the question, what does the Holy Alliance in and out of Congress mean to do with us on the Missouri question? . . . But let us turn from our own uneasiness to the miseries of our southern friends. Bolivar[316] and Morillo,[317] it seems, have come to the parley, with dispositions at length to stop the useless effusion of human blood in that quarter.

I feared from the beginning, that these people were not yet sufficiently enlightened for self-government; and that after wading through blood and slaughter, they would end in military tyrannies, more or less numerous. Yet as they wished to try the experiment, I wished them success in it; they have now tried it, and will possibly find that their safest road will be an accommodation with the Mother country, which shall hold them together by the single link of the same chief magistrate, leaving to him power enough to keep them in peace with one another, and to themselves the essential power of self-government and self-improvement, until they shall be sufficiently trained by education and habits of freedom to walk safely by themselves.

Representative government, native functionaries, a qualified negative on their laws, with a previous security by compact for freedom of commerce, freedom of the press, habeas corpus and trial by jury, would make a good beginning. This last would be the school in which their people might begin to learn the exercise of civic duties as well as rights.

---

316. Simon Bolivar (1783–1830). South American liberator and statesman. Born into a wealthy Venezuelan family, he studied in Europe where he was influenced by the work of eighteenth-century rationalists, especially Jean-Jacques Rousseau.

317. Pablo Morillo (1778–1837). Spanish general known for his brutal South American occupations. He was ordered by Spain to agree to an armistice with Bolivar.

For freedom of religion they are not yet prepared. The scales of bigotry have not sufficiently fallen from their eyes, to accept it for themselves individually, much less to trust others with it. But that will come in time, as well as a general ripeness to break entirely from the parent stem.

You see, my dear Sir, how easily we prescribe for others a cure for their difficulties, while we cannot cure our own. We must leave both, I believe, to heaven, and wrap ourselves up in the mantle of resignation, and of that friendship of which I tender to you the most sincere assurances.

Thomas Jefferson

89. JOHN ADAMS TO THOMAS JEFFERSON
February 3, 1821

DEAR SIR,

I have just read a sketch of the life of Swedenborg, and a larger work in two huge volumes of Memoirs of John Wesley by Southey. Your kind letter of January 22 came just in the nick of time to furnish me with a very rational exclamation: "What a bedlamite is man!"

They are histories of Galvanism[318] and Mesmerism[319] thrown into a hotch potch. They say that these men were honest and sincere. So were the worshippers of the White Bull in Egypt and now in Calcutta. So were the worshippers of Bacchus and Venus. So were the worshippers of St. Dominick and St. Bernard.[320] Swedenborg and Wesley had certainly vast memories and imaginations, and great talents for Lunatics.

---

318. Luigi Galvani (1737–1798). Italian anatomist who discovered "animal electricity," the electrically induced movements in a dead frog's legs. This led to the positing of electrical energy within humans and animals.

319. Franz Anton Mesmer (1734–1815). German physician whose work considering the possibilities of "animal magnetism," or mesmerism, led to the use of hypnosis. But Mesmer's original beliefs were that planetary movements affected bodily fluids somehow, perhaps magnetically. Mesmer reported some cures by using magnets to change bodily fluid movements or locations.

320. Dominic, founder of Dominican order of monks. Bernard, founder of Cistercian order.

Slavery in this country has been hanging over it like a black cloud for half a century, If I were drunk with enthusiasm as Swedenborg or Wesley, I might probably say I had seen armies of Negroes marching and countermarching in the air, shining in armor. . . . What we are to see, God knows! And, I leave it to him and his agents in posterity. I have none of the genius of Franklin to invent a rod to draw from the cloud its thunder and lightning.

I have long been decided in opinion that a free government and the Roman Catholic religion can never exist together in any nation or country. And, consequently that all projects for reconciling them in old Spain or new are utopian, platonic, and chimerical.

I have seen such a prostration and prostitution of human nature to the priesthood in old Spain as settled my judgment long ago. I understand that in new Spain it is still worse, if that is possible.

John Adams

90. JOHN ADAMS TO THOMAS JEFFERSON
   May 19, 1821

My dear friend,

Must we, before we take our departure from this grand and beautiful world, surrender all our pleasing hopes for the progress of society? Of improvement of the intellectual and moral condition of the world? Of the reformation of mankind? The Piemontese revolution scarcely assumed a form, and, the Neapolitan bubble is burst. What should hinder the Spanish and Portuguese constitutions from rushing to the same ruin?

. . . Can a free government possible exist with a Roman Catholic religion?

John Adams

91. JOHN ADAMS TO THOMAS JEFFERSON
September 24, 1821

DEAR SIR,

I thank you for your favor of the 12th instant. Hope springs eternal. Eight millions of Jews hope for a Messiah more powerful and glorious than Moses, David, or Solomon, who is to make them as powerful as he pleases. Some hundreds of millions of Mussulmans expect another prophet more powerful than Mahomet, who is to spread Islam over the whole earth. Hundreds of millions of Christians expect and hope for a millennium in which Jesus is to reign for a thousand years over the whole world before it is burnt up. The Hindoos expect another and final incarnation of Vishnu, who is to do great and wonderful things, I know not what. All these hopes are founded on real or pretended revelation.

The modern Greeks, too, it seems, hope, for a deliverer who is to produce them—the Themistocleses and Demostheneses—the Platos and Aristotles—the Solons and Lycurguses. On what prophecies they found their belief, I know not.

You and I hope for splendid improvements in human society, and vast amelioration in the condition of mankind. Our faith may be supposed by more rational arguments than any of the former. I own that I am very sanguine in the belief of them, as I hope and believe you are, and your reasoning in your letter confirmed me in them.

John Adams

92. THOMAS JEFFERSON TO JOHN ADAMS
June 1, 1822

When all our faculties have left, or are leaving us, one by one, sight, hearing, memory, every avenue of pleasing sensation is closed, and atony, debility, and malaise left in their places, when the friends of our youth are all gone, and a generation is risen around us whom we do not know, is death an evil?

When one by one our ties are torn,
And friend from friend is snatched forlorn
When man is left alone to mourn,
Oh! Then how sweet it is to die!
When trembling limbs refuse their weight,
And films slow gathering dim the sight,
When clouds obscure the mental light
Tis nature's kindest boon to die![321]

I really think so. I have ever dreaded old age. My health has been generally so good, and is now so good, that I dread it still. The rapid decline of my strength during the last winter has made me hope sometimes that I see land. During the summer I enjoy its temperature, but I shudder at the approach of winter, and wish I could sleep through it with the Dormouse, and only wake with him in the spring, if ever.

To turn to the news of the day, it seems that the cannibals of Europe are going to eating one another again. A war between Russia and Turkey is like a battle of the kite and the snake. Whichever destroys the other leaves a destroyer the less for the world. This pugnacious humor of mankind seems to be the law of his nature, one of the obstacles to too great multiplication provided in the mechanism of the universe.

The cocks of the hen yard kill one another up. Boars, bulls, rams do the same. The horse, in his wild state, kills all the young males until, worn down with age and war, some vigorous youth kills him and takes to himself the harem.

I hope we shall prove how much happier for man the Quaker policy is, and that the life of the feeder is better than that of the fighter. It is some consolation that the desolation, by these maniacs of one part of the earth, is the means of improving it in other parts. Let the latter be our office. Let us milk the cow, while the Russian holds her by the horns, the Turk by the tail.

Thomas Jefferson

---

321. Edward Young, *Night Thoughts on Life, Death, and Immortality* (1851).

93. JOHN ADAMS TO THOMAS JEFFERSON
June 11, 1822

DEAR SIR,

I answer your question, "Is death an evil?"

It is not an evil. It is a blessing to the individual and to the world. Yet, we ought not to wish for it until life becomes insupportable. We must wait the pleasure and convenience of this great teacher.

The globe is a theatre of war. Its inhabitants are all heroes. I believe the little eels in vinegar and the animalcule in pepper water, I believe are quarrelsome. The bees are as warlike as Romans, Russians, Britains, or Frenchmen. Ants or caterpillars and canker worms are the only tribes amongst whom I have not seen battles. And Heaven itself, if we believe Hindoos, Jews, and Christians, has not been at peace. We need not trouble ourselves about these things, nor fret ourselves because of evil-doers but safely trust the ruler with his skies. Nor, need we dread the approach of dotage. Let it come if it must. . . . The worst of the evil is that our friends will suffer more by our imbecility than we ourselves.

John Adams

94. JOHN ADAMS TO THOMAS JEFFERSON
QUINCY, March 10, 1823

DEAR SIR,

The sight of your well-known handwriting in your favor of 25th February last, gave me great pleasure, as it proved your arm to be restored, and your pen still manageable. May it continue till you shall become as perfect a Calvinist as I am in one particular. Poor Calvin's infirmities, his rheumatism, his gouts and sciatics, made him frequently cry out, Mon Dieu, jusqu'a quand! Lord, how long! Prat,[322] once chief justice of New

---

322. Benjamin Pratt (1710–1763). Massachussetts jurist appointed New York chief justice. The loss of a limb early in life led to a life of study. After collecting numerous documents, death precluded Pratt's writing a history of New England.

York, always tormented with infirmities, dreamt that he was situated on a single rock in the midst of the Atlantic Ocean. He heard a voice:

"Why mourns the bard? Apollo bids thee rise,
Renounce the dust, and claim thy native skies."

What are we to think of the Crusades in which three millions of lives at least were probably sacrificed? And what right had St. Louis and Richard Coeur de Lion to Palestine and Syria more than Alexander to India, or Napoleon to Egypt and Italy? Right and justice have hard fare in this world, but there is a Power above who is capable and willing to put all things right in the end; et pour mettre chacun a sa place dans l'universe [to put each in his place within the universe], and I doubt not He will.

John Adams by proxy

95. THOMAS JEFFERSON TO JOHN ADAMS
MONTICELLO, April 11, 1823

DEAR SIR,

The wishes expressed in your last favor, that I may continue in life and health until I become a Calvinist, at least in his exclamation of "Mon Dieu! jusqu'a quand!" [My God! How long?] would make me immortal. I can never join Calvin in addressing his God. He was indeed an atheist, which I can never be; or rather his religion was dae-monism. If ever man worshiped a false God, he did. The Being described in his five points, is not the God whom you and I acknowl-edge and adore, the Creator and benevolent Governor of the world; but a daemon of malignant spirit. It would be more pardonable to believe in no God at all, than to blaspheme Him by the atrocious attributes of Calvin. Indeed, I think that every Christian sect gives a great handle to atheism by their general dogma that without a revelation, there would not be sufficient proof of the being of a God. Now one-sixth of mankind only are supposed to be Christians; the other five-sixths then, who do not believe in the Jewish and Christian revelation, are without knowledge of the existence of a God!

This gives completely a gain de cause to the disciples of Ocellus, Timaeus, Spinoza,[323] Diderot and D'Holbach. The argument which they rest on as triumphant and unanswerable is, that in every hypothesis of cosmogony, you must admit an eternal pre-existence of something; and according to the rule of sound philosophy, you are never to employ two principles to solve a difficulty when one will suffice. They say then, that it is more simple to believe at once in the eternal pre-existence of the world, as it is now going on, and may forever go on by the principle of reproduction which we see and witness, than to believe in the eternal pre-existence of an ulterior cause, or Creator of the world, a Being whom we see not and know not, of whose form, substance and mode, or place of existence, or of action, no sense informs us, no power of the mind enables us to delineate or comprehend.

On the contrary, I hold, (without appeal to revelation), that when we take a view of the universe, in its parts, general or particular, it is impossible for the human mind not to perceive and feel a conviction of design, consummate skill, and indefinite power in every atom of its composition. The movements of the heavenly bodies, so exactly held in their course by the balance of centrifugal and centripetal forces; the structure of our earth itself, with its distribution of lands, waters and atmosphere; animal and vegetable bodies, examined in all their minutest particles; insects, mere atoms of life, yet as perfectly organized as man or mammoth; the mineral substances, their generation and uses; it is impossible, I say, for the human mind not to believe, that there is in all this, design, cause and effect, up to an ultimate cause, a Fabricator of all things from matter and motion, their Preserver and Regulator while permitted to exist in their present forms, and their regeneration into new and other forms.

---

323. Baruch Spinoza (1632–1677). Dutch philosopher and rationalist. His "God is nature" idea secured him an expulsion from Amsterdam's Jewish community. He rejected the dualism of Descartes and held that mind and matter are attributes of one substance: God. Wrote *Ethics* (1677).

We see, too, evident proofs of the necessity of a superintending power, to maintain the universe in its course and order. Stars, well known, have disappeared, new ones have come into view; comets, in their incalculable courses, may run foul of suns and planets, and require renovation under other laws; certain races of animals are become extinct; and were there no restoring power, all existences might extinguish successively, one by one, until all should be reduced to a shapeless chaos.

So irresistible are these evidences of an intelligent and powerful Agent, that, of the infinite numbers of men who have existed through all time, they have believed, in the proportion of a million at least to unit, in the hypothesis of an eternal pre-existence of a Creator, rather than in that of a self-existent universe. Surely this unanimous sentiment renders this more probable, than that of the few in the other hypothesis.

Some early Christians, indeed, have believed in the co-eternal pre-existence of both the Creator and the world, without changing their relation of cause and effect. That this was the opinion of St. Thomas,[324] we are informed by Cardinal Toleta, in these words:[325]

"God has been omnipotent forever, just as when he made the world. He has had the power to make the world forever. If the sun were in existence forever, light would have been in existence forever; and if a foot then likewise a footprint. But light and footprint are effects of an efficient sun and foot; therefore, the effect has had the power to be co-eternal with the eternal cause. Of this opinion is St. Thomas, the first of the theologians."

Of the nature of this Being we know nothing. Jesus tells us, that "God is a Spirit" (4 John 24), but without defining what a spirit is. Down to the third century, we know it was still deemed material, but of a lighter, subtler matter than our gross bodies. So says Origen: "God, therefore, to

---

324. Thomas Aquinas (c. 1225–1274). Christian theologian who attempted to reconcile faith with reason by positing the "Uncaused Cause" and the "Prime Mover." Wrote *Summa Theologica*.

325. Jefferson's letter contained only the Latin quote here from Tholen Toleta and the Greek for another quote. I have provided only the English translations from Lester J. Cappon's *The Adams-Jefferson Correspondence* (Chapel Hill: University of North Carolina Press, 1959).

whom the soul is similar, in consequences of its origin, is in reality corporeal. But, he is incorporeal in comparison with so much heavier bodies." These are the words of Huet in his commentary on Origen. Origen himself says, "The word, among our writers, is not used or known." So also Tertullian: "Yet who will deny that God is body, although God is spirit. Indeed, He is spirit of his own type of body, in his own image."

These two fathers were of the third century. Calvin's character of this Supreme Being seems chiefly copied from that of the Jews. But the reformation of these blasphemous attributes, and substitution of those more worthy, pure, and sublime, seems to have been the chief object of Jesus in His discourses to the Jews; and His doctrine of the cosmogony of the world is very clearly laid down in the three first verses of the first chapter of John, . . . which truly translated means, "In the beginning God existed, and reason [or mind] was with God, and that mind was God. This was in the beginning with God. All things were created by it, and without it was made not one thing which was made."

Yet this text, so plainly declaring the doctrine of Jesus, that the world was created by the Supreme, Intelligent Being, has been perverted by modern Christians to build up a second person of their tritheism, by a mistranslation of the word Logos. One of its legitimate meanings, indeed, is "a word." But in that sense it makes an unmeaning jargon; while the other meaning, "reason," equally legitimate, explains rationally the eternal pre-existence of God, and His creation of the world.

Knowing how incomprehensible it was that "a word" the mere action or articulation of the organs of speech could create a world, they undertook to make of this articulation a second pre-existing being, and ascribe to him, and not to God, the creation of the universe. The atheist here plumes himself on the uselessness of such a God, and the simpler hypothesis of a self-existent universe.

The truth is, that the greatest enemies to the doctrines of Jesus are those calling themselves the expositors of them, who have perverted them for the structure of a system of fancy absolutely incomprehensible, and without any foundation in His genuine words. And the day will come, when the mystical generation of Jesus, by the Supreme Being as His Father, in the womb of a virgin, will be classed with the fable of the generation of Minerva in the brain of Jupiter.[326] But we may hope that the dawn of reason, and freedom of thought in these United States, will do away all this artificial scaffolding, and restore to us the primitive and genuine doctrines of this the most venerated Reformer of human errors.

So much for your quotation of Calvin's, "Mon Dieu! jusqu'a quand!" in which, when addressed to the God of Jesus, and our God, I join you cordially and await His time and will with more readiness than reluctance. May we meet there again, in Congress, with our ancient colleagues, and receive with them the seal of approbation, "Well done, good and faithful servants."

Thomas Jefferson

96. JOHN ADAMS TO THOMAS JEFFERSON
QUINCY, August 15, 1823

Watchman, what of the night? Is darkness that may be felt, to prevail over the whole world? Or can you perceive any rays of a returning dawn? Is the devil to be the "Lord's anointed" over the whole globe? Or do you foresee the fulfillment of the prophecies according to Dr. Priestley's interpretation of them? I know not, but I have in some of my familiar and frivolous letters to you told the story four times over. But, if I have, I never applied it so well as now.

Not long after the denouement of the tragedy of Louis XVI, when I was Vice-President, my friend, the Doctor, came to breakfast with me alone. He was very sociable, very learned and eloquent, on the subject of the French Revolution. It was opening a new era in the world, and presenting a near view of the millennium. I listened. I heard with great attention and perfect sang froid. At last I asked the Doctor: "Do you really believe the French will establish a free demo-cratical government in France?"

He answered: "I do firmly believe it."

---

326. One of the many virgin birth myths/sagas of the pre-Christian world. Minerva, Roman goddess of wisdom springs (is born) from the head of her father, Jupiter.

"Will you give me leave to ask you upon what grounds you entertain this opinion? Is it from anything you ever read in history? Is there any instance of a Roman Catholic monarchy of five and twenty millions at once converted into a free and national people?"

"No, I know of no instance like it."

"Is there anything in your knowledge of human nature, derived from books, or experience, that any nation, ancient or modern, consisting of such multitudes of ignorant people, ever were, or ever can be converted suddenly into materials capable of conducting a free government, especially a democratical republic?"

"No—I know nothing of the kind."

"Well then, Sir, what is the ground of your opinion?"

The answer was: "My opinion is founded altogether upon revelation, and the prophecies. I take it that the ten horns of the great beast in Revelations, mean the ten crowned heads of Europe; and that the execution of the King of France, is the falling off of the first of those horns; and the nine monarchies of Europe will fall one after another in the same way."

Such was the enthusiasm of that great man, that reasoning machine. After all, however, he did recollect himself so far as to say: "There is, however, a possibility of doubt. For, I read yesterday a book put into my hands, by a gentleman, a volume of travels, written by a French gentleman[327] in 1659, in which he says he had been traveling a whole year in England, into every part of it, and conversed freely with all ranks of people. He found the whole nation earnestly engaged in discussing and contriving a form of government for their future regulations; there was but one point in which they all agreed, and in that they were unanimous: that monarchy, nobility, and prelacy never would exist in England again.

The Doctor paused; and said: "Yet, in the very next year, the whole nation called in the King and run mad with nobility, monarchy, and

---

327. Per Cappon, *The Adams-Jefferson Correspondence*, p. 595, this may well have been Samuel de Sorbiere's 1664 publication originally titled *Relation of a Voyage to England, touching on many things which look at the state of science, religion, and other curious matters.*

prelacy. I am no King killer, merely because they are Kings. Poor creatures, they know no better; they believe sincerely and conscientiously that God made them to rule the world. I would not, therefore, behead them, or send them to St. Helena, to be treated as Bonaparte was. But, I would shut them up like the man in the iron mask, feed them well, and give them as much finery as they pleased until they could be converted to right reason and common sense.

John Adams

97. THOMAS JEFFERSON TO JOHN ADAMS
MONTICELLO, September 4, 1823

DEAR SIR,

Your letter of August the 15th was received in due time, and with the welcome of everything which comes from you. With its opinions on the difficulties of revolutions from despotism to freedom, I very much concur. The generation which commences a revolution rarely completes it. Habituated from their infancy to passive submission of body and mind to their kings and priests, they are not qualified when called on to think and provide for themselves. Their inexperience, their ignorance, and bigotry, make them instruments often, in the hands of the Bonapartes and Iturbides, to defeat their own rights and purposes. This is the present situation of Europe and Spanish America.

But it is not desperate. The light which has been shed on mankind by the art of printing has eminently changed the condition of the world.

98. THOMAS JEFFERSON TO JOHN ADAMS
October 12, 1823

The circumstances of the times in which we have happened to live, and, the partiality of our friends at a particular period, placed us in a state of apparent opposition, which some might suppose to be personal also. There might not be wanting those who wished to make it so by filling our ears with malignant falsehoods, by dressing up hideous phantoms of their own creation, presenting them to you under my name, to me under yours, and endeavoring to instill into our minds things concerning each other the most destitute of truth.

And, if there had been, at any time, a moment when we were off guard, and in a temper to let the whispers of these people make us forget what we had known of each other for so many years, years of so much trial, yet all men who have attended to the workings of the human mind, who have seen the false colors under which passion sometimes dresses the actions and motives of others, have seen also these passions subsiding with time and reflection, dissipating, like mists before the rising sun, and restoring to us the sight of all things in their true shape and colors.

It would be strange indeed if, at our years, we were to go an age back to hunt up imaginary, or forgotten facts, to disturb the repose of affections so sweetening to the evening of our lives. Be assured, my dear Sir, that I am incapable of receiving the slightest impression from the effort now made to plant thorns on the pillow of age, worth, and wisdom, and to sow tares between friends, who have been such for near half a century.

Beseeching you then not to suffer your mind to be disquieted by this wicked attempt to poison its peace, and praying you to throw it by, among the things which have never happened, I add sincere assurances of my unabated and constant attachment, friendship, and respect.

Thomas Jefferson

99. THOMAS JEFFERSON TO JOHN ADAMS
MONTICELLO, January 8, 1825

I have lately been reading the most extraordinary of all books, and at the same time the most demonstrative by numerous and unequivocal facts. It is Flourens'[328] experiments on the functions of the nervous system, in

---

328. Marie Jean Pierre Flourens (1794–1867). French physiologist and professor at College of France, under patronage of Cuvier. She was the first to demonstrate localization of brain functions, that is, respiratory functions and muscular coordination.

vertebrate animals. He takes out the cerebrum completely, leaving the cerebellum and other parts of the system uninjured. The animal loses all its senses of hearing, seeing, feeling, smelling, tasting, is totally deprived of will, intelligence, memory, perception, etc., yet lives for months in perfect health, with all its powers of motion, but without moving but on external excitement, starving even on a pile of grain, unless crammed down its throat; in short, in a state of the most absolute stupidity.

He takes the cerebellum out of others, leaving the cerebrum untouched. The animal retains all its senses, faculties, and understanding, but loses the power of regulated motion, and exhibits all the symptoms of drunkenness. While he makes incisions in the cerebrum and cerebellum, lengthwise and crosswise, which heal and get well, a puncture in the medulla elongata [oblongata] is instant death; and many other most interesting things too long for a letter.

Cabanis had proved by the anatomical structure of certain portions of the human frame, that they might be capable of receiving from the hand of the Creator the faculty of thinking; Flourens proves that they have received it; that the cerebrum is the thinking organ; and that life and health may continue, and the animal be entirely without thought, if deprived of that organ.

I wish to see what the spiritualists will say to this. Whether in this state the soul remains in the body, deprived of its essence of thought or whether it leaves it, as in death, and where it goes? His memoirs and experiments have been reported on with approbation by a committee of the Institute, composed of Cuvier,[329] Bertholet,[330] Dumaril,[331]

---

329. Georges Cuvier (1769–1832). Vertebrate anatomist, paleontologist, and geologist. From fossil remains, he posited periodic extinctions of species. As a Protestant, he was regarded as an outsider. Wrote *Essay on the Theory of Earth* (1813) and *Discourse on the Revolutions on the Surface of the Globe and on the Changes they produce in the Animal Kingdom* (the third edition came out in 1825).

330. Bertholet Flemal (1614–1575). Flemish painter of mythological and religious subjects, including *Mysteries of the Old and New Testament* (Louvre).

331. Andre Marie Constant Dumeril (1774–1860). French naturalist. Wrote *Analytical Zoology, or a Natural Method of Classification of Animals* (1806) and *General Considerations on Classes of Insects* (1812).

Portal[332] and Pinel.[333] But all this, you and I shall know better when we meet again, in another place, and at no distant period. In the meantime, that the revived powers of your frame, and the anodyne of philosophy may preserve you from all suffering, is my sincere and affectionate prayer.

Thomas Jefferson

100. JOHN ADAMS TO THOMAS JEFFERSON
January 22, 1825

Your university is a noble employment in your old age, and your ardor for its success does you honor. But, I do not approve of your sending to Europe for tutors and professors. I do believe there are sufficient scholars in America to fill your professorships and tutorships with more ingenuity and independent minds than you can bring from Europe.

The Europeans are all deeply tainted with prejudices both ecclesiastical and temporal, which they can never get rid of. They are all infected with Episcopal and Presbyterian creeds and confessions of faith. They all believe that great principle which has produced this boundless universe, Newton's universe, and Hershell's universe,[334] came down to this little Ball to be spit upon by Jews. And, until this awful blasphemy is got rid of, there will never be any liberal science in the world.

John Adams

---

332. Antoine Portal (1742–1832). Anatomist and College of France Chair of Medicine. Wrote *Observations on the Nature and Treatment of Rickets and Curvatures of the Spinal Column* (1797).

333. Phillipe Pinel (1745–1826). French physician and psychiatrist. Opting for more humane treatments for mental illness, he did away with bleeding, purging, and blistering "treatments." Through Cabanis and Mme. Helvetius's salon he met Ben Franklin, Ideologues, and the ideas of John Locke. Wrote *Nosographie Philosophique* (1798), describing various psychoses, and *Medico-Philosophical Treatise on Mental Alienation or Mania* (1801).

334. William Herschel, or Herschell (1738–1822). German-born organist, composer/conductor, who, with his sister, Caroline, took up astronomy as a hobby. He discovered Uranus, which he initially took for a comet, and worked on double stars and astronomy maps. Wrote *Philosophical Transactions of the Royal Society* (1801).

101. JOHN ADAMS TO THOMAS JEFFERSON
QUINCY, January 23, 1825

MY DEAR SIR,

We think ourselves possessed, or at least we boast that we are so, of liberty of conscience on all subjects and of the right of free inquiry and private judgment in all cases, and yet how far are we from these exalted privileges in fact.

There exists, I believe, throughout the whole Christian world, a law which makes it blasphemy to deny, or to doubt the divine inspiration of all the books of the Old and New Testaments, from Genesis to Revelations. In most countries of Europe it is punished by fire at the stake, or the rack, or the wheel. In England itself, it is punished by boring through the tongue with a red-hot poker.

In America it is not much better; even in our Massachusetts, which, I believe, upon the whole, is as temperate and moderate in religious zeal as most of the States, a law was made in the latter end of the last century, repealing the cruel punishments of the former laws, but substituting fine and imprisonment upon all those blasphemies upon any book of the Old Testament or New. Now, what free inquiry, when a writer must surely encounter the risk of fine or imprisonment for adducing any arguments for investigation into the divine authority of those books? Who would run the risk of translating Volney's Recherches Nouvelles?[335] Who would run the risk of translating Dupuis? But I cannot enlarge upon this subject, though I have it much at heart.

I think such laws a great embarrassment, great obstructions to the improvement of the human mind. Books that cannot bear examination certainly ought not to be established as divine inspiration by penal laws. It is true, few persons appear desirous to put such laws in execu-

---

335. Constantin François de Chasseboeuf, Comte de Volney (1757–1820). Wrote *New Research on Ancient History* (1814) and *The Ruins: Meditations on the Revolutions of Empires* (1791). The latter stirred up religious skepticism in Europe and America, especially chapter 13, "Christianity, or, The Allegorical Worship of the Sun under the Cabalistic names of Chrishen, or Christ, or Yesus, or Jesus."

tion, and it is also true that some few persons are hardy enough to venture to depart from them; but as long as they continue in force as laws, the human mind must make an awkward and clumsy progress in its investigations. I wish they were repealed. The substance and essence of Christianity, as I understand it, is eternal and unchangeable, and will bear examination forever; but it has been mixed with extraneous ingredients, which, I think, will not bear examination, and they ought to be separated. Adieu.

John Adams

102. JOHN ADAMS TO THOMAS JEFFERSON
February 25, 1825

Have you read Genl. Smyth's Apocalypse?[336] I wish he had read Dupuis. This Genl. Smyth appears to have an ardent, inquisitive head. I like him much for his curiosity.

I wish your health may continue to the last much better than mine. The little strength of mind and the considerable strength of body that I once possessed appear to be all gone. But, while I breathe, I shall be your friend. We shall meet again, so wishes and believes your friend. But, if we are disappointed, we shall never know it.

John Adams

103. JOHN ADAMS TO THOMAS JEFFERSON
December 1, 1825

Mrs. Coolidge [Thomas Jefferson's granddaughter] deserves all the high praises I have constantly heard concerning her. She entertained me with accounts of your sentiments of human life, which accorded so perfectly with mine that it gave me great delight.

In one point, however, I could not agree. She said she had heard you

---

336. Alexander Smyth (1765–1830). Irish-born American legislator and soldier. Wrote *An Explanation of the Apocalypse, or Revelation of St. John* (1825).

say that you would like to go over life again. In this, I could not agree. I had rather go forward and meet whatever is to come. I have met in this life with great trials. I have had a father, and lost him. I have had a mother and lost her. I have had a wife and lost her. I have had children and lost them. I have had honorable and worthy friends and lost them. Instead of suffering these griefs again, I had rather go forward and meet my destiny.

I am, as ever, affectionately,

John Adams

104. THOMAS JEFFERSON TO JOHN ADAMS
December 18, 1825

You tell me she [Mrs. Coolidge] repeated to you an expression of mine that I should be willing to go again over the scenes of past life. I should not be unwilling, without however wishing it. And, why not?

I have enjoyed a greater share of health than falls to the lot of most men. My spirits have never failed me, except under paroxysms of grief which you, as well as I, have experienced in every form. With good health and with good spirits, the pleasures surely outweigh the pains of life. Why not then taste them again, fat and lean together. Were I indeed permitted to cut off from the train the last seven years, the balance would be much in favor of treading the ground over again.

Thomas Jefferson

105. JOHN ADAMS TO THOMAS JEFFERSON
January 14, 1826

I am certainly very near the end of my life. I am far from trifling with the idea of Death which is a great and solemn event. But I contemplate it without terror or dismay, "aut transit, aut finit," ["either it is a transformation, or it is an end."] If finit, which I cannot believe, and do not believe, there is then an end of all, but I shall never know it. And, why should I dread it, which I do not. If transit, I shall ever be under the same constitution and administration of government in the universe. I am not afraid to trust and confide in it.

John Adams

106. THOMAS JEFFERSON TO JOHN ADAMS
March 25, 1826

My grandson, Thomas J. Randolph, the bearer of this letter, being on a visit to Boston, would think he had seen nothing were he to leave it without having seen you. Altho' I truly sympathize with you in the trouble these interruptions give, yet I must ask for him permission to pay to you his personal respects. Like other young people, he wishes to be able, in the winter nights of old age, to recount to those around him what he has heard and learnt of the Heroic age preceding his birth, and which of the Argonauts particularly he was in time to have seen.

It was the lot of our early years to witness nothing but the dull monotony of colonial subservience, and, of our riper ones to breast the labors and perils of working out of it. Theirs are the Halcyon calms succeeding the storm which our Argosy had so strongly weathered. Gratify his ambition then by receiving his best bow and my solicitude for your health by enabling him to bring me a favorable account of it. Mine is but indifferent, but not so my friendship and respect for you.

Thomas Jefferson

107. JOHN ADAMS TO THOMAS JEFFERSON
April 17, 1826

Public affairs go on pretty much as usual: perpetual chicanery and rather more personal abuse than there used to be. Messrs. Randolph and McDuffie[337] have out–Heroded Herod. Mr. McDuffie seems to be swal-

---

337. George McDuffie (1790–1851). Served South Carolina as US congressman (1821–1834) and as governor. As a congressman, he, like Randolph, was a bitter opponent of the John Quincy Adams administration.

lowed up in chivalry. Such institutions ought not to be suffered in a Republican Government. Our American chivalry is the worst in the world.

It has no laws, no bounds, no definitions. It seems to be all a caprice.

My love to all your family, and best wishes for your health,

John Adams

Thomas Jefferson and John Adams both died on July 4, 1826.

ADDENDUM

A Sampling of Jefferson and Adams Writing to Others on Religion, Philosophy, and Morals

On October 18, 1756, just twelve days shy of his twenty-first birthday, John Adams wrote to his friend Richard Cranch of his decision to become a lawyer, rather than a minister:

"The frightful engines of ecclesiastical councils, of diabolical malice and Calvinistical good-nature never failed to terrify me exceedingly whenever I thought of preaching. But the point is now determined, and I shall have liberty to think for myself without molesting others or being molested myself."

Nine years later, in 1765, Adams wrote "A Dissertation on the Canon and Feudal Law." Therein, Adams wrote:

"Since the promulgation of Christianity, the two greatest systems of tyranny that have sprung from this original, are the canon and the feudal law. . . . But another event still more calamitous to human liberty was a wicked confederacy between these two systems of tyranny above described. It seems to have been even stipulated between them that the temporal grandees should contribute every thing in their power to maintain the ascendancy of the priesthood, and, that the spiritual grandees in their turn should employ their ascendancy over the consciences of the people in impressing on their minds a blind, implicit obedience to civil magistracy.

Thus, as long as the confederacy lasted and the people were held in ignorance, liberty, and with her, knowledge and virtue too, seem to have deserted the earth, and one age of darkness succeeded another until God, in His benign providence, raised up the champions who began and conducted the Reformation. From the time of the Reformation to the first settlement of America, knowledge gradually spread in Europe, but especially in England. In proportion as that increased and spread among the people, ecclesiastical and civil tyranny, which I use as synonymous expressions for the canon and feudal laws, seem to have lost their strength and weight. The people grew more and more sensible of the wrong that was done them by these systems, more and more impatient under it, and determined at all hazards to rid themselves of it. . . . The struggle between the people and the confederacy aforesaid of temporal and spiritual tyranny became formidable, violent, and bloody.

It was this struggle that peopled America. It was not religion alone, as is commonly supposed. But, it was a love of universal liberty and a hatred, a dread, a horror, of the infernal confederacy before described that projected, conducted, and accomplished the settlement of America.

. . . There seems to be a direct and formal design on foot to enslave all America. This, however, must be done by degrees. The first step that is intended seems to be an entire subversion of the whole system of our fathers by the introduction of the canon and feudal law into America."

On February 16, 1809, Adams wrote to Judge F. A. Van der Kemp:

"I hate polemical politics and polemical divinity as cordially as you do. Yet, my mind has been involved in them for sixty-five years at least. For this whole period, I have searched after truth by every means and by every opportunity in my power, and with a sincerity and impartiality, for which I can appeal to God, my adored Maker.

My religion is founded on the love of God and my neighbor, on the hope of pardon for my offenses, upon contrition, upon the duty as well as the necessity of supporting with patience the inevitable evils of life, in the duty of doing no wrong, but all the good I can to the creation, of which I am but an infinitesimal part.

Are you a dissenter from this religion? I believe too in a future state of rewards and punishments, but not eternal."

In 1814, Adams wrote to John Taylor:

"Turn our thoughts, in the next place, to the characters of learned men. The priesthood have, in all ancient nations, nearly monopolized learning. Read over again all the accounts we have of Hindoos, Chaldeans, Persians, Greeks, Romans, Celts, Teutons, we shall find that priests had all the knowledge, and, really governed all mankind. Examine Mahometanism, trace Christianity from its promulgation. Knowledge has been almost exclusively confined to clergy. And, even since the Reformation, when or where has existed a Protestant or dissenting sect would tolerate A FREE INQUIRY?

The blackest billingsgate, the most ungentlemanly insolence, the most yahooish brutality is patiently endured, countenanced, propagated, and applauded. But, touch a solemn truth in collision with dogma of a sect, though capable of the clearest proof, and you will soon find you have disturbed a nest, and the hornets will swarm about your legs and hands, and fly into your face and eyes."

In 1814 letters to John Taylor, Adams writes:

"What havoc has been made of books through every century of the Christian era? Where are the fifty gospels condemned as spurious by the Bull of Pope Gelasius? Where are the forty wagon-loads of Hebrew manuscripts burned in France by order of another pope, because suspected of heresy? . . . Have you considered that system of holy lies and pious frauds that have raged and triumphed for fifteen hundred years, and, which Chateaubriand appears at this very day to believe as sincerely as St. Augustine did?"

On December 27, 1816, Adams wrote to F. A. Van der Kemp:

"Christianity, you will say, was a fresh revelation. I will not deny this. As I understand the Christian religion, it was, and is, a revelation. But how has it happened that millions of fables, tales, legends, have been blended with both Jewish and Christian revelation that have made them the most bloody religion that ever existed?"

On July 8, 1820, at the age of eighty-four, Adams wrote the following to Presbyterian minister Samuel Miller:

"I must be a very unnatural son to entertain any prejudices against the Calvinists, or Calvinism, according to your confession of faith. For my father and mother, my uncles and aunts, and all my predecessors, from our common ancestor, who landed in this country two hundred years ago, wanting five months, were of that persuasion. Indeed, I have never known any better people than the Calvinists.

Nevertheless, I must acknowledge that I cannot class myself under that denomination. My opinions, indeed on religious subjects ought not to be of any consequence to any but myself. To develop them, and the reasons for them, would require a folio larger than Willard's Body of Divinity, and, after all, I might scatter darkness rather than light.

Before I was twelve years of age, I necessarily became a reader of polemical writings of religion, as well as politics. And, for more than seventy years, I have indulged myself in that kind of reading, as far as the wandering, anxious, and perplexed kind of life, which Providence has compelled me to pursue, would admit. I have endeavored to obtain as much information as I could of all the religions which have ever existed in the world.

Mankind are by nature religious creatures. I have found no nation without a religion, nor any people without the belief of a supreme

Being. I have been overwhelmed with sorrow to see the natural love and fear of that Being wrought upon by politicians to produce the most horrid cruelties, superstitions, and hypocrisy, from the sacrifices to Moloch down to those of Juggernaut, and the sacrifices of the kings of Whidah and Ashantree.

The great result of all my researches has been a most diffusive and comprehensive charity. I believe with Justin Martyr, that all good men are Christians. And, I believe, there have been, and are, good men in all nations, sincere and conscientious."

In response to the creation of Bible Societies in 1816, in addition to lamenting to Jefferson that the "corruptions" would not be removed from Bibles prior to world distribution, Adams had this to say in a May 30, 1821, letter to Stephan Sewall:

". . . these Bible Societies have been invented by deeper politicians still to divert mankind from the study and pursuit of their natural rights. I wish Societies were formed in India, China, and Turkey to send us gratis translations of their Sacred Books. One good turn deserves another."

The wrath of some clergy toward Thomas Jefferson in the 1800 presidential race was due in part to some statements Jefferson had made in his 1787 publication "Notes on the State of Virginia." Therein, for instance, Jefferson had written:

"By our own act of assembly of 1705, c.30 [codicil 30], if a person brought up in the Christian religion denies the being of a God, or the Trinity, or asserts there are more Gods than one, or denies the Christian religion to be true, or the scriptures to be divine authority, he is punishable on the first offence by incapacity to hold any office or employment ecclesiastical, civil, or military; on the second by disability to sue, to take any gift or legacy, to be guardian, executor, or administrator, and by three years imprisonment, without bail. A father's right to custody of his own children being founded in law on his right of guardianship, this being taken away, they may of course be severed from him, and put, by authority of a court, into more orthodox hands.

This is a summary view of that religious slavery, under which a people have been willing to remain, who have lavished their lives and fortunes for the establishment of their civil freedom. The error seems not sufficiently eradicated, that the operations of the mind, as well as the acts of the body, are subject to the coercion of the laws. But, our rulers can have authority over such natural rights only as we have submitted to them. The rights of conscience we never submitted; we could not submit. We are answerable for them to our God. The legitimate powers of government extend to such acts only as are injurious to others. But, it does me no injury for my neighbor to say there are twenty gods, or no god. It neither picks my pocket nor breaks my leg."

In 1786 Jefferson's Bill for Establishing Religious Freedom became law in Virginia. In his autobiography Jefferson tells us the following about that bill:

"The bill for establishing religious freedom, the principles of which had, to a certain degree, been enacted before, I had drawn in all the latitude of reason and right. It still met with opposition. But, with some mutilations in the preamble, it was finally passed. A singular proposition proved that its protection of opinion was meant to be universal.

Where the preamble declares that coercion is a departure from the plan of the holy author of our religion, an amendment was proposed, by inserting the word 'Jesus Christ,' so that it should read, 'a departure from the plan of Jesus Christ, the holy author of our religion.'

The insertion was rejected by a great majority, in proof that they meant to comprehend, within the mantle of its protection, the Jew and the Gentile, the Christian and Mahometan, the Hindoo, and infidel of every denomination."

On January 27, 1800, Jefferson wrote to Dr. Joseph Priestley:

"Pardon, I pray you, the temporary delirium which has been excited here, but which is fast fading away. The Gothic idea that we are to look backwards instead of forwards for the improvement of the human mind, and to recur to the annals of our ancestors for what is most perfect in government, in religion, and in learning, is worthy of those bigots in religion and government, by whom it has been recommended, and whose purposes it would answer. But, it is not an idea which this country will endure."

On March 23, 1801, Jefferson wrote to Moses Robinson:

"The Christian religion, when divested of the rags in which they [clergy] have enveloped it, and brought to the original purity and simplicity of its benevolent institutor, is a religion of all others, most friendly to liberty, science, and the freest expansion of the human mind."

To Dr. Benjamin Rush, Jefferson wrote on April 21, 1803:

"To the corruptions of Christianity I am indeed opposed, but not to the genuine precepts of Jesus himself. I am a Christian in the only sense he wished any one to be, sincerely attached to his doctrines, in preference to all others, ascribing to him every human excellence, and believing he never claimed any other."

In a January 9, 1816, letter to Charles Thomsom, Jefferson writes about his compilaton: "The Life and Morals of Jesus of Nazareth," a version of the New Testament he made while president, by cutting out and pasting only the segments of the New Testament he believed to have come from Jesus:

"I, too, have made a wee, little book from the same materials, which I call the Philosophy of Jesus. It is a paradigm of his doctrines, made by cutting the texts out of the book, and arranging them on the pages of a blank book, in a certain order of time or subject.

A more beautiful or precious morsel of ethics I have never seen. It is a document in proof that I AM A REAL CHRISTIAN, that is to say a disciple of the doctrines of Jesus, very different from the Platonists, who call me infidel and themselves Christians and preachers of the gospel, while they draw all their characteristic dogmas from what its author never said nor saw. They have compounded from the heathen mysteries a system beyond the comprehension of man, of which the great reformer of the vicious ethics and deism of the Jews, were he to return to earth, would not recognize one feature."

In a June 26, 1822, letter to Dr. Benjamin Waterhouse, after contrasting the doctrines of Jesus with those of Calvin and "Platonizing Christians" (Athanasian/Trinitarians), Jefferson asks:

"Now, which of these is the true and charitable Christian? He who believes and acts on the simple doctrines of Jesus, or, the impious dogmatists, as Athanasius and Calvin? Verily, I say these are the false shepherds foretold as to enter not by the door into the sheepfold, but to climb up some other way. They are mere usurpers of the Christian name, teaching a counter-religion made up of the deliria of crazy imaginations, as foreign from Christianity as that of Mahomet. Their blasphemies have driven thinking men into infidelity, who have too hastily rejected the supposed author himself, with the horrors so falsely imputed to him.

Had the doctrines of Jesus been preached as pure as they came from his lips, the whole civilized world would now be Christian. I rejoice that in this blessed country of free inquiry and belief, which has surrendered its creed and conscience to neither kings nor priests, the genuine doctrine of one only God is reviving. I trust that there is not a young man now living in the United States who will not die a Unitarian.

But much I fear, that when the great truth shall be established, its votaries will fall into the fatal error of fabricating formulas of creed and confessions of faith, the engines of which so soon destroyed the religion of Jesus, and made of Christendom a mere Alceldama [field of blood]; that they will give up morals for mysteries, and Jesus for Plato."

Thomas Sully painting,
Courtesy of the American Philosophical Association

Gilbert Stuart painting, *John Adams*, 1823,
Museum of Fine Arts, Boston

INDEX

Acta Sanctorum (Acts of the Saints), 120, 137, 146–52, 157

Adair, James, 29, 30, 32, 49, 50

Adam and Eve, 34

Adams, Abigail (Mrs. John), death of, 203

Adams, John Quincy, 37, 74, 80, 199

Adams, Samuel, 202

Addison, Joseph, 108

advances of the mind, 194

Agent, intelligent and powerful, 222

Age of Reason, 34

Alexander the Great, 95, 97, 119, 141, 220

Alexandrian Library, 71, 97, 98

Almighty, the, 27, 32, 34, 110, 205

altar, sacrifices on, 31

Ames, Fisher, 157, 180

Amours of Psyche and Cupid, 189

amphibologisms, 99, 121

angels, 211, 212

annihilation, 115, 124, 167, 169, 232

Antichrist, 24

Anti-Trinitarians, bill for relief of, 87, 90

Antoninus, Marcus Aurelius, 79

Apocalypse, apocalyptic, 61, 95, 158, 181, 185, 231

Apollo, 220

Apostles, of Jesus, 100, 111, 119, 139

Apostolic Fathers (ancient fathers), 96, 100, 208, 212, 223

Apuleius, 189

Archmagi, 30

Archytas, 126

Arians, 61

aristocracy, artificial (birth and wealth), 103–108

aristocacy, natural (virtue and talents), 103–108

Aristotle, 119, 120, 141, 151, 217

Arminians, 80

Arnobius, 120

Arrian, 84

arts and sciences (fine arts), 64, 153, 154, 155, 157, 161, 162, 189

Asiatic Society, 198

Assassination, Jesuitical, 186

Ass of Zeno (Cleanthes), 94

Athanasian Creed, 73, 93

Athanasian Divines, Athanasians, 91, 145

Athanasius, 136

Atheism, Atheists, 45, 60, 62, 76, 154, 161, 164, 173, 181, 197, 207, 211, 213, 220, 223

Athenagoras (saint), 212

atom, a molecule organique, 91

atoms of life, 221

Augustine (saint), 119, 212

Austin, Benjamin, 66, 76

Author of the Universe, 91

Auto-da-fe (act of the faith), burning of a heretic, 193

Babylonian captivity, 97, 110, 111

Bacchanalians, 45

Bacchus, 42, 215

Bamfield More Carew, king of Gypsies, 173

banks, mania, aristocratical swindling, funerals, 117, 180

Barlow, Joel, 77

Baronius, Cesare Cardinal, 120

Bartholomew's Day Massacre, 143

Barton, Benjamin Smith, 49, 50

Basil (saint), 212

basis of sensation, 211

Batteux, Abbe Charles, 88, 125, 133

Beast, Apocalyptic, 24, 81

Beatitudes, 26

Beaumarchais, Pierre Augustin Caron de, 172

Bedlam (English insane asylum) 77, 140

Bedlamite, 215

being, eternal, self-existent, 93, 94

Belsham, Reverend Thomas, 51, 70, 84, 90, 145

Berkeley, Bishop George, 198, 210

Bernard (saint), 215

Beverly, Robert, 43

Bible (Old/New Testaments), 28, 82, 97, 100, 104, 109–11, 127, 130, 132, 134, 135, 165, 230

Bible Societies, 185, 187

bigotry, 53, 64, 122, 127, 132, 175, 192, 194, 200, 215, 226

birth, virgin, 224

Blacklock, Thomas, 108

Blackmore, William, 181

blasphemy, blaspheme, 61, 132, 209, 220, 223, 229, 230

Blue laws, 132

body, without mind, most abhorrent of all human contemplations, 175

Bolingbroke, Henry St. John (viscount), 63, 81, 83, 95, 124, 167, 198

Bollandists, 137, 146–51

Bollandus, Joannes, 137, 150

book, never be afraid of, 197

book burnings, 71, 97, 109, 111

books that cannot bear examination, 230

Borgia, 156, 157

Bowditch, Nathaniel, 206

Boyer, Jean-Baptiste de, 125

Brahma, 128, 129, 134

Brahmins, 128, 140, 144

Brerewood, Edward, Indian origins, 49, 50

Brissot, Jacques Pierre, 60
Brocklesby, Dr. Richard, 124
Brucker, Reverend Johann Jakob, 98, 133
Bry, Theodor de, on Indians, 30
Bryant, Reverend Lemuel, 192, 196, 203
Buchanan, Joseph, 197
Budaeus, or Bude, Guillaume, 119, 130
Buffon, Comte de (Georges Louis Leclerc), 144, 169, 172
Bunyan, John, 114, 185
Burke, Edmond, 124, 145
Burr, Aaron, 114, 117, 133

Cabalistic Christianity, 140
Cabanis, Pierre Jean George, 209, 228
Caesar, Julius, 97, 115, 119, 141, 180, 193
Callender, James, 66, 76
Calvin, John, Calvinists, 59, 62, 80, 91, 161, 207, 219, 220, 221, 223
Camus, Armand-Gaston, 146, 151
cannibals of Europe, 218
Canus, Spanish prelate, 120
Cappe, Catherine, 52, 81
Carnot, Lazare Nicholas, 145
Catechism, 109, 202
Catherine the Great, empress of Russia, 161, 164, 169
cause, infinite and eternal, 92, 96, 169, 210, 222
cause, ulterior, 221
Causes Premieres, First Causes, 88
Cavalier, Chevalier (knight) of St. Iago de Compostella, 39, 51

Celtic, 30
cerebellum, life without, 228
cerebrum, life without, 228
chance, 90, 169
Chateaubriand, Vicomte François August Rene, 122, 146, 153
Checks and Balances, 60
Chew, Benjamin, 166, 174
children, grandchildren, great-grandchildren (help keep us alive), 192
chivalry, 234
Christ, 94, 127, 139
Christians, Christianity, 25, 41, 59, 60, 71, 77, 80, 81, 86, 89, 91, 94, 95, 98, 100, 101, 109, 120, 121, 124–26, 132, 133, 135–42, 146, 153, 157, 161, 165, 171, 185, 202, 211, 217, 219, 220–23, 230, 231
Church, 37, 40, 59, 116, 119, 120, 145, 157, 188, 189, 192, 195, 207, 211
Church, high, 39
Cicero, 71, 79, 98, 138, 141, 180, 193
Clark, Emily, 113
Clark, Samuel, 82
Cleanthes, Hymn of, *Hymn to Jupiter*, 94, 97, 98
clergy, 76, 104, 106, 116, 200
Cleverly, Joseph, 192
Clinton, De Witt, 117
Coke, Sir Edward, 171
Condorcet, Marquis de, 34, 60, 74, 82, 115, 119, 137, 144, 145, 169, 172, 191
Confucius, 78, 128

conjurers, 30
Consubstantialists, 87
Cooper, Thomas, 84
corruption, 26, 27
corruptions and impostures in religion, 188
corruptions of Christianity, 81, 89, 111, 185, 231
cosmogony (study of creation of universe), 196, 221, 223
Creation, 26, 34, 91, 93, 189, 223, 224
Creator, 124, 128, 184, 209, 211, 221–23, 228
creed, my creed of materialism (Thomas Jefferson), 211
creed and confession of faith, of John Adams, 208
Cromwell, Richard, 54
cross, the, as an engine of grief, 181
Crusades, 25, 158, 220
Cudworth, Ralph, 197
cures, prescribing for others, while unable to cure our own difficulties, 215
Cuvier, Georges, 228

Daemon(s), Daemonism, 99, 100, 111, 128, 129, 220
D'Alembert, Jean le Rond, 152, 161, 162, 164, 172
damnation, 91
D'Argens, Marquis, 125, 133, 145, 146, 173, 213
dawn of reason, 224
days of fire and fagot, 187
death, a blessing, 218, 219
death, as eternal extinction, 168, 169, 232

death, as evil, 217, 218
death, a transformation, 232
De Bry. See Bry, Theodor de, on Indians
Deffand, Marquise du, 169
Deism, Deists, 60, 79, 80, 82, 94, 173, 195, 213
delightful ignorance, 210
delusion(s), 28, 90
demi-popery, in Church of England, 195
demiurge(s), 100
democracy (will be revengeful, bloody, and cruel), 141
Democritus, 199
Demosthenes, 138, 161, 217
den of the priesthood, broken up, 194
Derham, William, pluralist, 142
design in the universe (impossible for human mind not to perceive and feel a conviction of), 91, 128, 222
despotism, ecclesiastical and imperial, 71, 188–89, 191, 201
devil(s), 23, 30, 33, 120, 135, 146, 168, 194, 224
devilisms, devilish, 125, 193, 194
D'Holbach, Baron, Paul Henri Thiry, 164, 169, 221
Diana of Ephesus, temple, 193
Diderot, Denis, 115, 141, 144, 157, 161, 162, 164, 169, 172, 221
disciples of Archbishop Laud, 38
disciples of D'Holbach, 221
disciples of Diderot, 221
disciples of Erasmus, 82
disciples of Ocellus, 221

disciples of Plato, 141
disciples of Pythagoras, 127
disciples of Spinoza, 221
disciples of Zeno, 94
Disraeli, Isaac, 159, 160
Ditton, Humphrey, 182
divine inspiration, 230
divines, 59, 63, 96, 143
divinity, 79, 204
Dominic (saint), 215
dread of annihilation, 124, 125
Druids, 30, 78, 144
Duane, William, 190
Du Barry, Comtesse, 113
Dumeril, Andre Marie Constant,
    229
Du Puis, Charles François, 135,
    136, 181–88, 191, 196, 198,
    230, 231
Dwight, Timothy, 200

Ebionites, 100
Ecclesia, 72
Ecclesiastic, Ecclesiastical, 23, 32,
    173
Edwards, Jonathan, 82, 142
election, corrupt, 116, 117
Ely, Ezra Styles, 82
Emlyn, Thomas, 82
Encyclopedists, 161
enemies of reform, 57
Enfield, William, 88, 98–100, 133, 213
Enoch, prophecy or book of, 129,
    135, 136
Epictetus, 78, 84
Epicurus, 78
Erasmus, 80, 83, 119
essence(s), 208, 210

Eternal, the (God of Shasta/Vedic
    texts), 128, 129
eternal preexistence of something,
    222
eternal preexistence of the world,
    222
ethereal gas (spirit), 212
Euclid, 82
Eustace, Reverend John Chetwode,
    191
evangelists, 99, 121, 122
evil, evil spirits, 30–34, 103, 124,
    136, 162, 172, 174, 181, 217,
    219, 220
existences, all might extinguish,
    169, 222
extinct, certain races of animals,
    222
extraneous ingredients mixed into
    Christianity, 231
exultation, in my own existence
    (Adams), 91

Faber, George Stanley, 24
fable(s), 29, 120, 181, 193, 199, 224
    classing virgin birth of Jesus as, 224
Fable of the Bees, 185, 187
Fabricated Christianity, 165
Fabricator of all things, 221
faction, in Church or State, 59
faculties, when all have left us, 217
faith, my (Jefferson), 89
Fall of Man (as allegory), 136, 181
False God (Calvin's), 220
fanaticism, 141, 157, 192, 200
Farmer, Hugh, 52, 129
farrago of falsehood (Acts of
    Saints), 151

Fast Day, John Adams's, 65
fasts, 29
fate, 169
fatalism, 207
feasts, festivals, 29–31
Flemel, Bertholet, 228
Flora, Roman goddess, 45
Flourens, Marie Jean Pierre, experiments on the nervous system, 227, 228
Fontanelle, Bernard de, 139
Forster, John Rheinhold, 49, 50
France, French king, nation, first of Ten Horns of the Beast to fall, 24
Franklin, Benjamin, 74, 113, 114, 118, 175, 216
frauds, ecclesiastical and imperial, 71
Frederick the Great, 33, 63, 144, 152, 161, 162, 173, 176
free government and the Roman Catholic religion, 216
freedom of religion, South America, not yet prepared for, 215
freedom of writing, speaking, thinking, 200
Freeman, Dr. James, 178, 183
friends of youth gone, 217
Fries's Rebellion, 65
Frog Land (Holland), 205
Fronde, the, 60
future state (life after death), hope for, belief in, 167, 168, 178, 205

Gadsen, Christopher, 202
Gallatin's Rebellion, 64, 65

Galvani, Luigi, 215
Gardiner, Sir Christopher, 39, 51, 195
Genet, Edmond, 65
Genlis, Comtesse de, Stefanie Felicite, 153
Gibbon, Edward, 59, 81, 124, 145
globe (Earth), as the madhouse of the universe, 141
globe, a theater of war, its inhabitants, all heroes, 219
Gnostics, 99
God(s), 33, 34, 40, 47, 49, 61, 63, 67, 73, 86, 90–92, 96, 97, 100–102, 123, 128, 130, 132, 136, 141, 144, 159, 162, 165, 169, 189, 190, 196, 198, 204, 205, 207, 208, 212, 216, 219–24
Goddess, 96
Godwin, William, 61, 115
Goethe, Johann Wolfgang von, 109, 110, 130
Gordon, William, 68
Gorges, Sir Ferdinand, 39, 41
Gospels, destroyed, 71
Governor of the World, 220
graves (of those we have known), 182, 183
greatest enemies to the doctrines of Jesus, 223
Great Principle of Christians, 95
Great Principle of Gentiles, 95
Great Principle of Hebrews, 95
Great Principle which produced universe, 229
Great Teacher (death), 203, 219
Gregory IX (pope), 111

grief, use/purpose of, 163, 170, 171, 174, 178–81, 192, 203, 204, 231, 232

Grimm, Baron von, Frederick Melchior, 160–62, 164, 165, 169, 172, 175, 178, 187, 191, 205

grossest fictions, immortalized in art, 189

Grotius, Hugo, 95, 96, 159

Guelphs, the, 144

Hallicarnassensis, Dionysius, 97

Hamilton, Alexander, 69, 85, 117, 180

Harrington, James, 82, 83

Hartley, David, 144

Hebrew(s), Hebraist, 29, 49, 95, 97, 98, 105, 111, 119, 121, 135, 136

Helvetius, Claude, 73, 172

Henry, Patrick, 204

Hera, 96

Heraclitus, 199

Hercules, 183

heresies of the Talmud, 111

heresy of immaterialism, 211

heretical divinity, my (Adams), 98

heretical works of D'Argens, 173

Herod, 233

Herschel's (Hershell's) universe, 229

Hesiod, 118

Hewes, Nimrod, 23, 28

Hindoos, 78, 134, 140, 141, 205, 217, 219

histories, annihilated, 71

Hobbes, Thomas, 184

Holley, Horace, 200–202

Holy Alliance (Massachusetts Constitutional Revision), 214

Holy Ghost, 144

holy leagues, 199

homonculus (little man), 165

Hopkins, Samuel, 82

Horace, 108, 193

human nature, perfectability of, 119, 158

human nature, total and universal depravity, Adams's lack of belief in, 192

Hume, David, 59, 63, 75, 81, 124, 142, 167, 198

Hus, John, 59, 143, 157

Hutchinson, Thomas 38, 42, 43, 68

Hymn of Cleanthes (*Hymn to Jupiter*), 94, 97

ideology, ideologians, 73, 74, 169, 186, 188, 190, 209

idolatry, 69

Ignatius of Loyola (saint), 153, 196

Immaterialists. *See* Spiritualists

immortality, of soul, 139, 168, 178, 220

improvement of intellectual and moral condition, 216

incarnation, 136, 217

independence of Church and Parliament, 202

Index Expurgatorius, 153, 156

Indian(s), American, 23, 24, 26, 29, 31–37, 41, 42

indulgences, sale of, 157

inequalities: moral, intellectual, physical, 114

infected with Episcopalian and Presbyterian creeds and confessions of faith, 229

infidels, 41
innovations, seen as heresies, 194
Inquisition, 133, 145, 146, 153, 199, 214
Inquisitor(s), 173, 193
instinct, unconsciously guiding, 184
Intelligence (Creator), 126, 162
intolerance, 200
Irish massacres, 143

Jarvis, Charles, 67
Jay, John, 80
Jehovah, 95
Jesuits, Jesuitism, 145–48, 151, 169, 173, 175, 178, 179, 185–87, 191, 193, 195, 199
Jesus, 60, 79–81, 84, 86, 88, 89, 99, 100, 111, 137, 139, 158, 165, 183, 194, 195, 217, 222–24
Jews, Judaism, 29–31, 79, 95–98, 109, 111, 136, 161, 165, 217, 219, 221, 223, 229
John (saint), 95, 224
Johnson, Samuel, 122, 124, 145
Jones, Sir William, 196, 198
Jove, 40, 95, 96, 174, 177
Jude (saint), 136
Jude, Epistle of, 129, 135
Juno, 96
Jupiter, 96, 101, 224
Justin Martyr (saint), 212

Keith, George, 43
Khan, Zingis/Ghengis, 34, 35, 49, 50, 141
Kingcraft, 39
King James Bible, 185
Kippis, Andrew, 52

knights-errant, of St. Ignatius of Loyola, 153, 156
Krebs, Nikolaus, 142

Lactantius, Lucius Caecilius, 212
Laertius, 120
Lafitau, Joseph Francis, 28, 30, 32
La Fontaine, Jean de, 139
La Harpe, Jean François, 83, 122, 172, 189
La Lande, Michel de, 161, 169
landjobbers (speculators in land purchases), 117
La Place, Marquis de, Pierre Simon, 206
Laud, ArchBishop William, 38, 39, 51, 60
Laudians, 39
League, the, 60
Le Clerc, Jean (Johannes Clericus), 197, 198
Leibnitz, Gottfried Wilhelm, 142, 165, 198
Leland, John, 82
Leo X (pope), 124, 157
Lespinasse, Julie de, 178, 205
Levy, David, 165
liberal science, 229
liberalism, advance of, 214
liberty of conscience, 229
library, ancient, 229
Lightfoot, John, 111
Like-substantialists, 87
Lindsey, Reverend Theophilus, 51, 52, 70, 80, 81, 84, 85, 143, 145
lives of the Caesars, 120
living life over again, 232
Livingston, Edward, 66, 67, 77, 117

Livy, 71

Locke, John, 63, 76, 159, 190, 209

Logos, of Plato (mistranslation of Logos as "Word," rather than "Reason"), 34, 93, 99, 198, 223

London, headquarters of Antichrist, 24

Lorraine, Cardinal, 59

loss over time, 232

Louis XVI, tragedy of, 224

Luke (saint), 71

Lunatics (Swedenborg and Wesley), 215

Luther, Martin, 119, 157

Lycurgus, 217

Macarius (saint), 212

Machiavelli, Nicholo, 109, 145

Macpherson, Christopher, 23, 25–28

Madison, James, 27, 95, 116, 192, 196

Magi, 30

Mahomet, 78, 196, 217

Mahometans, Mussulmans, 71, 141, 162, 196, 206, 208, 217

Maker (Creator) of the Universe, 90, 91, 125, 169

Malcolm, John, 186, 196, 198

malignant falsehoods, 227

malignant spirit, 220

Mamelukes, 205

Mandeville, Bernard, 185

Manilius, the astrologer, poet, 34, 198

Manu (Menu), laws of, 135

Maria Theresa (empress), 148

Mark Anthony (Marc Antony, Marcus Antonius), 180, 193

Marmontel, Jean François, 172

Marshall, John, 58, 68, 69, 133

Massachusetts Bay, 36, 39, 41–44, 46

materialists, 182, 197, 198, 208, 210–13

matter, 33, 34, 182, 209–12, 221, 222

Mayhew, Jonathan, 203

May pole, 41, 42, 45

McDuffie, George, 233

Mechanician of the universe, 34

medulla elongata (oblongata), puncture in means instant death, 228

Memoirs of the late Reverend Theophilus Lindsey, 51, 52, 56, 58

Merrymount (Mare Mount), 41

Mesmer, Franz Anton, 215

Messiah, 217

metaphysics, metaphysician(s), 32, 92, 142, 159, 162, 184, 209

metempsychosis (transmigration of souls), 128, 129, 134, 135

Middleton, Conyers, 89, 181

military cast, a Whitefield with a, 196

millennium, 24, 28, 217, 224

Milton, John, 82, 189

Minerva, 224

miracles, 28, 90, 91, 121, 137, 144, 207

misanthrope, can never be one (Adams), 193

missionary, 29, 188

Moisazor, 129

Moliere, Jean-Baptiste Poquelin, 179

monarchies, 24

monkish darkness, 194

Monroe, James, 196
Montesquieu, Charles Louis de Sec-
    ondat, 35, 186, 190, 191
moral(s), morality, 31, 32, 62,
    78–80, 86, 88, 98–101, 104,
    106–108, 113, 125, 128, 129,
    151, 154, 155, 158, 163, 187,
    189, 190, 197, 206, 214, 216
moral emancipation, 214
Morton, Nathaniel, 43, 48–50
Morton, Thomas, 37, 41, 43–48
Moses, 55, 78, 90, 94, 97, 98, 109,
    110, 130, 134, 136 165, 217
Mount Dagon, 42, 45
Mount Sinai, 90, 109
multitude and diversity (of sects), a
    security, 196
My Moral and Religious Creed
    (Adams), 187
mythology, 29, 196

Napoleon Bonaparte, 24, 73, 95,
    141, 143, 145, 157, 158, 162,
    186, 189, 198, 216, 220, 226
National Bible Society, 185, 187
Necker, Anne-Louise-Germaine,
    Baroness De Stael-Holstein,
    172
New English Canaan, or New
    Canaan, 37, 40
New England histories, 37, 38
New England Memorial, 43
Newton, Isaac, 63, 82, 159, 198
Newton's universe, 229
Nice (Nicaea), Council of, 121, 152
no-soul system, 89
Numa, Pompilius, 78

Ocellus, 88, 102, 125, 133, 145,
    162, 173, 213, 221
old age, dreaded, 217
Old Testament, compared with New,
    98
omniscience (God), 172
Ontassete, Cherokee orator, 31
Origen, 212, 223
Origin, of all Cults (Religions), 135,
    181, 185
original sin, 136

Paganism, modern, 89
Paine, Robert Treat, 48, 55
Paine, Thomas, 34, 66, 77, 141
Palestine, 220
Paley, William, 142
Pantheist(s), 207
Papebrock, E. G., 137, 147, 150
Parsons' Cause, 204
parties, political, 66, 70, 117
Pascal, Blaise, 173
passions and interests prevail, 191
patriarchs, 31
Paul (saint), 30, 96
personal abuse, 233
perpetual chicanery, 233
Peter (saint), 136
philanthropism, 195
Philo, 32, 33
Philonic Christian, 179
Pickering, Timothy 57, 69, 195
Pillnitz, Declaration of, 155–57
Pinel, Philippe, 229
Plato, Platonism, 32, 34, 89, 93,
    100, 119, 125, 126, 128, 135,
    138–41, 179, 198, 212, 217
Platonic Christianity, 100, 101, 109, 139

Pliny, 193
Plotinists, 99
Pluralist, Pluralism, 142
Plutarch, 97
Plymouth (Plimouth), 39, 43, 46, 47
politics, weary of, 23
polytheism, abolish, 206
Pomham, Aaron and Moses, 35, 36
Pompadour, Marquise de, 113
Pompey, the Great, 97, 117, 119
Pope, Alexander, 69, 94, 95
pope(s) (Roman Catholic), 71, 111,
    113, 119, 122, 124, 137, 144,
    146, 152, 157, 173, 182, 187,
    188, 192–95
population, original of America, 32
Portal, Antoine, 229
possessions, demoniacal, 135
posterity (posterity will judge), 27,
    57, 64, 195
powder plots, 143
power, above, 220
Pratt, Benjamin, 219
prayer, rendered futile and absurd
    by fatalism, 207
predestination, 89
prejudices, ecclesiastical and tem-
    poral, 229
Prepuce, of the Savior, 137
Preserver of all things, 221
Price, Reverend Richard, 52, 53, 92,
    93, 115, 153, 154
priest(s), priesthood, 29–31, 35, 36,
    60, 71, 80, 87–89, 99, 133, 139,
    141, 144, 145, 152, 153, 157,
    158, 167, 176, 187, 190, 191,
    194, 206, 226
Priestcraft, 39, 53, 87, 167, 194

Priestley, Dr. Joseph, 24, 52–54, 56,
    70, 73, 77, 80, 81, 83–90,
    94–96, 98, 115, 121, 124–28,
    133–37, 142–45, 165, 181, 182,
    198, 224, 225
principles, 57
Progress of the Human Mind, his-
    tory of, 34, 76, 82, 119, 144
prophets, prophecy, 23–29, 32, 61,
    90, 136, 137, 156, 158, 178,
    217, 224, 225
prostitution and prostration of
    human nature in Spain, 216
Protestant Popedom, 194, 195
Proverbs of Greek poets, 118
Psalms of David, 108
Puritans, 38
Pyrrho, pyrrhonism, 90, 213
Pythagoras, Pythagoreans, 78, 88,
    102, 125, 128, 135, 140, 179,
    180, 198
Pythagorean Christian, 179

Quakers, 59, 88, 145, 190, 195, 218

rabbis, 71
Ramsay, David, 68
Randolph, John, 67, 73, 77, 233
Raphael, Raphael's Moderator, 189
Rapin, Rene, 76
Ray, John, 142
Reform, Reformations, 23, 26, 99,
    143, 156, 186, 206, 207, 216, 224
Reformer, Jesus as, 99, 224
refutation, of prophets and prophe-
    cies, 25
regeneration of all created things
    into new and other forms, 221

Regulator of all things, 221
religion, 32, 52, 53, 76, 77, 80, 87,
    91, 114, 116, 120, 127, 130,
    132–34, 143, 145, 157, 161,
    185–90, 192, 193, 200, 201,
    205, 206, 215, 216, 220, 230
religious freedom, law/act, 106, 133
Republicanism, 24
resurrection of Connecticut to light
    and liberality, 194
Resurrection of Jesus, 60, 80, 81
resurrections, two, of the dead, 165
Revelation(s), 84, 86, 90, 101, 132,
    133, 204, 217, 220, 221, 225,
    231
revelation, of nature, 90
Rhode Island, 116
Richard the Lion-Hearted, 220
riddles, spirit and matter remain,
    198
right of free inquiry, 230
risk of translating, 230
Robespierre, Maximilien François,
    60, 162
Rochefoucald, François de la, 59,
    74, 137, 158
Roman Catholicism, 39, 62, 121,
    122, 191, 201, 216, 225
Romans, Bernard, 49
Rousseau, Jean Jacques, 63, 73,
    115, 141, 144, 161, 164, 172
Ruler, the, 94
Rush, Dr. Benjamin, 48, 55, 77, 78,
    84, 86, 89, 90, 94, 122

Sachems, 25, 33, 36
Sanchoniathon, 78, 128
Sages, Grecian, 71

Sanskrit, 128
science(s), 28, 31, 32, 53, 57, 62,
    86, 105, 107, 143, 229
Scripture(s), 29
Search, Edward, pen name of
    Abraham Tucker, 82
Sedgewick, Theodore, 57
self-existent universe, 223
Seneca, Lucius Annaeus, 78, 79, 97,
    193
Separatists, 39
Septuagint, 97
Sermon on the Mount, 182, 185
Sewall, Jonathan, 68
Shandy, Tristram, 108
Shasta, 128, 129, 135, 162
Shays's Rebellion, 64, 75
Shekinah, 90
Shiva, 129
Simplicius, 84
slavery, 216
Smyth, Alexander, 231
Society for the Propagation of the
    Gospel, 48
Socinians, 62
Socrates, 78, 101, 119, 139, 179
Socrates, compared with Jesus, 84,
    86
Solon, 217
Sorbonne, French theological school
    (Sorbonite), 153, 156, 172, 193
sorcerers, 30
soul, 85, 211, 223, 228
Spinoza, Baruch, 221
spirit, defined, 182, 210–13, 222
spirit, good, 36
spirit, great, 26, 31, 33
spirits, evil, 30, 31, 220

Spiritualists, 142, 182, 197, 198, 207–12, 228
Stagyrites (Aristotleian), 99
Standish, Captain Miles, 47
Stewart, Dugald, 208, 209, 211
stocks, putting prophets in, 28
Suetonius, 120
suicide (methods), 169
Superintending Power maintains universe, 222
superstition, superstitious, 25, 26, 29, 64, 122, 132, 157, 189, 191, 196, 200, 201
Supreme Being, 95, 96, 134, 165, 223
Supreme Intelligence, 126, 223
Swedenborg, Emanuel, 142, 216
Swift, Jonathan, 94, 181, 193
Sydney, Algernon, 76
syllabus, 89, 93, 98, 108
Syria, 220
system founded in hopes, not fears, 202

Tacitus, 71, 97, 157, 193
Talmud, 98, 111
Tatian, 212
Tecla (Thecla), Acts of, 122
Temple of Diana, 193
Ten Commandments, 109, 110, 130, 182, 185
tenets of Church, 37
Tenskwatawa, prophet of the Wabash, 24–27, 144
terror, terrorism, 25, 28, 36, 64–67, 90, 155, 193, 232
terrorism, of the day, 64
Tertullian, 212, 223

theist, theism, 164
Themistocles, 217
Theocritus, 82
Theognis, 96, 101–103, 106, 113
theologians, Christian, 91
theologians, in general, 35
theology, 125, 142, 160, 162
Thomas Aquinas (saint), 142, 222
thorns on the pillow of age, 227
thought, freedom of, 224
thousand-years' reign, 217
Thucydides, 82
Ticknor, George, 175
Timaeus, 88, 125, 126, 145, 162, 173, 213, 221
Tippecanoe, Prophet of, 32
Toleta, Cardinal, 222
Torrey, John, 114
Towers, Dr. Joseph, 24, 137
Tracy, Comte Destutt de, Antoine Louis Claude (Analysis of Dupuis), 183–87, 209, 211
Tracy, Uriah, 57
Transubstantiations, 73
Trinitarians, 61, 80
Trinity, 88, 90, 126, 135
tritheism, 223
Trojans, 49
Tucker, Abraham, 81, 82, 187
Turgot, Jacques, 74
Turks, 71
tutors and professors, European vs. American, 229

Unitarians, Unitarianism, 70, 80, 87, 95, 195
Universalists, 62
Universal Providence, 95

Universal Toleration, 188
University of Virginia, 229
Uranologia, 187, 188

Van der Kemp, Francis Adrian, 83, 175–77
Vassal, William, 168, 174, 179
Vedas, Vedams, 134
Vendee, 67
Venus, 42, 215
Vergil, or Virgil, 109, 193
Veronica (saint), 137
Verres, Caius, 118
virgin(s), virgin birth, 189, 224
virtue, efforts in favor of, 171, 197, 208
virtue, essence of, 184
Vishnou, Vishnu, 128, 217
Vives, Juan Luis, 119, 120
Volney, Constantin François Chasseboeuf de, 230
Voltaire, 55, 81, 122, 144, 152, 161, 162, 167, 169, 172
Vulgate, 187

Wabash, Prophet of the. *See* Tenskwatawa, prophet of the Wabash
Washington, George, 69, 85, 116, 117, 180

Watchmaker of the universe, 34
Waterland, Daniel, 82, 89
weary of philosophers, theologians, politicians, and historians, 35
Wesley, John, 216
Wharton, Joseph, 24
Whiskey Rebellion, 65
Whiston, William, 182
White Bull, worshippers of, 215
Whitefield, George, 123, 142, 196
winter nights of old age, 233
Witch(es), Witchcraft, 25, 30, 132
wizards, 30
Wolcott, Oliver, 57
Wollaston, Captain, 36, 41–43, 48
Wonder Working Providence of Zion's savior in New England, 37
Woods Prospect, 37
Wycliffe, John, 143, 157

Xenophon, 72, 179

Young, Dr. Thomas, 76

Zaleucis, laws of, 127
Zeno, 94
Zinzendorf, Nikolaus Ludwig von, 142
Zoroaster, 78, 128